Praise for *The Ancestor*

"From the icy opening battle of man vs. wolf, you feel yourself in the hands of a master storyteller and that feeling never lets up."

—SJ Rozan, bestselling author of *Paper Son*

"This thrilling novel is rich in descriptions of the vast, snowy, and deadly wilderness of Alaska; it ably captures the type of person who chases gold."

—*Foreword Reviews*

"A story that blends the familiar and the supernatural in a manner that calls Stephen King's work to mind. That said, Goldberg's book possesses a flavor all its own—a distinctive mélange of the sincere and the strange."

—*Kirkus Reviews*

"Beautifully written, and capturing the unforgiving grit of Gold Rush Alaska, Lee Matthew Goldberg's *The Ancestor* is a thrilling page-turner with an ache in its heart. I'm a huge fan."

—Roz Nay, author of *Hurry Home*
and *Our Little Secret*

"*The Ancestor* is more than a novel. It's an ode to the rich tradition of adventure storytelling...seasoned with ample spice of love and violence and greed."

—Matt Phillips, author of *Countdown*
and *Know Me from Smoke*

"In *The Ancestor*, Lee Matthew Goldberg masterfully weaves together a story involving family and violence set against the backdrop of an unforgiving Alaska of both past and present."

—Andrew Davie, author of *Pavement*
and *Ouro* *os*

D1427446

THE ANCESTOR

BOOKS BY LEE MATTHEW GOLDBERG

Novels
Slow Down
The Mentor
The Desire Card

Novellas
Satellite of Love
Middle of Nowhere

LEE MATTHEW GOLDBERG

THE ANCESTOR

Down & Out Books
3959 Van Dyke Road, Suite 265
Lutz, FL 33558
DownAndOutBooks.com

Cover design by Zach McCain

ISBN: 1-64396-114-4
ISBN-13: 978-1-64396-114-9

For Dad, and all the ancestors we've loved and lost.

According to Greek mythology, humans were originally created with four arms, four legs and a head with two faces. Fearing their power, Zeus split them into two separate parts, condemning them to spend their lives in search of their other halves.
— Plato, *The Symposium*

Every man is a quotation from all his ancestors.
—Ralph Waldo Emerson

1

One eye open, the other frozen shut. He knows what an eye is, but that other "I" remains a mystery. Mind scooped out and left in ice. Words slowly return. Blue sky, that's what he sees. The sun twinkling like a diamond. Tundra, there's another recalled word. Packed snow on all sides as if the world succumbed to white. The air a powerful whistle. A breeze blows, not a friend but a penance. It passes right through and chills to the core, this enemy wind. Limbs atrophied, no idea when they last moved. Boil of a sun thaws and prickles. Tiny spiders swinging from leg hairs, biting into flesh. He cries out but there is no sound. For it feels like he hasn't spoken in centuries.

Back of throat tastes of metal. Blood trapped in phlegm. A cough sends a splatter of red against the stark land, a streak in the form of a smile. When was the last time he ate? His stomach growls in agony, a good sign. Organs working, or at least attempting to work. His one eye scans to the left and the right, no sign of anyone, not even an animal. No chance for a savior or sustenance.

He gums his jaw, the first inkling of movement. Aware of his scraggly beard coated in frost. Crystals spiral from his chin, collect in his lap. Now he sees his hands, luckily in gloves except they are a thin brown leather, rather useless. Bones crack as he maneuvers to remove the gloves. Fingers tremble once hit with fresh air and numbness subsides. Massages his legs, gets the blood flowing, an injection of life. The spiders accelerate and then relent, toes wiggle, and he sits up. Around his neck rests a notebook and a fountain pen, the tip crusted in flakes. He feels an object in a front pocket and pulls out a silver compact mirror, the back embroidered with floral patterns, ladylike. *This is not my mirror*, he decides, but then has a more important realization. *Who am I?* With trembling hands, he brings the

1

mirror up to his face for a glance.

The reflection of a stranger. All beard save for a few features that emerge. A bulbous but authoritative nose, green eye flecked with gold, a mane of dark hair cascading to his shoulders. Handsome in a grizzled way. Shades of a bear in the roundness of his cheeks and a wolf in his stare.

"I am…" his lips try to say, but there is no answer. Often one can wake from a dream and the dream seems real for a moment, but a sense of self never vanishes. Whoever he was is long gone, unlikely to return anytime soon. At least while he remains freezing in the wilderness.

I must make it out of here.

It's relieving that he thinks of himself as an "I." Whoever he is, he *is* someone. A mother birthed and fed him from her breast. A father taught him…taught him what, exactly? Survival skills? How to hunt? If he had a father worth his while, he'd know how to do this.

And then, a caterwauling from the depths of his soul, a fawn-in-distress call that plants a trap for curious predators. He knows this sound well, meaning he's lured prey before. His daddy schooled him like a good man should.

The waiting game. Another call erupts, a coyote's howl this time. He can recognize the difference. Then it comes to him that he needs to know what to do should an animal appear. He pats down his pockets, no weapon but his fists. And then, the clinking of sharp nails against the ice sheet. A majestic wolf, eyes like the sky, shimmering coat the color of clouds. Its charcoal nose twitches; the blood he hacked up in plain sight. He and the wolf lock into a dueling stare, neither wanting to be the first to flinch. A vision of death with baring teeth, or the start of his new life if victorious. The wolf doesn't give him a chance to contemplate, lunging with a mouth full of saliva. He catches it in a brutal embrace and is knocked off his heels, slamming his back against the hard ground. They skitter down a slick snowcap, snapping at each other like angry lovers. The wolf is relentless, a worthy opponent, a test of wills. He gets the beast in a headlock, trying to crack its neck, but the wolf is too slippery. Breath fumes from other kills circle into his nostrils—this wolf has never lost a battle before. Blood splashes, no clue which of them has been wounded. They spin in the snow like a tornado. He makes a fist, jams it in the wolf's mouth. Teeth scrape against his knuckles as he rams his fist farther down the wolf's throat, seconds of painful warmth. The wolf heaves, chokes, attempts to chew off his hand, but its strategy is futile. It has only come across other animals, never a human mind that can think steps ahead.

Now he attempts a headlock again with his left arm, squeezing off circulation. The wolf lets out a whimper that reverberates through his wrist. They lock into another dueling stare, except this time he does not see the many kills of the wolf through its gaze. He visualizes its sadness, its inevitable end. And then, the sound of the wolf's neck breaking, his blood-soaked fist removed from the back of its throat. Its dead tongue lolling out of its mouth against the icy bed. He pets its beautiful coat, this formidable foe, now a present wrapped with a bow. Delectable to quench his all-consuming hunger.

He needs the clearest block of ice he can find. Using the wolf's teeth to carve a fine, translucent, round piece, he creates a magnifying glass. He rubs the dirt away and keeps rubbing until enough moisture flecks off. There's a bed of whittled grass at the slope he and the wolf ended up in, and he holds the ice over the dry grass, propping it against two logs until a brilliant rainbow prism shoots through and he blows and blows until a fire ignites. He rips off all the breakable branches he can locate to stoke the flames. While it spreads, he procures a rock to blunt out the wolf's teeth, then uses them for the painstaking task of skinning the fur. He does it carefully so a semblance of a coat remains, which he dips into a nearby brook to wash away the lingering blood and sinew. The sun has mostly dipped behind the mountains and he wears the wolf's coat to mask the chill, then roasts its carcass over the roaring fire, breaking off legs and gnawing while the true flesh still cooks.

The meat is a godsend to his empty stomach and also an immediate poison that his body rejects by throwing up. He sucks on some ice and the queasiness diminishes. By the time it's fully cooked, darkness reigns and he feels like a shell. With each chew, he becomes human again, but the loneliness isn't as easy to fight off. There are souls that feel lonely, he assumes, but at least they have themselves for company. They can rely on memories to help them through cold nights. He searches his mind for a wisp of the past, any nugget, wading through a never-ending sea. The horizon seemingly attainable, but with every stroke just as far away. He'd cry but the tears are frozen in his ducts, one eye still sealed shut.

When he has eaten enough of the wolf, and his belly distends like a newly pregnant woman, he feeds the fire with more broken limbs and curls up to its warmth, his only confidant in this harsh wilderness, possibly his only companion forever—a lifetime of attempting to be caressed by flames and nothing more. He wraps himself tightly in the wolf's fur, hoping that when he wakes again he'll know who he is. The nightmare vanished along with the sun rising like a bride's pretty little hand on his grizzled cheek.

2

Travis Barlow knows that the key to hunting caribou is with your head rather than your legs. This has been passed down to him and his buddy Grayson Hucks from their fathers and their fathers' fathers all the way back to when both families settled in Alaska. The Hucks clan came from Anchorage, migrating from Ireland prior to the Civil War where a ton of brothers met their end before the last surviving one escaped as far north as he could. Travis's history traces back to his grandfather Papa Clifford, born in Nome but only vaguely knowing where his ancestors came from. Papa Clifford took both boys out early on along with Travis's brother Bobby, giving them each a .30-06 rifle with heavy bullets to counterbalance the wind. The trick is to observe the movement patterns of several herds before intercepting a suitable ambush point and aiming downrange.

The boys have been friends for over twenty years now beginning in the schoolyard when they banded together to fight back against a bully that targeted both. Neither was studious and often met the teacher's questions with a befuddled stare, so this bully labeled them dunces and beat the pulp out of them during recess, alternating between the two until the dunces finally retaliated with loose bricks that nearly killed their tormentor. A month of detention later an unbreakable bond was formed.

While others might use Sundays for religious observance, the caribou hunt has become the men's church, a better workout than most get and a way to put food on the table. They drive out at the first hint of spring in Travis's pickup with him at the wheel, some country tunes on the radio, dip tucked in their bottom lips, and two six-packs of ice-cold Molson beer.

"Shit, I didn't tell you me and Lorinda broke up," Grayson says, spitting a glob of brown into an old plastic bottle.

"What was it this time?"

Grayson reaches over to shake Travis, causing the pickup to veer from its lane. But there are no other cars on the winding road to the wilderness.

"You wanna cop to pull us over?" Travis laughs.

"Can't pull myself over. And I believe I have it in good with the other fellas in blue in town, so I think we'll be okay."

"Anyway," Travis says. "So, Lorinda. What happened?"

"'Munication issues."

"Meaning?"

"Meaning, I never talk and she talks too much."

"She's too good for you."

"That's what I told her! And then, she left. She ain't like Callie."

"Callie got her own issues, like any other."

"Callie's carved from gold and you know it."

Travis wipes away a grin, knowing his better half is the one who got the raw deal in their relationship.

"Got to give a girl credit to fall in love with a nose like yours," Grayson says, cracking open a beer, the froth staining his mustache.

"My mom always said I had a presidential nose."

"Cora's just too kind. That's a nice way of saying monstrous."

Travis pounds Grayson's shoulder, hard enough for it to burn. Grayson whaps him back.

"All right, all right, Gray. Don't send us off the road."

The winter has been harsh so Callie forbade any hunting, mostly out of fear for the unsafe roads due to avalanches. The cold months hit Travis harder than usual this year, being out of work and alone most of time with their toddler, Eli. He'd had a difficult time relating to the child as an infant, but now the majority of his days consist of every possible question Eli can ask, most of which he has no idea how to answer. So his bones ache for springtime when he can finally feel free and wind his way up to the Preserve. The sensation of bringing back a caribou for his family to feast on is greater than any drug.

Though the sun shines and April's in the air, it's deceptively cold when they emerge from the pickup, a little wobbly from the beers. They sling their .30-06s around their backs and look for tracks, knowing caribou have glands between their hooves that deposit a scent with each step.

"Did I tell ya that goods store has been seized for never paying their rent?" Grayson asks, while keeping an eye peeled for any creeping creatures.

"The one on Platen? No one ever went there. Think it was a drug front."

"It was. Anyway, should be cheaper to have the state as a landlord."

Travis rubs his goatee, not as a mode of contemplation but to give his fingers something to do.

"I'm not there yet, Gray."

"When will you be?"

"When I have the kind of funds to make that decision," Travis says.

"We need a good fish shack, like a luncheonette. You've got all the hungry fisherman who dock their boats and are tired of the Pizza Joint."

"Fisherman don't want to eat more fish."

"That's where you're wrong. If you excel at fish, the word will spread."

"Town's small enough that we don't need to do much for word to get out there."

"So what's keeping you, buddy?"

"Diapers are expensive. Yeah, Eli's still in 'em. Mortgage on the house. Fuck, I still owe my parents from the down payment."

"What about Callie's folks?"

"They're pissed enough I stole their girl from California. They ain't gonna invest in no fish shack."

"No Travis's Tugboat?"

"That was always a stupid name and made no sense. My name don't gotta be in it."

"There's always police work," Grayson says, one eyebrow raised. There'd been a time years ago when Travis thought he might pursue that line, his dad being the sheriff and all, but he never had the calling. He didn't rebel like Bobby did in the stereotypical way that sons of the law might, but he cares as much about protecting and serving the people of Laner, Alaska as he does dancing (which he hates).

From the pickup, Travis takes out the proper clothes and gear. KUIU attack pants and guide jackets, insulated gloves, Merino wool sweaters, bandanas, and a neck gaiter. A 65mm spotting scope, binoculars, Havalon Piranta hunting knife, and a license should they run into any parks department officials. They dress in silence, the start of their meditation. Puffy and snug, they hike up a slope until the pickup is far away but still close enough so they can drag a heavy, dead caribou.

Travis spies a track first, the indentation of the hoofs sparkling clear. The scents that caribous release draw other herds. This one's fresh, probably from early this morning since it's beginning to lightly snow but the track has yet to be covered. Grayson taps his shoulder.

"Wolves," Grayson says, pointing into the distance. Sure enough, a pack encircles a thin band of smoke that streams toward the sky.

Travis nods and aims his gun at that same sky, lets off a few rounds. The wolves spook and scurry away, traveling farther from the sound.

"Who lit a fire?" Travis asks.

Grayson shrugs. "Out of range from the binoculars. All I see is smoke."

Travis squints into his own pair but can't make out anything more either.

"Probably someone like us gone hunting at the first sign of decent weather."

Hunting requires patience and that's Travis's favorite part of the sport. His home's full of noise; he never gets a moment's peace. Out here, he gets to dive within—only the smacking sound from the dip in Grayson's lip audible. What he loves about fishing too, except fishing has turned into something more sinister than just a day of serenity. The fish shack has been a dream for some time, one he thought he could bring to fruition. He'd been saving all the years he worked at the oil refinery on the outskirts of town, but when he was gutted in a slew of layoffs no one saw coming, all those savings had to be poured into everything but the dream. Life always hit you with a one-two punch, so of course he'd been laid off just as he had a newborn. Callie's tips from waitressing were barely able to cover formula after the baby refused breastmilk. So fishing makes him sad now as opposed to calm. And he doesn't think that'll ever change.

The caribou arrive as the wind ramps up, making a shot more of a guesstimate. He'll only get off one or two rounds before the gunfire scares them. Three waddle over to their ilk's track, caribous rarely traveling in large herds. One could feed his family for almost two weeks between all the cuts. To be a true hunter, you never waste a morsel.

Maybe Grayson knows Travis needs this so he lets his best friend fire the first shot. The bullet slopes down, carried by the burgeoning breeze, and narrowly misses.

"Again," Grayson whispers, lining up the dispersing animals in his own scope but allowing Travis another chance.

Travis fires, the bullet careening right in the ear of one unlucky caribou. The other two take off in distress. After a few rounds, Grayson hits them both. They fall into each other, pressed together like they're cuddling.

"Woo hoo," Grayson cheers, patting a beat against Travis's back. But Travis never celebrates, since death is never a celebration. It brings him closer to his own mortality—that one tiny slip could cause destruction. This feeling lingers in the lump in his throat until he swallows and passes it on.

The caribou ran some distance, so they bring the pickup nearer. After putting away the binoculars, Travis finally allows a celebration with a cracked-open Molson, frigid against his chapped lips. Grayson does a touchdown dance over the dead carcasses while Travis grabs the rope and ties them up. With every ounce of exertion left in them, they hoist two caribous into the back of the pickup, not enough room for the third. Flurries are beginning to fall, and they cover the kills with a heavy tarp.

"I'm gonna take a leak 'fore we head out," Grayson says, trotting away.

"Why you going so far?"

"Okay, it's a massive dump. Mind yer biz."

Travis watches Grayson's blond head become smaller and smaller until he passes behind a snowy bank. He takes off his baseball cap and stands over the lone caribou they must leave behind. He places the cap over his heart and gives thanks for the meals they've procured, not to any type of god because he believes in nothing like that, but to the law of nature, which requires sacrifices for one to survive. He hopes other hungry animals find the carcass and make a good meal so its death is justified.

A twig snaps over yonder and he cranes his head but he's left the binoculars in the pickup and doesn't bother to get them. It might be a critter coming to observe this funeral, nothing to be concerned about. The sky absorbs his focus, blue like the eye of a wild and beautiful bird, blue like the wallpaper in Eli's room, sweet Eli who should be waking from his nap by the time he gets home.

"I must hug him more," he says, surprised to vocalize this out loud but glad he does. That way it's truly out there in the world, this massive love he feels for another human being even when the little terror sometimes makes him wish he was deaf. "I must love them all more," Travis says directly to the clouds, the same ones passing over Callie and his son so the essence of his words might trickle down as vapors into their hearts.

3

Right eye jolts open, the lid flapping like a pulled shade, the left still frozen. The fire has extinguished; he's not surprised. To keep it stoked, he should've only allowed himself an hour of sleep at a time, but rest was more important than warmth. Limbs have tightened up again, difficult to move so he rolls from side to side to get the blood flowing. Out of the corner of his good eye, a wolf sits poised, staring with a piercing blue gaze. His first thought being that this is the wolf he already killed and consumed. It has returned as a vision, a terrible oasis. But the reality of the wolf's growl tells a different story, one filled with its pack circling around their prey. Four of them, teeth bared, impossible to fight all, the end near. He swears he'll go out swinging.

"Come at me, sumbitches," he snaps, morphing into a wolf now too.

One attacks by bearing its teeth and going for his arm, but then a gunshot rings out, the echo like a door slam. He scans for the source but is too afraid to truly move. The wolves all do the same, their necks pivoting in unison toward the distance. Another round goes off and this gets them scared. They vanish as a unit, scampering down a hill until they are gone.

This time he can tell the direction of the gunfire, due east, curious how he knows that phrase. A rocking ship on uneasy waters lingers in his consciousness, but this is not the moment to search for memories. Whether the bullets come from friend or foe, he'll die out here soon enough if he doesn't investigate.

Silently, he pursues the gun owner, hazy from dehydration, each step a lifetime. He's adept at not making a peep. This is a skill he's practiced and excelled at before. Atop a bluff stands a man holding some sort of hat over his heart, a dead caribou at his feet. The man wears unfamiliar clothes very different from his own Mackinaw coat and trousers with rubber boots. The gun slung around the man's back is one he's never seen before. But he doesn't know much of what he's seen before, so it isn't much of a shock.

When the man turns from the caribou, he can make out his profile but the man does not see him. This man believes he's alone. His good eye zeroes in on this first human. Dark, shaggy hair kept long, prominent nose and absorbing green eyes with flecks of gold. He removes the embroidered mirror from his pocket. He brings it up to his face to look at himself again. Then his gaze goes to this doppelgänger, this replica of himself except for a scraggly beard. Is he so far gone from thirst and hunger that he's envisioned a duplicate? He shakes his head back and forth so the vision might disappear, but it remains more vibrant than ever—his past or future self, long-lost twin, or whoever it might be. He nearly soils his pants, manages to keep his colon tight.

"Was all backed up," he hears another voice call out. A fair-haired man pops up over the bluff.

"I didn't need to know that," his duplicate replies.

"Shat out a moose I tell ya. You got to see it."

"I ain't looking at your shit, Gray."

"No man, this one is, like, legendary. Size of a baby's arm."

"You need more fiber."

"C'mon, Trav. Indulge me."

"All right, you degenerate."

The two disappear over a hill. He's motionless, mind whirling, unable to decide the next step. He peers past the dead caribou over to some large metal thing on wheels resembling a carriage but without any horse. He makes a break for it and dives into the back, tucking himself tight under the tarp, nose-to-nose with two dead carcasses starting to reek. Barely enough room to squeeze in. He hears the two other men return and hop in the front. A puttering noise is followed by a reverberation under his body, and then he's in motion: soaring, gliding.

"Take me away," he whispers to the dead animals. He closes his one eye, exhausted from the trying morning where he almost died before he was brought to life again.

His dreams, fragmented and untethered, full of images but nothing coalesces. Staring into a dirty hanging mirror, running a comb through his thick hair. This mirror existed in a place he called home, except nothing exists beyond his reflection trapped in a black hole. Does it lead to a bedroom where a wife and child lay? He senses a presence of something greater than himself in his heart, a pure love, yet who he loves remains an enigma. Somehow, he has found the first key to open the first door, now he must discover the rest.

The carriage stops with a jolt. His head bangs against the metal bed. The dead caribous jostle. He hears a muffling conversation from the two men in the front. They must not find him in the back so he slides out like an eel, slithering into a puddle on the ground. The front doors are opened and he scurries under the wheeled monstrosity, just enough room to fit. He stares at their boots.

"I don't mind carving up the meat," one man says to the other. "If you want to pick it up later."

"You don't have to do that, Trav."

"Keeps me busy. You sure you don't need a ride?"

"I'm gonna pop into Elson's. Have me a brew."

"You call a cab if you need it. Don't be getting in your patrol vehicle."

"Thanks, Mom. Will do."

"Fuck you, kindly."

"Solid hunt today."

"Wouldn't have expected anything else, Gray."

A whirring buzz resonates and he can see a large door opening upward and a room filled with tools and such. His doppelgänger, who has been called "Trav," hoists the caribou inside one at a time. This Trav is strong, like himself. Once both caribous have been brought in, the door closes. He wiggles out and stands, bones cracking.

He observes the space where Trav has entered, no window to peer inside. A home is built around this entrance and he hugs the siding until he reaches glass he can see through. A small child lies on his stomach, feet kicked up in the air. The child focuses on a large box with moving pictures, mouth agape. The window has been open a crack and the smell of apples and cinnamon wafts into his nostrils. Stomach churns, saliva drips, longing occurs. A bite of something sweet seems an impossibility, a morsel of anything would be a gift from God.

"Eli," a voice says, sugary like that dream. The boy doesn't avert his eyes from the box as a woman joins him.

His heart stops beating, then beats faster, organs out of whack. The woman has reddish-orange hair, wild like a fire, clipped back in a ponytail that hangs down to the small of her back. A kind face, the tips of her cheeks rubbed red, freckles dancing across her forehead. All her teeth show when she smiles. He can tell she smiles a lot.

"Daddy's home," she tells the boy, who then becomes alert. The boy jumps up, feet tapping away. "Give him time, he's in the garage."

She pets the boy's hair, gently sitting him back down. She tucks him to her chest, his legs crossed over her own. They stare at the curious box with the moving pictures.

From their fireplace, flames crackle and whistle, and he wants more than anything to be a part of their coziness. The love in this house full and simmering. Remote yet familiar. His head feels like a blown-up balloon, and he has to grab onto the windowsill for support. The world gets small like he's looking through the wrong side of binoculars, then widens again, stretched out and surreal. A different woman and a different child appear in his mind. A similar fire cooks. The child and the woman are dressed in recognizable clothes. She wears a floral dress buttoned up to her neck with lace around the trim, not much skin exposed unlike the woman he just witnessed. Her hair less orange, redder, even fierier. She sings to the child, tucked beneath her bosom, who's barely able to keep his eyes open. "To-ra-loo-ra-loo-ral, too-ra-loo-ra-li, too-ra-loo-ra-loo-ral, Hush, now don't you cry." It's an Irish melody, this he knows. Ireland is a country, and he's not there now. He's in America; he can tell from everyone's accent. He's uncertain if he's been to Ireland, if that's a part of his history.

He dives further into this vision, afraid it might disappear. The woman has a name that rests on the tip of his tongue, but for now, that's where it will stay. The same with the child. These aren't strangers, he surmises. They are certainly a part of his past. Is this the wife and son he craves? He waits to feel his heart swell with love but it's been frozen for too long like he has.

Frozen.

At that thought, his sealed eye twitches. How long had he been trapped in the wilderness unable to move? This unsettles him, the notion that he's farther away from home than he ever could have imagined, no mode of transport to take him back.

"To-ra-loo-ra-loo-ral, too-ra-loo-ra-li, too-ra-loo-ra-loo-ral, hush, now don't you cry."

The song settles into his soul, but he doesn't heed its advice. Tears the size of raindrops plop from his socket, collect in his beard, and leave a salty tang on his lips.

The woman and the child morph back into the ones in the house before him, cruel imitations since he believes the others to be his actual family. Why else would they sink into his mind? Are they fretting right now as to where he could be? Do they cry similar tears from being apart? A stabbing pain in his stomach warns him that he might never know. He squeezes his good eye shut to conjure them again, but they have faded, possibly never returning. The lullaby remains trapped between his ears while he stays trapped in this voyage to a new world, this hell on Earth.

In the house, Trav enters the room and the boy squeals, leaps into his father's arms. They spin around in delight, shower each other with kisses, each one causing the pain in his chest to stab even harder. He wants to burst in and replace Trav, experience the sensation of a kiss, a foreign entity since it's been so long. Eons have seemingly passed without a hug and this has whittled him down to a nub.

"Got a whole caribou," Trav says, and the woman gives her thousand-toothed smile and now they kiss, long and hard, melting into each other.

He must turn away, unable to watch their happiness anymore. He folds into his sleeve, the tears continuing to stream. But in horror, he forces himself to look back, since he knows the only way to return to his loves will be to keep this family in his sights.

So he glues his rheumy eye to the glass, knowing at least one thing about himself.

He is tenacious. And no one should stand in the way of what he wants.

4

Trav calls her California. A strange name for a woman, the man thinks. He rests his ear up against the crack in the window so he can fully hear their conversation. The boy is still absorbed in the odd box with the moving pictures where tiny people speak from out of it like they're alive. California is a place that this man has known; it rings true in his mind. He's seen it before, traversed its land, although he's unsure how it looks. Not cold like where he stands now, this he knows. Items from his past traveling to his cranium in pieces, but he will be patient. He must.

California comes to Trav with envelopes in hand. These envelopes bear bad news. The man can tell from the worried dimple that has formed between her eyes.

"And I was having such a good day," Trav says, folding into a chair.

She hugs him from behind. "I hate being a buzzkill."

"Mortgage. Water. Electricity. Phone." Trav chucks the envelopes on the table. "Which is the least important?"

"We could take out a second on the home?" California says, but her voice strains and she does not mean it.

He waves her away. "'Least we got meat for the next two weeks."

"I'll get Lorinda to give us some pizzas. She's always willing."

"Maybe not. Her and Gray broke up."

"Shit," California says, blowing her bangs away from her face. "Cheated on her?"

"That's not what he told me."

"Doesn't mean it isn't what happened."

A lull laps around their conversation. They watch their son watching the box, craving his naiveté to the woes of adulthood. The man sees this in their frowns.

15

"Have you been...looking?" California asks, then it's obvious she wishes she didn't say anything. Trav cuts her with his sharp eyes, doesn't respond.

"I bet Elson could get you a shift behind his bar," she says. "Place has been hopping since the layoffs."

"Glad Elson's doing so well."

"Now, now," California says, changing her tactics. She curls into Trav's lap, rubs his meaty thighs, tickles his neck with her nose. "No one's got it better than us Barlows."

Barlows.

The man tries the word out on his tongue and it seems to fit. He's said it before, many times. Us *Barlows.* A last name? Does he know these people somehow? Maybe he *is* Trav's twin, although they don't seem concerned that he might be missing. Maybe he's been missing for so long that they've stopped caring.

On impulse, he goes to knock on the window and let them know of his existence. But then he stops, recoiling, afraid of their reaction. If he's a stranger, he'll ruin his spying and any chance of getting back to the visions from before.

"Do you want me to tell Stu and Cora not to come over for dinner tonight?" California asks.

"No, it's Sunday. I'll make a stew for Stu."

"It's so odd that you call your dad...Stu."

"I came out the womb calling him that."

"Oh, I didn't tell you, my folks are putting in a pool."

Trav raises an eyebrow, but he's clearly uninterested.

"Maybe we can go down with Eli when they finish," she says.

Trav spins out of his chair, disappears for a moment, and returns with a frosted beer. He cracks it open and indulges.

"Who's paying for the flight?"

"I'm sure they will if we ask."

"But nothing comes free with them, Callie. You know that."

"They miss me is all."

Trav chugs another long swig. "How in the hell did you wind up in buttfuck, Alaska with a loser like me?"

"Because...I was on a cruise and we docked for the day and I saw this tree trunk of a man slicked with oil on his overalls, hair like a lion's mane, tearing into a sandwich like it did him dirty, and I said, 'This will be my future.' Saw it in lights."

She takes the beer from his hand, sips, and leaves it on the table out of reach. She kisses him sweetly, which makes the boy finally look up from the box and cover his eyes, saying, "Gross!"

"I love you, California," he says, the first real grin on his face that the man has seen.

"I love you...most of the time, Travis."

Trav picks her up and rocks her in his arms. She glides through the air. Her arms bare and the top of her breasts peek out, which startles him. He knows he's used to women being modest, this girl flashy. Some stirring rumbles beneath his waist, the first true sign of life since he opened that one eye. He's beginning to form again and this brings him joy.

"I need to start carving up that caribou if we're gonna have a meal ready by the time my folks come," Trav says.

Trav places her down, cheeks flushed. She looks at Trav like he wishes she would do to him. And for one tiny moment, he believes that she does, gaze flickering over in his direction as he crouches down low, afraid he's been caught. But when he pops back up, Trav and California have both gone. Only the child remains, focusing on the box with moving pictures, as if it's an oracle that could read a map of all of their futures.

He holds Trav and California tight in his mind, back flush against the house, traces of their conversation still batting around. Hallucinations run wild, likely from hunger. The wolf has long passed through his digestive system and he's ravenous. Squeezes his eyes shut until what he truly craves spirals back, not Trav and California but the woman and child he once knew intimately.

He can feel the notebook he found earlier pressed between his heart and coat. He holds it in his filthy fingers, opening the cover for the first time. Pages have been torn out, likely never to be retrieved. At the top of the first page, someone has written 1898 in a calligraphy script. With a pen attached to the notepad, he rewrites the date, the handwriting exact. It is 1898, he decides. He's relieved to know the year, a start to unlocking some doors.

"*Focus*," he tells himself.

All of his sudden he rushes along a wave, stomach churning and bile dribbling from his lips. The sensation of being on a ship familiar. He has traveled this way many times prior. Have the oceans taken him here? Are

17

they his only chance of returning home?

So he builds this ship in his brain, piece by piece until completion. The sails wave mightily as he sets off for treasure. The waters are rough and hard to traverse. He arrives to land sick and doubled over, vomit crusted in his clothes. He wanders until he reaches the home he remembers. At the door, she stands in an apron, flour on her nose, tiny child in arms.

He's sucked back from this vision once again, but this time he grabs the pen to illuminate his inspiration...

I see my beloved at the door, red hair worn up like a Gibson Girl, all swooshes and poofs. She has been making a cinnamon pie, rather my favorite. I know our time is limited for I am set to travel soon. Where to? This I do not know yet. But I understand that I've left her before and will leave her again, in pursuit of mystery. I'll be leaving a child as well. A bright boy with apple cheeks, prone to fits. Yet my love for him is like a soup pot boiling over, ever simmering.

"But must you go?" my beloved asks. Her voice musical, lilting. She has questioned my pursuits before, but never convinced me to stay. My blood full of adventure, this I am certain.

"It awaits," I tell her, a glint in my eye.

"But you've never..."

Her voice trails off because she can see that these words hurt. As an explorer, I'd searched before, probably came close to my dreams, but always awoke before they coalesced.

What are those dreams? I want to ask. But that is never a conversation she and I actually had, so I am unable to bring it to life with this fine pen. What could possibly have taken me away from my loves, this wicked enough object the devil dangled just out of reach?

"But what about Joseph," she says, "you missed his first steps, his first words. What more will you miss?"

Finally, a name! A connection to my past. Joseph. Yes, I've said this name many, many times. Little Joe, that's what I called my son. Little Joe with the wide eyes, apple cheeks, and fair swirl of hair. Little Joe who liked to play stick and hoop. Who could keep his hoop rolling longer than anyone. And his toy horse that he'd pull with a string. The one he slept with. The one he called Baby.

"Adalaide," I say. "I go for us."

Another name! My sweet Adalaide. Tough woman at home on our farm. Yes, we had a farm! Unafraid of getting dirty with the sheep we raised. Often found by our loom making the most lovely wool clothes she'd sell around town. I can even recall their smell—a touch of lilac perfume just like she wears.

Now I beg that she'll say my name, give me a sense of self to complete the puzzle. It buzzes on her lips, waiting to be released. Please, my darling, I beg. Please, help me get back to who I used to be.

"No," she says instead. "You go for you." She hides her teeth, not giving me that smile I desire so. "You pretend it is for us, but it's your restlessness. And you'll never be quenched."

"This is the last time," I plead with her. I attempt to hug, but she has no interest. Neither did Joe, she's turned him against me. They have made it on their own without me and will do so again, for even longer than they can imagine. Days will become months and soon years, a telegram never arriving. She'll wait by frosted windows and then grow weary of a miracle. I'll be a memory she'll keep in a locked box, turning to it when the nights are long and cold. And there aren't enough logs in the world to stoke the fire and keep her warm.

"Oh, Wyatt," she'll proclaim, when she's old and withered without a husband to replace me. Joe will leave her to start his own family and the nights will become longer and even more fitful, her own restlessness overwhelming, the cause of death being a shattered heart.

I lament.

"Wait...I have written my name! Wyatt. Yes, Wyatt Barlow. It flows so naturally. I am Wyatt Barlow, born 1860, a part of the Civil War generation, old enough then to remember how all the men in town returned as ghosts.

"I am Wyatt Barlow," I say, under my breath as if it's a secret. Then I shout it out loud and proud, "I am Wyatt Barlow!" I tell the earth, and the sky, and the hidden stars, and the hide-and-go-seek sun, and any woodland creatures who have come to witness my awakening. I have woken in so many ways these past few days, but this one the most revolutionary. No longer a specter of a human, a hollow shell clanging around. A man with a strong and true name. A man who must get back to his family by whatever means possible.

A black dog surges from the house rushing after a Glaucous gull, tongue dancing in its mouth.

"Chinook!" a voice calls after it. One that Wyatt recognizes as Trav's.

Wyatt leaps to his feet, a great charge of energy. He hightails it out of there before any reunion could occur, not ready for whatever outcome may arise. He whips his head back and can see his duplicate watching his flight through a thicket of thin trees, unaware how the two are connected.

"C'mon, Chinook," he can hear Trav saying, but by then he gets far enough away.

He will come back for more windows into who he was.

Their address burns across his forehead. 201 Elk Road.

"I am Wyatt Barlow, I am Wyatt Barlow," he says, over and over, in case his broken mind decides to lose it again.

5

Elson's Pub. The doors just opened for the day, cool breaths of flurries winding their way inside. The town not much more than a long street with slender pathways shooting off from the main artery. A Pizza Joint simply called that. Feed Store. Bait and Tackle. Grocery. Clothes Mart. Hunting & Ammo. Docks running parallel with a few lolling boats. Ice-capped mountains cutting off the distance. And Elson's, the name ringing a fine bell for Wyatt since he heard it being mentioned by his doppelgänger.

Midday and it's already pretty packed, only room at the bar. Sawdust on the floor. On a hanging screen, there are blurring images of tiny men shooting across ice with sticks. Stink lines may be rising from Wyatt's body, but Elson's is full of fishermen stopping in for lunch with their own sour smells. He wedges between two of them, their eyes reddened from a few empties surrounding their finished plates.

There's music in the air. Where it comes from he does not know. Sounds like it's playing from the heavens. Some singer saying he's "Got Friends in Lowly Places," whatever that means. A rounded man with a beard down to his chest cleans a glass with a towel and asks him, "What you want?"

Wyatt blinks in confusion. It's the first human contact he's had and he's not quite comfortable with using his voice box yet. He tries but remains unsuccessful so the man tosses him a menu.

He attempts to read the words. A good a chunk of them don't seem like actual words.

"Go with the burger," one of the fisherman says. The one with two chins. "Elson's known for his burger."

The fisherman pokes the menu with his plump finger under the words, *Mondo Hamburger.*

"Comes with chili cheese fries," the other fisherman says, skinny as a fishing pole, Adam's apple bobbing up and down. "You from around here? Feel like you remind me of someone."

Wyatt shakes his head.

"Elson," the fishing pole says, to the man behind the bar. "One Mondo and a tall Molson."

"Ale?" Wyatt manages to ask.

The larger one rubs his stomach in a circle. "Yes, ale."

"Much obliged," Wyatt says.

"So, where you from?" the fishing pole asks.

"Yonder," Wyatt replies, waving at the distance as if he actually knows.

The two look at each other and then burst out laughing.

"You sure talk funny."

Wyatt begins laughing too, since he doesn't know what else to do. The beer arrives in a stein, sweet foam spilling from the sides. He takes a hearty gulp and can't stop.

"Slow down there," the larger one says.

Wyatt finally lowers the beer after it's half empty.

"Good." He blinks at them. "Wyatt." He extends his hand, his cheeks turning rosy from saying his actual name.

"I'm Tuck and that's Jesse," the larger one says and they shake. "We fish wild coho. The morning was a windfall so we celebrating."

"Our boat is full of pink," Jesse says.

Wyatt has no idea what they mean but he nods.

"So what brings you to Laner?" Tuck asks.

Wyatt points at the floor like he's questioning if this is Laner.

"Shit, man, this guy doesn't even know where he's at," Tuck says. "We're closest to Nome. That's where most out-of-towners want to go. About thirty miles east. Is that where you wanna be?"

"Nome."

"Well, might as well get some grub in ya before you go there. Gonna be cheaper here at Elson's."

The Mondo Hamburger arrives, a fat patty dripping with grease. A side of chili cheese fries stacked high. Wyatt digs in. Tuck and Jesse are still talking but he doesn't care. His world being that burger. With each bite, his energy skyrockets. He practically licks the plate clean.

"Holy moly," Jesse says. "You should enter Elson's eatin' competitions. Don't think I've ever seen a fellow swallow food that fast."

Wyatt replies with a truncated belch. His stomach spasms, the massive amount of food working its way through.

"I got it," Tuck says, snapping his fingers. "He looks like Stu's son…the other son."

Jesse nods, but Wyatt can't see straight.

"Outhouse?" Wyatt asks, and the two reply with a guffaw. They motion to a hallway.

Wyatt fumbles his way to the bathroom. Luckily, it's empty. He sees a white porcelain seat and sits down, lets out a flood. There's a ream of thin white towels he assumes to be better than leaves. As he rises, he feels full and empty at the same time.

When he returns, another man has joined the fisherman. Wyatt recognizes him as Trav's hunting friend. He's in a uniform and appears to be a man of the law. As Wyatt sits, Tuck pats his shoulder.

"Wyatt, this is Deputy Grayson Hucks. Stopped by to have a tall one…or *five* with us after his early shift ended."

Wyatt extends his hand, but when Grayson shakes it the deputy asserts his dominance. Grayson's eyes seem to narrow, untrusting this new vagrant who has stumbled into town. Grayson's drunk to the point of rocking on his heels.

"Haven't ever seen you before," Grayson says, slightly crushing Wyatt's fingers.

Wyatt doesn't know if he's relieved or saddened that this man doesn't see the resemblance between him and Trav. Might be the beard. Or that Grayson seems pickled.

"I'm an explorer," Wyatt says, puffing out his chest.

"What are you exploring in Alaska?"

"Alaska," Wyatt repeats quietly. The frigid terrain finally making sense. High up north at the edge of civilization. What could have possibly brought him here?

"Gold?" Tuck cackles, and all three of them laugh.

This triggers a twitching in Wyatt's good eye. Could gold be what brought him all this way? A quest that pulled many men of his generation. And does it mean that everyone else in the bar hunts the same shiny prize?

He reaches into a pocket and discovers two tiny nuggets. Leaving one, he pulls out the other, holding it in his dirt-caked palm.

"Well, fuck me. That is gold," Grayson says. He rips the gold piece out of Wyatt's hand to inspect it in the light. Out of instinct, Wyatt grabs the deputy's wrist forcibly. The two eye each other like they're about to enter a duel.

"Here, here," Grayson says, giving it back. "I ain't after your nugget."

"Did you find that nearby?" Jesse asks. "Damn, people haven't been searching for gold in these parts since the turn of the century. Last century."

The three of them begin talking about their ancestors who came to the area in the hopes of finding fortune. Wyatt tunes them out, goes far within. Too much of this Alaska doesn't match up with any recollection of the place where he'd traveled. He doesn't have memories of it yet, but this new flashy world seems far from where he came from. Like he'd stepped in some time machine.

"Newspaper," Wyatt says, not to anyone in particular. "What's the date?"

Tuck removes the newspaper from under his plate that's covered in grease stains.

With shaking hands, Wyatt reads the date. April 4th, 2019.

2019!

He nearly faints, the room cants, his feet unsolid on the ground. He holds his arms out for balance, almost comes crashing down. He clutches the newspaper as if it's a life preserver.

"No, no, no," he says, turning toward the door.

"Hey, hey, where you going?" Grayson asks. "Hey, you gotta pay."

He hands the gold nugget to Grayson, his eyes pleading to let him go.

"What a nutter," Wyatt hears Tuck say, but he's already at the door, the brilliant cold slapping him in the face.

He stares down at the date on the newspaper again. Running his finger across the print as if he's trying to erase and see if it's been a prank. But the date stays firm. *2019.* One hundred and twenty-two years past the date he wrote in his journal.

He can barely catch his breath, the universe spinning. Falling to the ground with trickling tears, he asks the snow bed as if it might hold the answer, "Where's the dratted time machine?"

Managing to scurry to the back of Elson's, Wyatt works to get his bearings. The newspaper hasn't left his hands, joints locked, tears still flowing like mad. The year 2019 etched into his skull. No chance of it being untrue. If he weren't from the past, how come none of this new future makes any sense? Nothing seems familiar. And if it's all true, it means that Adalaide and Little Joe are long dead. What had propelled him before was to find them by any means possible, now only their graveyard a destination.

He punches his leg, curses at himself for being weak. He must seek answers. Even if Adalaide and Joe are gone, he needs to discover everything he can about them. Could the date written in the journal be a mistake? No. He knows too many facts from that era. William McKinley was president. The City of Greater New York had recently been created. The Spanish-American War was being fought. Joshua Slocum completed a three-year solo circumnavigation of the world. All these facts are easily accessible where everything afterwards remains a blank.

But what does this mean? Had he chased a golden fortune in the wilds of Alaska and somehow frozen in time for over a hundred years? That doesn't make any logical sense. However, it does explain why his twin Trav wasn't at all concerned with his disappearance. But if Trav isn't his twin, who he is then?

"I'm his ancestor," Wyatt decides, his mouth wide in the shape of an O. He sucks in a hit of icy air. This revelation sits with him, earns its place in his mind until it swears to settle in for good. His grandson? No...his great grandson? He starts counting out the years on his fingers, reaching the conclusion that it's likely his great-*great* grandson. This brings him a flash of unabashed glee—that his surname has stuck for four generations. But that mirth soon gets zapped with unbearable melancholy taking its place. All the life moments that passed by while he was trapped in ice. The unfairness of this plague.

"Why me?" he howls, bits of the digested wolf still burning inside.

A lonesome howl bellowing through the afternoon, continuing until night drops its dark and heavy cloak.

6

Callie's been preparing caribou stew all day in the slow cooker. The lean meat diced medium, Holy Trinity of carrots, onions, and celery along with potatoes, tomatoes, garlic, a bay leaf, beef stock, flour, thyme, rosemary, and butter. Practically everything they have in their pantry, most of the goods taken from Pizza Joint. Lorinda never minded, although that might change now that she has it out with Grayson. Selfish to think this, but money has been so tight and Travis too stubborn, proud, or whatever to take a job beneath him. She'd mentioned to Stu and Cora about hinting at fishing work on a boat. If she brought it up, Travis would refuse, but Stu has a way of shutting down any arguments fast.

She's been into crystals for some time, always believing in energies but never practicing. She's learned to tell the crystals what she wants. Back in California, she used to wish for success as an actress. A childhood dream like other Los Angelans before its improbability reared its head. Now a healthy family always comes first. She's wanted the crystals to watch over Papa Clifford for some time since his health started declining. She doesn't have to worry about her own folks because they had her so young. And health-wise, Eli and Travis are all right, although mentally Travis has been slipping into a belabored funk.

Travis enters the kitchen splattered with blood from carving the caribou. Startled, she swivels around, some freshly diced onions drop to the floor.

"Five second rule," Travis says, swiping a beer from the refrigerator.

"I just mopped, the onions would be covered in Mr. Clean."

She scoops them into the trash.

"I imagine you're gonna wash up before your folks come," she says, eyeing the blood.

"Nah, I was hoping to give them a horror show."

She chuckles but it's stilted. She finds herself doing this more, forcing things between them. What used to come easy now feeling like they're acting out roles. Something her parents had warned her about.

"You'll get bored up in Alaska," her mother said, sucking a hit from a freshly rolled joint.

"It's pure up there," Callie responded, because she'd caught the Alaska fever. Wide-open spaces, room to breathe. She had felt so stifled in California, her friends caught up in bullshit. Dating apps and dressing up, putting on a show. They lived close enough to L.A. to get lost in the Hollywood spillover. Each of them attached to this hot director, that model, this cute actor. She was guilty of it too but started to find it nauseating.

"There's no smog there," she said, running out of defenses.

"We'll get you an air purifier."

"I'm in love."

This had been something she'd vocalized before with other boyfriends, but more because she'd been with them for long enough it seemed she had to. If she wasn't in love like they were, then she was to blame. Cold and heartless Callie. With Travis, it felt magnetic, essential.

"Someday, you'll come back to California," her mother said. "It's in your name. It's written in the stars."

But she was convinced Alaska would be her new permanent home. Vast and welcoming, uncharted and bursting with adventure. Full of good, true energy, and a crazy thing called love.

Stu arrives with a six-pack dangling from his finger, Cora with a Bundt cake. Travis showered and shaved, smelling of musk. He knows Callie likes a forest scent, anything animalistic. He's found her distant lately, but maybe it's because he's been receding too. What is a man beyond his work and his ability to provide for his family? Right now, he feels like sludge, a percentage rather than a whole.

"Grandma, grandpa," Eli yells, tackling Stu's leg. Stu always hesitant with the boy, like he'd been with Travis and Bobby. Cora the opposite, made of hugs.

"There's my favorite sweet little boy," Cora says, plying him with lipstick kisses and leaving marks. Eli fawning over the attention.

Chinook starts barking like crazy so Travis takes him out to the dog-house with kibbles and water to last him the night.

Afterwards, they settle in the den. The men talk of Travis's hunt over beers. The women sip a sherry that Cora gifted last winter. Eli draws a moose.

"That's lovely, Eli," Cora says, patting his head.

"I know."

"This hair color," Cora says, fingering a braid of Callie's. "A bottle won't get me close to it."

"I was once told as a child that redheads have no soul," Callie replies. "Kids can be so mean."

"So a herd came by pretty fast?" Stu says, pivoting because of his bad leg. He gives the slightest wince, but Travis knows it hurts worse. Shot in the line of duty about ten years back, the first and only time.

"Yeah, I think the caribous get bold after the winter when there's no hunters around. You should come with Grayson and I next time."

A futile attempt, like usual. His father not going hunting in years, too much pain connected to those olden days.

"Papa Clifford wanted to come, but didn't have the energy," Cora says.

"We'll do Sunday dinner at your place next week so we can see him."

"He'd like that," Cora replies, catching Stu's eye to get him to respond, but Stu focuses on a painting of a mallard over the mantle as if he's studying fine art.

"Shall we eat?" Callie asks, directing them to the dining area.

She'd brought out the good plates they'd gotten from the wedding. It was a small affair, held in Nome. She didn't even invite any of her friends, already feeling distant from them. Her parents insisted on coming. The attire was casual and her father wore a reindeer sweater. He spoke of it throughout the night like it'd been a charity he donated to. He and her mom calling Alaska "quaint" multiple times. They hid in their liquors and fled at sunrise.

"I hope everyone likes stew," Callie says, and Travis gives her a wink.

"Smells of heaven."

"It's all the crockpot. I did very little."

"Nonsense," Cora says. "Travis, I always said she had a knack for cooking. I'd bet you'd make a great caterer."

"Who would I cater for around here?" Callie asks, and then nibbles on her tongue.

They settle into the meal. Eli loves the "boo," which is what he calls the caribou. Stu stays quiet like usual, never one for much conversation, even worse over the years. Cora monopolizes the flow, a role she took on long ago.

"Did you hear about that goods store?" Cora asks, puffing up her curly hair that resembles a biker's helmet. "Closed down."

"Heard it was a drug front," Travis says into his near-empty beer.

"That's not public knowledge. But yes. Heroin."

Stu's voice cracks as he says this. The table goes silent except for Eli who's singing a song he made up about a boo.

"I didn't mean..." Cora begins.

Stu holds up his hand, gives a firm nod. "Son, I wanted to talk to you."

Travis digs at the remnants of beer in the bottle with his tongue. "Yeah, Stu?"

"I had a conversation with Smitty the other day. Runs the *Cutthroat* boat. Northern pike, rainbow trout. Salmon, of course."

"I know Smitty, tell him hi."

"Sure. I will. So Smitty's been looking for a guy."

"A guy for what?"

"Help on the boat. Old Charlie was making trips with him. But Old Charlie is getting, well, old."

"Stu, listen..."

"Now, son, you got a family and money doesn't sprout from trees."

"Smitty probably pays in coins."

"It's something."

"And what does he need? He does all the fishing."

"Mostly the cleaning."

"Well, that's..." Travis makes a fist. "That's...I'm thirty years old. I'm above scooping out guts."

"No one is above nothing. We do what we must. I'ma tell him yes. You go out there for a day and see how it goes. Maybe he'll let you fish some."

"Whoop-dee-do."

"*Don't.* You hear me? Don't backtalk me."

Stu points an imposing finger, and even a fighter like Travis goes quiet. As a kid, he may have posted up against Stu, but not anymore. Now it'd just be cruel.

"I'm sorry. I'll...okay. You can tell Smitty yes."

"I already did," Stu says, and heads into the kitchen for another beer.

"That was good," Cora says, her smile trembling.

Callie takes Travis's hand. His is cold because he runs cold, always has. She rubs his hitchhiker's thumb.

He spins out of his chair and wobbles a little to the kitchen. Stu stands by the window over the sink staring at the moon. The moonlight silvery. The kitchen appliances buzzing. A faint tear lingering at the corner of Stu's eye, barely noticeable except to Travis, since his father never cries.

"Pop," he says, with a heavy hand on his father's back.

"Sink's dripping," Stu replies, still transfixed with the moon.

Travis wants to say something like, "He's watching, he's with us," but words never suffice.

Stu doesn't wipe away the tear as it builds in power and trickles down a wrinkle in his cheek. His face full of lines, not in the past but deep grooves now. A short and solid man, hard as stone. Crewcut, lips so thin they're hardly there, a Barlow's nose.

Out of the window, they hear a snap followed by a rustling. It doesn't sway his father's gaze, but Travis peers into the swell of darkness. Its blue-black lure. Alaska populated by black holes, places where matter disappears. Their home surrounded by animals, but this doesn't sound like one. A human rustling, since humans are restive creatures. Animals more patient even though their time on Earth more limited.

"Do you hear that?" he asks Stu, who lets out the universe's longest sigh.

"Let's go back 'fore your mother talks Callie's ear off."

When Travis returns to the dining table, Eli has fallen asleep over his moose drawing. Callie scoops him up to take him to bed. Cora bathing him in more kisses.

"Dinner was delicious," he tells Callie, their sleeping son between them. She seems tired so he'll let her sleep in.

"Honey, we'll do the dishes," Cora says, beginning to clear the table. She nods for Stu and Travis to help.

They stack plates and convene in the kitchen. The pull of the window absorbs Travis again. A dark silhouette flitting against the already dark night.

"Do you see that?" he asks his folks, but they're too busy scraping the plates into the garbage.

"Bobby?" Travis says, so quietly, not out loud, only in his heart. The silhouette turns, sparkling from the moonlight. Beamed down from above, or likely from below since that was probably its final destination.

He watches its dance, knowing it stays alive the more he conjures its spirit. He holds the clout. That's what he wants to tell Stu, who squelches that spirit deep down, its tar-like substance glue in his guts, begging to be released, begging its host to finally release.

7

A desire to return to 201 Elk Road so Wyatt can invoke his wife and child again. Their memories already beginning to recede. Faint morsels, translucent and undefined. Her lyrical voice rounded with an Irish brogue. Little Joe muted, too much of a newborn to have a voice. Had he only known his son as a bleating baby? Wyatt's legs, however, have given up the fight. Jellied and unable to trek through the woods again. With belabored steps, he peels off of the main strip down an unexplored lane. An abandoned goods store calls forth. Yellow police ribbon in an X across the entrance. A hole in the front window the size of a fist. He reaches in and twists the lock open.

Inside smells damp, the place unlived. The floors stripped bare, no trace of any goods. Shelves thick with dust and grime. A ceiling dripping moisture. Only a hair warmer than outside, but he'll take it. Behind a counter, he folds into the fetal position, knees to his chin, pinwheeling his legs to get circulation going. He'll rest for a moment and then begin his journey to Elk Road, but sleep has another idea. Within seconds, he's under its spell.

A quaint house sways atop a small hill. Browned and in disrepair but immediately home. He's drawn there, wanting to wrap his arms around what it represents. A farm surrounds. A few sheep, a chicken coop, pig sty, myriad of vegetables, a tractor idling. The sun an orange cracker in the bone sky. A fire cooks in a hearth, a pot of heated water beside. Adalaide with a child in her arms, no longer a newborn but still a little boy. A steaming washcloth to the kid's forehead, his chills making him look like he's seizing.

"He's so cold he's like an ice block," she says, the music gone from her voice.

"Should I call the doctor again?" he hears himself ask.

"The doctor," she says, as if she's given up. "He comes in, puffs out his feathers, and leaves without any change."

"Maybe this time will be different."

"I'm tired of your naivety," she says. He scratches his head because he doesn't know what this means. "He's always cold, even in the boiling summer."

"Lemme stoke the fire more."

He pokes at the flames, just to give him something to do. That morning he was already out the door, ready to vanish for an indeterminable amount of time. An expedition, no longer to California anymore, which had been overrun and depleted of all its gold, but to Alaska, a new frontier full of shiny nubs. And then, this.

"You can go," she says, but she really means, *don't you dare.*

"If I bring back a fortune we can get him real doctors. Not just Dr. Greeson down the way."

"What if he's not here when you return?"

"Dr. Greeson? His family has lived here for generations."

"I mean Joseph."

At the sound of his name, Joe pops his head from out of the heavy quilt. Face pale, cheeks sunken.

"Are you g-going away, Papa?"

He kneels beside his child in his wife's arms, not allowing any of Adalaide's scorn to infiltrate.

"Remember how I told you how a man is measured?"

The boy manages to nod, teeth chattering and sounding like his mouth is full of glass.

"This is my calling. Always has been. As a boy like yourself, I dreamed of gold in far off lands."

"You did?"

"Sure," He holds the boy's cheek in his palm. Instantly, his own hand goes cold as if it has siphoned some of the boy's chills. "Some men get a calling to the priesthood like Father McDaniels, or to the law like Officer Langley, but lemme tell you, Joe, once you see gold, nothing else seems to sparkle."

Now he falls in line with Adalaide's daggers.

"Don't blunt the truth, Wyatt," she says.

"That is the truth. You don't understand. You can't understand. I'm restless, unfulfilled."

"Finally. A glimmer of you speaking from the heart. We're not enough for you."

"No, you misunderstand. I don't feel like I've fulfilled the promise I made to you on our wedding day."

"Health and happiness, that's all I need."

"We don't have neither. We're barely scraping by. The home needs fixing. That's why Joe's sick. It's drafty all the time. I want to tear it down and start again."

"You're already out the door. And nothing I say will change anything. So go. Leave us."

"Not like this."

"You can't have it both ways. Make a decision. Stay here and be miserable or leave us in misery. What's most important to you?"

He'd already set his pack by the doorframe full of provisions and hiking and camping gear. He had a ticket to a docked ship stuffed in his pocket, which cost more than he pretended it did. He'd invested in this journey, to turn around now a terrible admittance of defeat. Is that what he wants to teach his son?

"I'm gonna call on Dr. Greeson to come by today to give Joe a look."

"Go."

He attempts to hug them but she turns her cheek. He has a horrible vision that her profile will be the last image he'll have of her. Little Joe has closed his eyes, exhausted from a day of fits. When he kisses Joe's head, it's frigid, like kissing a tombstone.

He barrels out of the house before he can change his mind. Warning himself not to be weak and give in. Certain that when he finds his way back with fistfuls of gold, it'll solve all their woes. A strained relationship. Joe's forever chills. The riches will create miracles.

The sun setting by the time he steps outside. The crackling fire from within the greatest source of light as he makes his way through the gloaming. Passing homes full of families warming in front of similar fires until the town recedes so far in the distance it barely registers as anything at all.

Slept but not rested. Wyatt awakes curled up, joints aching. Sliver of sunrise illuminating the dust mites. A dream and a nightmare fading: emboldened by envisioning his wife and child, tortured from realizing he'd been an abandoner. Chosen gold over them. It pained him to think that their last encounter ended with friction. He shuts his one eye to return, hoping that he couldn't have fled when his son needed him most. But deep down where thoughts live but stay hidden, he knows he's truly this monster punished by many lifetimes in ice.

Again, Adalaide and Joe dissipate even more. Shades of their features vanishing. Unfair that he didn't travel back to happier times. He needs the drug that will bring him there. The Barlow family on Elk Road.

Morning brings out the fishermen along the docks. Pungent smells lining the air. Bristly beards and heavy gear to stave off the sleet. If he'd been looking closer, he would've seen Trav getting on one of those boats. He passes by not ten feet from his supposed ancestor, his possible great-great grandson. But hunger gnaws at his stomach, his brain full of too much soup to be fully aware. The woods have his attention, the precise route to get him to Elk Road.

When he arrives, the dog is mewling in its little house. Water bowl bone dry, a few kibbles hardened to the sides. It licks its lips as if Wyatt might provide breakfast now that dawn has broken through.

He looks in the window at the living area, no trace of California or the boy. Passing around, he emerges at their bedroom. Mother and child nestled in bed and snoring away. She's even more beautiful in sleep, an angel sent. Red-orange hair sprawled across the pillow almost aflame against the white sheets. The boy with cherub cheeks and a cowlick dreaming of something sweet. Oh, how he wants to crawl into bed with them and never wake. The window has been shut, locked from within. He surmises that is probably for the best. He doesn't know what he might do if he had the ability to enter. This is the life he left behind and he swears not to make the same mistake twice.

They could be his. They deserve to be his. They just don't know this yet.

But they will.

They will.

8

Smitty runs a small operation. Not quite a commercial fishing boat like some of the others based along the dock that go out for days at a time. It'd been him and Old Charlie for the longest time. But Old Charlie's rheumatism had gotten really bad and he's known in town as a pretty miserable drunk. Too much of a hindrance so likely Old Charlie'll be spending his days making bathtub gin.

Travis stayed away from the waters for the past two years. Stu knew why, keeping the same distance. The fact the town is rimmed by ocean doesn't help. But fears need to be faced. Travis had gotten up at four a.m. when it was still dark. The quietude of pre-mornings energizing. Poured two separate thermoses of black coffee and caribou soup. Callie and Eli still fully asleep, which made him glad. He'd have been upset if he woke her when she obviously needed solid rest.

Took the pickup down empty roads. The sun flirting with rising, traveling in long orange fingers across the earth. The blackness of the sky turning a bewitching purple. Clouds like puffs of endless smoke. The air redolent of quaking aspens and white spruce as he sipped his boiling coffee, the sludge warming. He held his breath when he arrived.

The docks are full of life unlike the barren roads. Fisherman hauling out for the start of the season that picks up even more once summer blossoms. The winter a time of packaging, smoking, and shipping off the catches of the year. He visualizes his fish shack for a second, a beacon off the docks. Full of regulars like at Elson's. Bisques and fresh catches of the day with Callie either cooking or waiting tables and Travis getting together the menus, his role the face of the place. Eli coming in after school, munching on his favorite fish sticks. He lets the vision go, whipping himself enough.

Smitty's all smiles when Travis gets to the boat. A small affair but enough to get the job done. Smitty with his stringy hair, bushy eyebrows, a hooked nose, and a swirl of a beard. Fingers always slicked with oil and palm lines blackened, hands pink and raw.

"Ready to bust your ass, greenhorn?" he asks Travis, his voice gritty from a lifetime of cigars. One already chewed down, tucked between his bottom teeth and lip, a thin line of smoke blowing from the cherry.

The waters are choppy and Travis's stomach unused to the abuse. The black coffee sloshing around. He helps with letting the skiff go to set the net. Waits for the skiff to close the net. Piles the web while not letting it tangle up. Uses the hydraulics to haul the catch onto the deck. Rather paltry bounty, not being fully in season yet. Repeats the whole chain. Sifts through and tosses all the garbage, cans and plastic bottles, refuse and gunk. Hands smelling of salt and sewage by the second go around, fingernails black.

"How's Papa Clifford been doing?" Smitty asks, still at work on his cigar even though it's no longer smoking.

"Much the same. He's moved in with my folks."

"That's probably for the best."

"He's ninety-three."

"Oh, God bless. That is a life. And all his time in Alaska. He's a sourdough."

"Doesn't see much, hearing's pretty gone. But he's still sharp. Mind clearer than most."

"Fought in World War II, didn't he?"

"Yup, front line. Shot in the ass and actually kept going. Had the bullet taken out, stitched up, and then went right back."

"Different generation they were. Built of brick. Not a pansy among them. Kids these days so sensitive. Got a nephew who makes crying his job. Wouldn't be caught dead out on a boat like this. How's your son by the way?"

"Eli's great. We're all great."

"C'mon, help me pull this in."

They hoist in the net, a few salmon flapping in the grooves. Travis hunches down to sort away the flotsam. His stomach roiling, doing backflips.

"I think I might puke, Smitty."

"Do it over the stern."

Travis crawls to the back of the boat, focusing on a lighthouse along the horizon to keep him grounded. A swell of bile creeps up his throat but manages to stay intact. He spits it out, leaning over the edge, the waves rollicking below. This ocean that brings the town life, but has taken it away too. The final resting place for his brother who went out high on bad shit. He never stood a chance, not even from birth. His body missing for the longest days ever experienced.

Now Travis vomits tar-black due to the coffee, sour on the back of his tongue, watching it break apart and float away into the void of the Arctic.

The workday moderately successful. Cooler full of cleaned fish. Travis tired in his bones. They dock the boat and crack open beers, Smitty getting froth all over his beard. Travis blinking away any queasiness. Feeling good, worthy, semi-formed again. Stu had been right as usual.

"Got a few fish packed away for your family," Smitty says, nodding at a tiny cooler beside the giant one.

"You don't have to, Smitty."

"I know. You earned it." He clinks his bottle against Travis's. "So tomorrow again at the ass crack of dawn?"

Travis grins. "Yeah. Cool, man."

"I tell ya, you're a lot more reliable than Old Charlie and smell a ton better."

Travis sniffs his collar. "Woof, jury's out on that."

"Finish your brew so I can get these salmon to The Angler in Nome."

Smitty raises his nose with his dirty finger at the mention of the place.

On the way home, the inside of the pickup full of a wafting fish aroma. The winding road empty like in the morning, but not lonely, simply still. Travis's fingers stiff on the wheel, blistering pink. His eyes swelling with tears, the alien salt stinging. Not tears of sadness, this he decides. He won't let them be anything more than a body's way of letting go.

9

For two days now, Wyatt has developed a pattern for studying the Barlows. He leaves the abandoned goods store long before dawn. The trek through the dark woods a contemplative meditation. Fingernail of the moon guiding the way. From behind a thicket of bushes, he watches Trav parting before sunrise. When he's ready, he'll follow to see where he goes. But California and the child are the immediate spotlight.

The child joins her in bed once the father has gone. She's more loving with him, extending her arms to the boy as opposed to curled up in the fetal position with Trav present. Maybe Trav makes love to her at night, but never in the morning. If she were Wyatt's, he'd make love to her at all times.

Mother and child remain in that haze between sleep and reality until the sun makes its presence known, careening into the bedroom and bathing it in a glow. They snuggle for a while, the child usually with his eyes closed, California running her pale fingers through his hair. Wyatt wonders if his own family had mimicked the same ritual in his absence.

They wake and separately urinate. She makes eggs and uses an instrument that browns bread, smears it with butter. Fruit sits in a type of cold box, always fresh, a daily miracle. She clutches a steaming cup, allows the aroma to enliven her senses.

The first day he waited until they came back with the sun about to set. He decided he'd use the sun as a marker, giving it another day to be positive that their absence for many hours isn't a fluke. The second day became a duplicate of the first. Now on the third, he takes a chance and enters.

From studying the house, he assesses its penetrability. A back door with a screen. Sometimes she leaves the door open with only the screen as a blockade, but only when home. If she's gone, it stays shut and locked. The dog could pose a problem, but instead of barking it barely acknowledges him at the door, more interested in its flavored bone.

He's aware of his putrid smell so he must be careful. California disappears into the room where she urinates, the child occupied in front of the box with moving pictures. He slides in, slithering down to the basement. Knowing she has never gone down there before, at least on his watch. He lingers until the water rushing through the pipes settles. Her bath is done. She puts on music. He hears the sound of footsteps across the ceiling, then a door slam and lock and the pitter-patter of their car starting. He has learned this word when he asked about it to someone in town. The man responded with a curious eyebrow, thought he was joking. Wyatt feigned drunkenness and so the man explained about a car, a magical vehicle that uses gasoline to move people around. Horses seem to be no longer necessary. The future—a wheel spinning through everyone's palms. It both scared and excited Wyatt, unsure which feeling affected him more.

He ascends from the basement. The home beams the after-scent of her perfume, not lilac like his beloved, even sweeter. California douses herself in candy. These past few days he's lost Adalaide and Joe more and more, desperate to get them back. This intrusion necessary for his sanity. Swearing to be as careful as possible, he attempts his first move. A bath of his own. Wanting to rid of the stench he's carried for too long. He carefully strips naked, placing his clothes in the machine he's seen her use. She always adds some type of liquid, and in a half an hour, the clothes are washed then put it a different machine to dry. He presses a few buttons until it whirs, the echo of his old rags slapping around.

In the bathing room, he decides it should be called an in-house since all he knows are outhouses. He tests out the spigots that pour forth water. First too hot, then too cold. Finally, just right. He slides his battered body in once the water reaches a level to his liking. Instantly soothing, his muscles relax, stress dissolving down the drain. He squeezes the bottles surrounding the rim into the water and delights at the bubbles arising. Washing every nook and cranny. Washing away the last hundred years of immovability.

Drip-drip from the faucet, no clue how long he's pruned. Imagining he could stay here in this home of bubbles, California returning to witness all of him. Standing up with his manhood swinging from side to side, her eyes fixated, tongue lapping—this simulacrum who looks like her husband, kept on ice and alluringly revealed. She'd join their never-ending soak, nipples pink and upright, skin like cream, vagina a lighthouse bringing him in from the dark. "I love you, Wyatt," roaring from her songbird lips. A new Joe incubating in her belly afterwards.

A bell rings and startles, breaking his fantasy. Wrapping a towel around his waist, he searches for the source. An instrument bleats, attached to the wall. He's seen her talking into this like a madwoman. Eventually, it stops. The wash is complete so he moves the clothes into the drying machine, wet towel included. He paces the house naked, envisioning himself as the owner of these walls. On the mantle, a photograph of the family begs to be stolen. He removes it from the frame to find a duplicate copy, which he'll keep. That way he could be transported back to his era at any moment. He bends the picture so Trav isn't visible anymore. The dryer finishes and he takes out his clothes, cotton-scented clean. Even caked snow and gunk no longer on the rubber boots.

The dog joins him on the rug, curl of its tongue hot against his cheek. Does it believe him to be Trav? Regardless, the first contact of any kind sets him afire. Blood running warm again. He tickles the dog behind the ears and it goes crazy. Pawing at him, wrestling around. He hugs it for security, for sanity, weeping at anything that shows love, this other species who sensed his blues.

He ends the day in their bedroom, a quick nap on the bed, the sheets heaven. Outside the sun bobs lower, indicating that it's time to go. He curses at its insistence but knows it's wiser than he. Retracing his steps, he makes sure he has not left any sign of his intrusion. He gives one last look at the Barlows' lives, avowing that soon he'll be invited inside so he can truly work at infesting.

The door slams shut as if only the wind had knocked it closed.

10

Miss Evelyn's craftsman home has a heavy-columned front porch, front-facing gables, and overhanging eaves, a nod to the early twentieth century. To Callie, it always appears cozy, another reason she approves of Eli spending half the week here ever since Travis started working again. For the other two days, she drops him off at the Huskie Day Center where he gets to socialize with a dozen other toddlers. But Callie likes Miss Evelyn better since she watches him free of charge.

Miss Evelyn's been widowed as long as Callie has lived in Laner, her husband having a debilitating stroke he never quite recovered from before passing. Her twin children go to the university in Anchorage but only visit on breaks. She lives off Harry's pension, the mortgage on the home already paid, a lifestyle far from lavish. If Callie ever felt Eli becoming an imposition, she'd insist on paying. But Miss Evelyn appears overjoyed to babysit so she assumes it a fair trade.

"There's my little monster," Miss Evelyn says, as Eli marches inside like he owns the place.

"Grrrr," Eli says, turning his hands into paws.

Callie finds Miss Evelyn has a gracious aura. Cheeks like a gopher, permanent stretched smile, hair sometimes in pigtails like a small girl. When she chuckles, her whole body seems to roll. And she chuckles a lot.

"I made a boo drawing!" Eli says, whipping out a piece of paper that looks like dark smears instead of an animal.

"Caribou," Callie tells her. "We've been eating it all week. Travis hunted one."

"Oh my!" Miss Evelyn chuckles. "What a boo! Was it yummy?"

Eli rubs his stomach while humming.

"I have a new book to read to you that came in the mail yesterday,

Eli. It doesn't have a caribou in it, but it does star a wolf!"

"I like wolves too. Chinook is a wolf."

"Oh, precious," Miss Evelyn says, tousling his hair.

"Thanks as always, Miss Evelyn."

"Nonsense. Can I make ya a coffee for the road? Seem tired this morning."

Callie nods at Eli who's already running around the area rug pretending he's a wolf. "Every morning."

"Ah, he'll be as tall as you before you know it. Then gone."

"I know, I know. Thanks for the coffee but gotta run."

"Bye, Mommy!" Eli howls. "I'm a wolf!"

"Bye, my wolf," she says, blowing a kiss.

Pizza Joint does a barebones breakfast but has its regulars. Callie likes the early shift, home by no later than six. The tips might not be as good as the dinner rush but it's easier on her feet. They do an egg sandwich, or a bowl of oatmeal, sometimes pancakes if the cook is feeling generous. Mostly catering to fisherman in after their first haul for a hot coffee, or some of the elderly townsfolk eager for conversation.

Lorinda's owned the Joint for a decade, long before Callie arrived in Laner, Lorinda's family going back three generations here. Everyone in Laner seems to have a story of their Alaskan heritage except for Callie. In some ways this causes people to be drawn to her, but it also keeps her at a distance. Always seen as a Cheechako. She'll never quite be one of them.

"Girl, we *need* to talk," Lorinda says, grabbing Callie's arm and whisking her away from the cook at the counter. Roy's old and mostly mute, keeps his head down and his eggs and pizza dough fluffy.

"What is it, Lor?"

She finds herself enraptured by Lorinda's jet-black hair, so silky smooth, straight out of a shampoo commercial. Lorinda always ready for the runway, as Callie would say.

"This requires a cig," Lorinda says, squeezing her eyes closed. "Roy, we're taking five."

Roy waves them away without looking up from the eggs on the grill.

Outside the wind whips, Callie chilly in her fleece since she left her coat inside. Lorinda in a tank, impervious to the cold. *Alaskan blood,* Callie thinks.

"Grayson was texting me all night!" Lorinda cries, frustrated from being unable to light her cig.

"I got you." Callie cups her hands around the lighter as the flame finally sticks. The cherry glows and Lorinda inhales hard.

"Stalker much?" Lorinda laughs, and Callie knows that Lorinda enjoys complaining about something. Lorinda holds up the phone as evidence, bubbles of never-ending texts one after the other. She flips through them. "I love you, I want you, I need you. You're making a huge mistake. Blah, blah, blah. Like this is my fault."

"You never told me why he—"

Tuck and Jesse appear as if invoked out of thin air.

"Didn't mean to startle," Jesse says, hands shoved in his pockets, never able to meet Callie's gaze.

"Well, go inside, fellas," Lorinda snaps. "We're talking girl things." She kicks Tuck in the butt as the two men scooch inside the Joint.

"That Jesse has eyes for you," Lorinda says.

"Travis would murder him."

"I don't doubt it." Suck, blow, ash, repeat. "So, I caught Grayson at that…house of ill repute. The one all the police boys go to."

"Was he just there or did you catch him…in the act?"

"Girl, I don't give a hard rat damn. I'm older than you by almost a decade and I got about six years on Grayson. Things are starting to go south."

"Lorinda, you're a knockout."

"Every girl at that place is in their early twenties. Asses you can bounce dimes off of. Even if he only entertained…"

"You don't think the two of you can work it out? You guys have had ups and downs before."

"Exactly," Lorinda says, poking the cigarette at the breeze. "Too many hills and valleys with that prick. And just so you know, his prick ain't all that. He's all bark."

"Travis says he's distraught."

"I'm surprised Gray even knows the definition of that word. Point is, that ain't the only time he was at that house. I was talking to one of the girls. Aylen. Pretty little thing. Native American."

"She lives with that sketchy cousin of hers on the mini reservation on the outskirts, right?"

"Whole family is a bunch of sketch. Anyway, for twenty bucks, she spilled. He comes in for hand jobs. I'm like, you *moron*. Who the hell even wants a hand job? I never even attempted them since I didn't think we were in eighth grade. He could've just told me that's what tickled his fancy."

"It's the thrill of the secret," Callie says. "That's what tickles him."

"Well, it ain't no secret that his clothes are in a snow heap on my porch. And he can keep his dumb cat too. That bitch is always giving me the side-eye."

"Give me one of those," Callie says, snatching a cigarette and relishing in a drag. Lorinda's still cackling away but Callie has tuned her out. The snow coating the trees beginning to melt and Callie can finally see green. What she misses the most about California, if she's honest. Alaska encased in white for too much of the year, the sensation of being trapped—like she's been on ice too. The longer she stays, the more claustrophobic she feels.

"Girl, where has your mind gone?" Lorinda snaps, knocking knuckles against Callie's skull.

"Travis went back to work."

"At the oil refinery? I thought there were no openings."

"Smitty's boat. Cleaning fish."

"Well," is all Lorinda has to say about that.

"It's a job," Callie says. "I admire him for putting his ego aside."

"He still moody as fuck?"

"Lorinda! No, he...he's actually been better this week."

"I'm teasing. I'd kill for a man like Travis. At least he's home with you and not out chasing all kinds of poontang."

Lorinda ashes the cig against the door, then swings it open and stomps inside. Callie stays, enjoying her solitary moment, one of the few she ever gets. When she was younger as an only child, she sought company every chance she had. Now she finds herself longing for stillness, of a day without anyone to talk to, nestled up in her own head with the delight of letting her thoughts roam. They float to the land of *what ifs*, since she can travel anywhere. Maybe she never left L.A., still went to castings, still tried to make it. She was talented. She knew it, but so was every girl in their twenties. She'd played Emily in her high school production of *Our Town* and her acting teacher said she had potential. She scored a line in an indie movie after graduating, skipped college, but never landed an agent or another role. Did some modeling and always felt like she was slumming. Rejections became nuisances. That's what the Cali sun started to represent, a spotlight of failure. So she drifts back to the here and now, blinking to a cascade of flurries. Docked in her white world. Oceans away from who she used to be.

She inhales one final drag. Inside she tends to Tuck and Jesse's table. Tuck does all the talking. Egg sandwiches with ham and American cheese for both, monster coffees heavy on the caffeine. She smiles and jokes and flips her hair, keeping Jesse in her gaze. He's younger, barely more than a teen, lean muscles and shy eyes. In a flash, she's mounted him, no idea where that mindfuck came from. She and Travis haven't made love in a while. He was acting too glum when bedtime rolled around, too wiped from work this week. Tonight, she'll seduce him, even if his fingernails still smell of fish guts.

"Orders coming up, boys," she says, giving them a show as she bounces over to the kitchen. A little spice sprinkled in an otherwise bland Thursday. No harm, no foul.

"Owoooo," she howls at a low hum, picturing Eli prancing around Miss Evelyn's as a wolf.

She can be one too.

11

A surprise for Travis, that's what he's been promised. First Callie orders a bath once they put Eli down. Not just a shower, a full scrub. The ocean heavy in his pores, body overloaded with salt, fish guts etched in fingerprints. He hasn't taken a bath in ages, the last time probably with her pre-Eli. When they lived more impulsively. When routine hadn't gotten in the way of lust. The soap bar finds every last bit of grime. He's gentle with the scars along his chest from when he was a little boy and a stray cat on their property scratched him up good. He had gone to pet the cat, not realizing it was protecting its baby kitten, a tiny wet nub of fur.

When he finishes, he wraps a towel around his waist and finds Callie in lingerie on the bed striking a pose like a mermaid rising from the sea.

They don't speak, words only killing the mood. Any distance between them eradicated by exploring tongues, contorted positions. But they never look at each other, pleasure overriding a true connection. He lies in a pool of their sweat wanting to vocalize his fears as well as his yearnings. She's his best friend and also his greatest mystery. He knows that's what they have most in common—she can say the same.

She rests in the crook of her arm, hair cascading over her throat. When she miscarried after having Eli, she didn't want to be touched. But they waded through that, or at least he thought. He'd mourned the idea of the child, but she dealt with the physical loss, the awful draining. He gave her the space she required, let her be the one to circle back. And she did, just like now. But was she ever really present, or does she tag a duplicate in their bed while she escapes into her mind? Traveling beyond their little Alaskan lives. It kills him to imagine her tanning on a California beach. Would she have been happier if they never met?

"I love you, Cal," he says, but not all words have meanings. His are empty sounds, hanging in the air anticipating the same response. And so, she does. She always will. He knows she loves him more than she's loved anyone else, save Eli. But sometimes love just ain't enough. He's heard her singing that song before. He's sung it himself like a hymn.

He turns the lamp off, and they both shiver from the soaked sheets.

A warmer day on the *Cutthroat*. Travis holds onto the good from last night, discards the bad. Callie had made an effort and he didn't pull away. That's a start. Tonight's another chance to link. Smitty boasting a tall tale of the biggest salmon he's ever caught, size of a big kid. Net wouldn't cut it so he had to reel that sucker in. Both fighting for their lives, since the fish might've been strong enough to yank Smitty overboard, send him into the pounding waves. And then a divine intervention—hand of God taking his side—the salmon not standing a chance. Wouldn't eat that fish once it was caught for anything. After photo ops, he keeps it mounted on a wall, a reminder of touching greatness.

"We only get a few of those in life," Smitty says, leaving black oil stains on his sandwich but eating it without regard.

"Few of what?" Travis asks, gnawing at a caribou bone.

"When we leave our bodies and watch wonder unfold. Those moments we go back to, again and again when we need them the most. When times get tough."

"Yeah," Travis says, trying to think of his own. Wedding day. Eli's birth. But everyone has those similar moments. Doesn't he have any that are unique? "Yeah," he keeps saying. Figuring that if he agrees, Smitty will let it go faster.

He gnaws on the bone until no flesh remains.

Beers afterwards at Elson's. The sun hasn't set yet as they inch closer to spring, in breakup season now. Tuck and Jesse already at the bar, only suds left in their steins. They speak of the day's catches, the successes and failures. Discuss purse seines and cork lines, lead weights and which boats are best. Which fish are already seeming bountiful this year and which may be endangered. Grayson moseys up like he's stepped out of some Western, laying his holster on the counter.

"Keep 'em comin' tonight, Elson," Grayson says, his eyelids twitching.

"Worked a double."

"And what were the people in Laner up to today?" Tuck asks, signaling Elson for another.

"Hiker got lost in Burr woods, damn near lost a toe from frostbite. Speeder on Route 78. Moose sighting on Main."

"No shit?" Jesse asks, face-palming.

"I said, *sighting*. Turns out it was Old Charlie wasted off homemade hooch, no actual moose."

"I cut him off around two in the afternoon," Elson says.

"You know it's worse cutting him off," Grayson says.

"I ain't gonna be responsible for alcohol poisoning," Elson says, spitting into a glass and signaling the end of that conversation.

A few beers later, the men are all toasty. Leaning on each other and singing whatever song's on the juke. Grayson veers between exuberant and hateful, alcohol often bringing out the best and worst of his personality. He picks at Jesse's virgin-like ways. Tuck's spare tire. Smitty's hobo beard. Everyone but Elson, his beer supplier.

"I think you've had enough, buddy," Travis says, when Grayson tries to order. Travis eyes Elson, and Elson agrees with a blink.

"I'm the law," Grayson thunders.

"Yes, yes we know this," Travis says. "And you have the biggest dick of us all."

"Want me to prove it?" Grayson says, starting to unzip.

"No, no, no," Travis says. "That's all you need, man, is for someone to video it. Don't give Stu any ammunition."

"Your dad's a cock," Grayson says.

"Now I know you don't mean that. You love him like he was your own father."

"Yup, I do," Grayson slurs. "Oh shit—*her*."

"What?"

"Her!"

A wavering finger points toward a young woman at the end of the bar alone on a stool. Long black hair down to her waist. Elegant neck with a jutted chin, hazelnut eyes, tanned and exotic skin.

"What did you tell her?" Grayson shouts. Before Travis can restrain him, Grayson bounds toward the woman's stool. She responds by pivoting in place. He grabs her elbow and she yanks it back.

"I don't want to be involved," she says, baring teeth.

"Too late. Lorinda said she talked to you."

"I don't tell lies."

"What happens in that house should stay in that house," Grayson says, his face angry red. "She broke up with me."

"It's not my problem!"

She grabs her denim purse, leaves ten bucks on the bar, and swivels out of his grasp.

"Watch your friend better," she tells Travis, as she whisks past. The door swings open wildly and she's gone into the night.

"Fucking bitch," Grayson slurs.

"What's this about?" Travis asks.

"You get him out of here," Elson yells.

"C'mon, c'mon, buddy," Travis says. He pays their tab and drags Grayson to the door. He's afraid of encountering the woman once they get outside, but she's smart enough to vanish. He knows of this house where she works. Run by a madam named Raye, full of roaming girls. He's driven by before to big band music pumping from the windows, a relic of another time. Raye liking her place to be steeped in the past. Cell phones required to be left at the door. At least from what he's heard.

"Car's over there," Grayson says, sticking his chin into the wind.

"Sorry, buddy, but neither of us are capable of driving. Walk'll be good."

They head through the woods, Grayson's house about a half mile from Travis's. Band of moon lighting their way. Crackle of ice and snow melting. Trees unfreezing and breathing again.

"I loved her," Grayson says, falling back on his ass and struggling to get up like a turtle on its back.

"You don't know what love is," Travis tells him.

"Enlighten me."

"You wouldn't have gone to a house like that if you loved her."

"Why do sex and love always have to be intertwined?"

Travis bursts out laughing, never hearing his friend speak so poetically before.

"I mean, I can love Lorinda, right? But I can get pleasure from another. Why is that not okay?"

"It just isn't."

"C'mon, you ain't never thought of another woman other than Callie? You're no saint."

"I've never strayed."

"You never would?"

The question lingers, the woods preventing it from escaping. The answer being *no*, but could that question ever be answered honestly? Circumstances change, opportunities arise, love fluctuates.

"Let's get you home, bud," Travis says, pulling Grayson to his feet.

"You're my bud, Trav. My one true bud. This world is better because of you."

"All right now."

"There should be multiple yous," Grayson says, outlined by the moonlight, a blue phantasm. "So you can help solve all of our problems. So you can help solve all the world's problems."

"Are you done?"

Grayson gives a definitive nod.

"Yes, yes I am, sweet Trav. Sweet Trav aplenty."

12

Routine grows tiresome, or maybe Wyatt's just reached a type of exhaustion he's unable to return from. Awake with dawn, no shades covering the windows to block the intrusive sun. A picture of California and the boy tucked in a groove on the kitchen counter, the first thing he'll spy upon opening his eye. By having their photo so close, Adalaide and Little Joe should permeate his dreams. But his dreams have been a void, motionless and lacking any substance. Stomach growls once he has the energy to stand. Limping to Elson's Pub to rifle through the trash before it's picked up. A mish-mash of food, unable to discern what he's eating. Only that it's cold and doesn't nourish.

He's wanted to trek to the Barlows' house, but the journey through the woods has become an impossible task. He's too weary to attempt. A common beggar now, vacillating down Main Street from store to store, cracked palms out in supplication while heads turn away. Back to the abandoned goods store for a nap that lasts until dark. The night streaming in primed to destroy any progress, encasing him back in a frigid jar.

After a few rounds of this torture, he's zapped with a tiny bolt of extra energy one morning. Elson's trash also supplies better food than before, not only scraps but almost a full leftover meal he consumes with fury. Wavering between heading to the Barlows' and trying to scrounge for change, he opts for the money. A warm meal more beneficial than all else. This is his mission. And he accepts.

Not many folks are out and it's colder than last week. The wind whipping. Green leaves hiding behind layers of silt snow. Shivering outside of the pub, hoping for a drunk soul to take pity. All of them with booze on their minds and nothing else.

And then he sees a woman leaving Elson's. She's tottering from side to side. Long hair like a curtain swept over her left shoulder with a viscous thickness. Neither a smile nor a frown, emotionally indifferent, already battered by the day. Injun look to her, not that he minds. The idea of distancing himself from Adalaide for a moment of reprieve. She wears a multi-patterned coat, hexagonal shapes interspersed with what appears to be wind sails, hallucinatory. She can tell he's watching, averts her lips a millimeter into more of a smile.

"You seem cold," she says, crouching down until she's at his level.

Cold is all I know, he wants to tell her. But he phrases it with more levity: "I'm an ice man."

"Well, Mr. Ice Man. I can help you get warm."

She maneuvers the curtain of hair to her other shoulder, combs it with her fingers like it's a loom.

"You're beautiful."

His teeth chatter, limbs trembling beyond control.

"Come with me," she says, this brilliant buoy that's found him adrift. She hoists him to his feet, catching his large body in her woolen arms. "I know a place that can make you toasty again."

An old Victorian house, paint chipped and crumbling facade. The interior full of scented wax, sharp perfumes. Shutters closed as if the world doesn't exist outside. Nearly brings him to tears, this newfound cocoon. There's a cobwebbed bar by the entrance, liquor bottles tinted with dust. A blond woman smokes from a cigarette holder, the vapors clouding her face. His paramour leads him upstairs, each step a whining creek, a dimly lit hallway and a room at the end with yellow light pouring from the doorjamb.

Smell of sweet sweat when they arrive. A bed sagging in the corner, sheets in disarray. A heater spits steam. He runs his cracked hands over the mist, hot air shooting through his bloodstream, a great melting occurring. She strikes a match, touches it to the wick of a candle. A woodsmoke aroma torches the room.

"It's a hundred for whatever you want, Ice Man."

"This is a brothel?"

She cackles into her fist. "Best in Laner, possibly in all of Alaska."

"I have no..." He takes a deep breath that robs all of his energy. "I have no money."

Now her lips slant downwards, a serious frown developing. "Should've known you were homeless and not just a drunk drifter." She blows out the candles in disgust. Hazelnut eyes filled with ire. "Out," she says, with her thumb directed at the door.

The ground swells. He finds standing laborious, longing to lie in her messy sheets and turn off his mind. Digging through his pockets, he procures the last golden nugget he owns.

"It's real," he pleads.

She hops over, disbelieving. Once she holds it in her hands, her face tells a different story.

"Gotta be worth more than what you usually charge," he says.

The door had been left open but now she closes it. She pockets the gold, thrusts a fingernail between his eyes.

"I'm only doing this because it's a slow day and you're so pitiful."

She wrenches off her coat like it's a chore. A shirt gets tossed in a pile next. Stands before him without a bra, nipples dark and large as stones.

"No, no, I…" Struggles to formulate his thoughts. "Can we simply lie in bed together?"

She scrunches her face. "No nookie?"

He crawls on hands and knees to her bed, folds himself inside, the sheets like clouds. A pillow cradling his head after not being supported for over a century. Stiff neck doesn't even begin to describe the pain.

She shrugs, eternally bored. Lying beside him while the heater whistles a dirge. He pets her never-ending mane of hair.

"What's your name?"

"Aylen."

"Is that your real name?"

She studies her nails, more enraptured with them. "Only one I've been given."

"Wyatt Barlow here."

"You're certainly strange, Wyatt Barlow."

"I'm sure I've been called worse."

"Is that a challenge?"

"I'm not from here," he says, looking out of the window as if it could guide him to his past.

"Where from?"

"A different time."

She cackles again, a bird-like toot through her nostrils. "Is that so? And what time was that?"

"Long before you or your father or your father's father or even his father was born."

"My father was a dick and I'm sure his father's father was the same. Lots of drunks. Walked out on me when I could barely crawl. You sure you don't want to touch me a little? Lot more fun than yapping."

"I...like talking to you. I haven't really had company in a long time."

"There you go speaking of *time* again. I think you've got a fixation."

"I just want to get back to when I'm supposed to be from."

She cups his massive hands, directs one toward her breast. She does the fondling for him.

"I have a wife."

"So do most of the men that come here. I don't judge."

"I love her."

"I'm sure you do. This don't mean you love her any less."

"You have an Injun look to you. That's the first thing I thought when I saw ya."

She lets go of his hand, her mouth grasping for what to say. "No golden nugget is worth some racist bullshit."

"I don't know those words. I...was makin' an observation."

"We're not called Injun, asshole. It's Native American."

"Doesn't make sense."

"You don't make no sense."

She fishes for the golden nugget from her pocket, ready to give it back.

"No, no, please. I apologize. I told you, I'm not from your time. I don't know the right things to say. Please lie back down."

He pats the bed. She hesitates, but gold trumps all else. He's been poisoned just as much by its lure.

"All right. Native American, that's what you're called in 2019. I won't make the same mistake."

"This is something you should've learned long ago. But I'll play along with your time travel story. When are you from?"

"1898. Came to this area for the Gold Rush and believe I never left."

"What have you been doing since then?"

"Thawing."

She plays with her areolas, pinching until the nipples harden.

"You don't have to do that," he says. "Really."

"Men back then didn't like sex?"

"I told you I love my wife."

"If your story's true she'd be about one hundred and fifty. Hate to break it to you, but don't think she's still around."

A layer of frost coats the window blurring the outside. Between the lit candles and a song playing downstairs from what sounds like a phonograph, he's transported. Modern world disintegrated. No Adalaide or Joe—but their bed materializes. What it was like to descend into its sheets after a long and arduous expedition. The caress of home after one has been beaten. Covered in hot towels to soothe aching limbs. Adalaide beside him with a bucket tending to his sores. Maybe abandoning them wasn't the last time he saw either one. He could've returned only to leave again, hopefully with her blessing.

"Where did you go?" Aylen asks, snapping her fingers in front of his nose.

"I saw her," he says, enchanted. Reaching for Adalaide, but she's already dissolved.

"Who's that, honey?"

"My wife."

Salty sting of tears, figuring he's wept more in the past few days than in a lifetime prior. He wipes them away, ashamed.

"I'm sorry for crying."

"You ain't the first to do that in this bed. Usually it's after sex though."

This entices a smile out of him.

"Ah, you can express emotions other than grumpy." She digs an elbow into the mattress, rests her head in her palm. "Tell me about her. What was her name?"

"Adalaide."

"Very pretty name. What was she like?"

He goes to say what should come naturally, but finds himself at a loss. How to describe someone who only exists in a few memories? She's nothing more than a fog.

"I don't know." His hands shake and this scares him, her too. "I'm trying to get back to her, my son as well. I believe the last time we spoke I wasn't kind."

"Memories aren't always what really happened. I'm sure you're being hard on yourself."

"My son was sick. He's always cold and we don't know why. Instead of being there for him, I came here. For gold!"

"Did you find that gold at least? Beyond a nugget?"

He has a fantasy of digging through snow. Fingers blistered. Fear throbbing throughout his chest. A hole in the earth and gold shoved deep down. Its brilliant shine covered until it was fully unearthed. He surfaces from this passage, head spinning, nausea creeping. Clinging to Aylen just to maintain.

"I have these visions," he says, gumming his dry mouth. "But you say that memories aren't always what happened, so I don't know if they're real."

She pulls him to her bosom as if he's a tiny child. "Come. Rest."

His cheek sticks to her breast from the boiling temperature of the room. They are fused together. She massages his temples, sends him into a deep sleep, further down than since he awakened. There's a tunnel he finds, a direct line. A giant ship docked that he runs to catch, its sails flapping from battering gusts and welcoming him aboard. But the tunnel only allows a picture of this like he's staring at a painting. He's unable to board, however it's more real than any mirage he's had thus far.

This ship being what brought him to the present, that he's certain. He must find a way to get on for it holds clues to where he departed from and possibly what happened once he arrived.

"Hush, Mr. Ice Man," he hears a lovely siren sing from the sky. "Rest your weary eye."

13

Travis drives his family five miles through an unseasonably late blizzard for a Sunday night dinner at Stu and Cora's, since Papa Clifford wasn't feeling well enough to make it to their house last week. The weather proving fickle. Eli difficult to bundle up again after being free from his snowsuit for days. Callie cursing the blinding whiteness. Travis wondering if the *Cutthroat* will be able to head out tomorrow.

"You're liking the job, aren't you?" Callie asks. She clutches a jade crystal hanging from her neck.

"Tell your crystals to make the snow go away."

"They don't work like that."

He knows he's joking, but can see it hurts her some. Callie believes wholeheartedly while Travis lives fully by logic. He's never been able to stretch his mind.

"It's only been a week or so," he says, squinting to see the road ahead. All he needs is a moose to pop out of nowhere. Laner filled with stories of car crashes related to wildlife on dimly lit roads. "But yeah, I'm doing well. Smitty's got me fishing some, as well as scooping out guts. And we shoot the shit all day. I've really missed being out on the water."

"I know you have. I could tell."

"Hey, Little Man," Travis calls out behind him. Eli's iPad bathing his face in artificial light. "You miss me?"

No response.

"That damn iPad. Eli, I'm gonna throw it out the window."

Travis reaches behind, fumbling to try to grab it.

"Nooooooooo!" Eli screeches.

"Travis, let him play," Callie says.

"Stu would've smacked me when I was Eli's age if I didn't respond."

"Well, we don't smack kids no more. That's not a thing."

"Everyone's so sensitive now. No one can say boo to their kids anymore."

"Boo!" Eli screams, making them both jump.

"Eli, keep your voice down."

"Boo!" Eli yelps, as Travis slams on the brakes inches from a moose in the middle of the road. Staring back as if it could care less if they'd run it over.

"Jesus titty-fucking Christ," Travis says, gulping his breath. His fingers fusing to the wheel. He pries them off.

Callie had lunged for his arm, gripping it tight. She too unclenches. The blipping noise from Eli's iPad the only sound except for the spiraling flakes against the hood.

The moose smacks his gums and sashays into the woods, thoroughly unaffected by the ordeal.

"Are you all right?" Travis asks. "Is everyone okay?"

Callie swivels around to find Eli just as impervious as the moose.

"He's fine," she says. "He doesn't care."

"I was thinking about a moose," Travis says. "Right before it happened."

"Let's just get going before the car stalls."

She massages her forehead, as if she's working on a burgeoning headache.

"Right before. I thought about a crash, Callie."

"Okay. So? You foretold this. Is that what you're saying? You're the one who never allows yourself to believe in the uncanny."

Callie fingers her crystal and looks over at Travis, but he's gone inward. He plays out the crash in his mind. The moose weighing more than the car and standing firm while the car is thrown into the woods. A giant tree slicing through the windshield. A thick branch spearing through Callie and Eli like a skewer.

And Travis, left behind to sweep up their pieces.

At Travis's folks' place, Callie can't stop talking about the moose. How it appeared out of nowhere. How Travis braked inches from its snout. They're all waiting while the stew Cora made heats up: Stu with a Rob Roy aperitif, Travis lost in a cold beer, Eli scribbling doodles, Papa

Clifford in the bathroom since they arrived.

"Is he okay?" Callie asks, indicating the bathroom.

Cora blushes. "Stopped up from all the new meds he's taking. Sometimes he'll go through the whole *Alaskan Dispatch* in there."

"Cora, you don't have to paint a picture," Stu says, spinning out of his seat. "I'll check on him."

Once Stu's out of ear range, Cora's voice drops *sotto voce*. "He's been so sensitive about Papa. I think the fall really scared him."

"It was scary for all of us," Callie says.

They look over at Travis who's circling the rim of the bottle with his pinky.

"We lost you there, Travis," Cora says.

When Travis finally glances up, he appears as if he has no idea who he is or where he's landed.

"Baby," Callie says, tracing his thumb.

The toilet flushes, causing the hairs on the back of Callie's neck to sharpen. Stu leads Papa Clifford outside. In the scant days since they've seen him, Papa Clifford has withered. His arms riddled with sores, face sunken in. Thin where he used to be robust, a belt cinched tightly in an attempt to hold up his pants. Stu sees them start to slide down and catches in time.

"Hey Papa, it's good to see you," Callie says, raising her voice but still Papa doesn't hear.

Stu gets his father situated in a special chair at the table that supports his back.

"Everyone can stop gawking now," Papa Clifford says.

"No one's gawking," Cora says. "We're all just happy to see you."

He twists his lips at her and waves to Eli. "There's my boy."

Eli's still doodling but Callie lifts up his chin. "Eli, say hi to Papa Clifford."

"Hi, Papa."

"What'cha drawing?"

Eli shrugs. "Boos and stuff."

"The kids were almost in an accident on the ride over," Cora says. "Moose on the road."

"Huh?"

"*Moose* on the road."

"A caboose? Haven't rode one of those since the fifties."

"No, a..."

"I heard you the first time. Just fuckin' with ya."

The table all chuckles.

"Dad, you'll never change," Stu says, his hand on Papa's shoulder like he's afraid of letting go.

"And you, sonny?" Papa says to Travis. "What's your deal?"

"Sorry, Papa," Travis says, spiraling back to normal or at least faking it well.

Cora fetches the stew she made, bison with red wine and sweet bay. Callie wants to say she's been eating caribou all week and could barely stomach the idea of more wild game, but she nibbles mostly at the potatoes and carrots so as not to hurt Cora's feelings. Cora's too busy trying to feed Papa Clifford to notice.

"They told me you got a new job, Travis," Papa says, swatting Cora's hand away when she tries to come at him with a fork. "Lady, I can do it myself."

"We've gotta put meat on your bones," Cora says, but Stu gives her a signal to let it go.

Callie spies the three empty bottles by Travis's plate and the fourth in his hand, figuring she'll be the one driving home.

"It's work," Travis says.

"Good you're back on water," Papa says. "Barlows are meant to be on water. That's how we got to Laner."

"You want to tell us the story?" Cora asks.

"I don't know what *the* story is, but I can wrestle through my mind for one. Father traveled up from Washington State, this was in the twenties. Said the land pulled at him to come, at least that was what my mother told us. Never really knew the man. But we settled and almost a hundred years later, we're still here. Then Mother caught pneumonia while I was stationed in Germany fighting the devil. Returned to my sister Rose gone mad. She wound up in an institution over in Juneau, shock treatments and the like but they never took. I met Frannie the day Rose was taken away. That good woman saved me. And now she's in high heaven. None of you can know what it's like to be the oldest person you know. I've lived too long."

"Don't say that, Papa," Cora chides, shaking her head.

"I don't mean I'm ready to string up a noose and call it a day. But I'll..." He stops, eyes creaming over. "I'll wake up sometimes and for a second I'm young again. When I'm still connected to my dreams. But then my body reminds me of its decay. Worst feeling ever."

Cora massages Papa's veiny hand, the blood rushing to her face.

"Now, now, Papa. Maybe we can think of a better story."

"No, I shouldn't complain. Isn't a full life what we all aim for? I look at someone like Bobby and think, now that's just not okay. That's enough to make you truly ask God why."

Stu sucks at his cheek, then quietly gets up. He pushes his chair into the table and exits the room.

"Papa," Cora says, in a nagging tone.

"What?" the old man asks.

Her mouth trembles. "Why did you have to…?"

"Ah, sorry, sometimes my mouth goes to where my mind tells me not to. Foolish, foolish of me."

Callie wants to say anything to help the situation, but understands that no words could suffice.

So she gives Papa a wink that makes him smile again.

"I'm gonna get a beer," Travis says, wanting to be far away from that table, his family, even lucidity.

In the kitchen, the cool of the refrigerator with the door open allows him to transport. He's out in the tundra where the world stills. He hasn't thought of Bobby all week ever since that first day out on the *Cutthroat*. Not to fault Papa Clifford, but his brother's the last thing he wants to think about tonight. Their entire clan swallowed up by the loss—Stu the worst. He bets Stu's down in the basement now, a madman's shrine devoted to any possible conspiracy.

Sure enough, when Travis descends, Stu's hunched over a crowded table lit by a tiny cone lamp. Browning newspapers surrounding like wallpaper. Bobby's name multiplied in Helvetica bold. Stu doesn't hear him come down, that's what madness does. Traps you. Better to recede up those stairs than join the funeral. So he leaves his father who's got his notepad out, marking up the margins with a black pen that never leaves his side. Travis longs to snap that pen, end the mystery by allowing the tragedy to remain an enigma—as callous as that might be.

Bobby never deserved this kind of obsession. Yet Travis's entire life had been centered around his parents attempting to prevent what had been destined to occur. And what destroyed him more than anything was thinking that his brother's death shouldn't be mourned, but justified.

Sometimes he wants to yell that in Stu's ear, except he doesn't have the heart to watch a man crumble.

14

Aylen injected life into Wyatt, but also robbed him even more of Adalaide. Upon exiting her house of women, he has even less a sense of his love. She withered in the night, a sacrifice for his sin. And he'd not been truly aberrant, holding onto Aylen's body but rebuffing advances for anything more. He surmises that the men who partake of her services must not be too kind because she let him lie there for hours. Downstairs, they could hear clientele getting drunk and frisky. But she remained burrowed in his bear arms, telling him stories of long ago that had been passed down to her from generations.

"Are you part of a tribe?" he had asked, still transfixed with her hair. How it ran through his fingers like silk.

"Tlingit...but not since I was a child." She'd rolled a cigarette, and in the dim dusk light, her face became obscured from the smoke. "There are very few of us left in this area. It's a matrilineal society and my mother has passed. I don't plan on having children so it ends with me."

"Why don't you want children?"

"In case you haven't realized, I'm a whore."

"You don't have to use such a crude term," he said. "And you do not have to do it forever."

"There's not much opportunity around these parts." She exhaled the smoke as if she were disgusted. "But Raye, the madam, is good to me. All of us. We're a family. I never had a family."

"I miss my family," he said, choking up. The words like nails in his throat.

"You really have a child?"

"Had."

"Oh, I'm sorry."

"Like you said, he would be well over a century old. There's no way he's still alive."

She scrunched up her nose. "You can drop the act."

"I do not know what that means."

"This time travel story. It was amusing, but you can be honest."

"I am."

She ashed her cigarette. "It's getting old. I'm growing tired of it."

"I didn't travel through time. Right before I left, I recall a book that came out titled the *Time Machine*. That's not what happened to me."

"All right, I'll humor you. What happened?"

"I was frozen. This I believe. I went hunting for gold in these parts and became suspended."

"Okay, but why did you unfreeze now?"

"This I do not know."

"So what's your goal?"

"Goal?"

"Your purpose. What do you want now?"

"To solve the mystery of who I am. Yes. I am slowly forming into my old self. I can feel him creeping back. But I still have a long way to go. And if I did discover gold before, I want to find it again."

"You're about a century too late."

"This I am afraid of. And I have accepted that. But the memories of my wife and child are the true gold I want to attain."

"That's rather lovely," she said, getting up and wrapping herself in a see-through lavender shawl. "I can bring you up a plate of food if you want. You look like you haven't had a good meal in about a hundred years."

She was out the door and he felt a stirring down below, but the stirring was not for Adalaide. He pictured Aylen floating through the sky cocooned in her lavender shawl. And before he could do anything, he came on her sheets, mystified by the arousal.

He quickly dressed and left before she could notice, forgoing a hot meal to protect his pride.

Back at the abandoned good store, the night passes in a fit. Wyatt clutches the picture of Adalaide and Joe but no memories resurface. He senses they exist in his brain but he's been denied access. It's been days since he's seen the Barlows, and he decides this must be the cause. Worth it to sacrifice sleep and trudge through the woods so he can arrive to their house as soon as possible.

The moon, his only friend, lights a glowing path. He follows its come-hither beckoning. Having made this journey multiple times, he can do it without much stress. The fear lies in the fact that the trick might not work anymore. The memories he's been given of Adalaide and Joe the only ones he's allowed.

The little house sits quietly. A creek bed lapping behind its yard. The curtains closed, denying any view. This he finds insulting. The doghouse empty and he's chilled so he crawls inside, a crudely made bed better than what he's been lying on in the abandoned store. Sleep proves difficult but he's not shivering since the doghouse has a flap for a door that blocks the wind.

He goes under momentarily, casting along choppy waters again. Shoulder to shoulder down below the deck with a hundred other wishful seekers. Stomach bloated with worms from turned fish for supper. His pack kept close to his chest for fear of it being stolen. No chance of turning back, destiny awaiting. Fantasies of glint gleaming in all their wide-awake eyes.

Coming to, his frozen eye causes pain. He's attempted to separate the top lid from the bottom but no measure has proven sufficient. The sun breaks through the cold morning, shining along the hoarfrost on the yard like it's lit with gold. His ear twitches at noises from inside the house. He could camp out and watch California and the child like always, but that's simply a bandage to the wound. He must follow Trav and figure out a way to ingratiate himself into the family.

Knowing Trav takes the pickup each morning, he dives in the back and covers himself with the tarp like before. Usually Trav has left prior to dawn breaking so he's lucky he didn't miss his chance. Door slams soon enough. The scruff of boots against the snow.

"See ya, Chinook," he hears Trav call out. A minute later, Trav gets in the pickup and they're off.

Trav likes music this morning, and Wyatt can identify with the singer's yearnings. A love gone lost. After a hundred years, nothing really changes. But he won't weep anymore, since he's doing all he can to get closer to his beloved.

The pickup stops amidst a din of gruff voices. Rollicking waves cutting. The air full of salt and fish. Cusp of the ocean. He peeks out of the tarp through a hole to see they've reached the docks. Burly fisherman mingling, their faces eaten up by beards like his own. Some drink from steaming cups. Others get their boats ready to attack the waters. The motor shuts off and he hears Trav step outside. After a moment, Trav's legs appear. Trav reaches down to tie a shoe, and while the two lookalike men don't lock eyes, Trav glances in his ancestor's vicinity. Wyatt clamps his breath shut, praying to a higher power that Trav doesn't remove the tarp. The shoe-tying seems endless, likely due to Trav's frozen fingers that can't get a good grip on the loop. Trav rubs a fleck of dust from his eyelash, and once it's discarded, he doesn't stare at Wyatt anymore. Their chance meeting thankfully postponed until the optimal time.

With lunch under his arm, Trav makes his way to a particularly burly man with an impressive beard and gut. The two appear jovial with each other, slapping each other playfully on their arms. Once they are far enough away, Wyatt jumps out from under the tarp and follows them down the dock to a boat called the *Cutthroat*, white bottom with a red trim. The men load up their supplies while Wyatt gets a chance to study Trav close up. He props himself on a bench no more than twenty feet away.

Now that he's seen his own reflection multiple times since his awakening, he's able to put it up against Trav's visage. He feels the slope of his own nose, both of them with an indented line down the middle. Prominent cheek bones and an identical touch of rosacea. Trav's beard maintained and trim but with the ability to sprout into a massive masterpiece like Wyatt's. Thick hair short and clean in the front and tickling the back of Trav's neck. Wyatt's fingers get caught up in the knots of his own mane. Thick thighs and stocky torso, strong shoulders made for physical labor like Wyatt's. A smile that nearly cuts Wyatt in two, this great-great grandson of his with no idea how close the past idles beside him. Wyatt longs to give him an engulfing hug, but he has more important plans. As Trav hops on the *Cutthroat* and the boat becomes untethered, rocking from the churning waves until it becomes a speck along the horizon amongst a dozen others, Wyatt takes out his notebook and flips to the front page with the date of 1898. He touches pen to paper, closes his good eye, and lets loose an outpouring. Tapping into over a century ago, his past illuminates—a brilliant show of colors and ancient but familiar sounds, tales of death-defying adventures that hopefully lead to elusive treasures.

15

I embark! After traveling by train from our Washington farm to Seattle, I board the *G.W. Elder*, a steamboat that will wind up the Panhandle and stop in Victoria, Nanaimo, Tongos, Wrangell, Juneau, Douglas, and Sitka. From there, I will make my way to where inklings of treasure are thought to be held. I am not a novice at this kind of expedition. The California Gold Rush persuaded many men like myself to leave behind their families in search of a prize, my own father one of them. But I was born too late to truly catch history. By the time I arrived in Sunshine, California, all I found was dust and despair. Others had been lucky enough to haul off with glint in their palms after tapping the Earth's well dry.

Alaska will be different, for its land is more untouched. The average prospector won't take their chances at failure again, especially since its terrain is not as easy to traverse. A regular unfit hobo could meander down to California and stumble across gold, but in Alaska, only the adventurous seekers will be rewarded.

In preparation, I have exhausted all of my funds on clothing, gear, and the ninety-four dollars for the ship's passage. I realize I am leaving Adalaide and Joe with meager money to live, but it is a risk that must be taken. We've carried on hand-to-mouth for too long and if Joe's doctor bills keep getting more expensive, without this windfall we won't stay afloat.

While I was not pleased with how things ended with Adalaide before my departure, to linger and chase her affection again would've been too dangerous. Adalaide has a talent for swaying one's mind, and I do fear that since I'm not the youngster I used to be, this jaunt will be my last. Because of that, it's destined to be the one that's finally a success.

The ship, magnificent. Three tiers high with a smokestack puffing gray clouds into the sky. Ivory white with wraparound decks on each floor. Men like me with calluses on their hands board along with religious missionaries and those heading to Alaska for work in the brand-new fish canneries. Smiles peek out of beards and mustaches. Songs of the sea pass from their lips. I clutch my ticket like it's a lifeline, relieved once I'm finally on board waiting for the ship to leave port. There are wives along the dock with babes in one arm, waving handkerchiefs with another. Townsfolk arrive just to watch the ship go, the excitement of the journey palpable to all. I imagine Adalaide and Little Joe shouting their love to me, but alas, they are a mirage. I remove a picture of them from out of my coat pocket. A photographer took it outside of our farm the week Joe was born. My wife and I hold the baby between us, not smiling because it wasn't a custom at the time. Both of us believing a ghost robs our souls a little every time a photograph is taken. Joe wrapped up in a blanket given to us by Adalaide's mother, a little cocooned caterpillar against my forearm, tiny as a bug. I miss them already, the pieces of me I had to leave behind.

The *G.W. Elder* blows its horn and we set sail, the sun hot against my cheek. I've dressed for Alaska but I'm sweating from the summer heat, so I strip down to just a shirt and stuff the rest in my pack, which nearly overflows. We are directed down below where we're shown our bunks, rows and rows of thin mattresses with a few inches between them. Most men have already claimed theirs, the smart ones settling in corners or by the dusty windows right below the ceilings. I am left with a dark mattress I can barely see, even in the daylight. A man has already placed his pack down at the adjacent bed. His pack resembles mine and I know he's not a missionary or fisherman. He is after the same hope.

"Watch out for that one," says a different man to my left. His face reddened from drink and obesity, little wisps of hair stick up from his head, his full beard the color of mustard. He's missing a tooth or two but has an affable smile. His pudgy fingers rest on my shoulder. "Just a word of advice," he adds, with a wink.

"Why do you say that?"

"I recognize his pack. CFL stitched on the inseam." The pudgy fingers move from my shoulder to indicate his evidence. "Been on a ship with him before. Pickpocket."

I instantly check my pockets as if this unseen man may have already been sneaky.

"I should move," I say, gathering up my pack. The man shakes his head, the lines in his protruding neck disappearing and reforming.

"All out of beds I'm afraid. Looks like we'll have to sleep with one eye open."

He widens the eye that previously winked. Bloodshot veins cloud the white part.

"Frank Allard." He shoves his meaty hand in mine, squeezing rather tight. "Good to have another pair of eyes on your side, don't ya think?"

"Wyatt Barlow. Pleasure to meet you."

The boat tilts, forcing me to hold onto the wall for support. With his stocky frame, Frank stays firm.

"Gonna be a lot of that so you better get used to it," Frank says, with a laugh that jiggles around the phlegm in his throat. "You headed up north for gold, religion, or fish?"

"What do you think?"

Frank takes a step back, as if to take all of me in. Satisfied, he nods and replies, "Gold."

"What gave it away?"

"There ain't a stench of fish or God on ya."

I laugh at that. For a moment, I miss Adalaide and Joe a little less, having found a confidant so quickly.

"Fish for me, that's my gold," he says, picking out a bite of food from between his teeth. "For fish are real whereas gold is fantasy."

I clench my fists and chew on my lip. "I'm gonna find it."

His laugh jiggles around more phlegm. "Okay, Wyatt. You let me know when you start rubbing elbows with Mr. Rockefeller."

We head over to get some food into our bellies. A mushy meat along with hard bread, cheese and relishes, and a small piece of cake. Frank laps his up, nary taking a breath between each bite. The rocking of the ship has affected my stomach, and it feels like whatever I consume might come back up. But Frank tells me that meals are only served twice a day, and since we boarded after breakfast, this will be all for the night.

"So, Mr. Gold," Frank asks, "got a sweetheart at home?"

At first, I don't want to talk about Adalaide out of fear of missing her more. But when I begin to speak of her appearance, her luscious warmth, how doting a mother she is, I am filled with a swell of comfort I've lacked since I left.

"I have a good woman too. Rosalie. Two children as well. If there's work in Alaska, I'll wire some money down so they can join me."

"Times been tough for you?"

"The panic of '93 nearly bankrupted us. Couldn't get a loan to save our life. Was working in a shingle mill at the time. All of 'em closed. McKinley's brought things back to normal somewhat, that's what a conservative will do, but Rosalie and I are still buried by loans and IOUs. Had a friend doing well up in the fishing canneries around Sitka. Said he'd introduce me."

"I wish you all the best, my friend."

"And you, Wyatt? Always been a gold hunter?"

I ponder this phrase. I've been a hunter my whole life. Learned it early on from my pap, who fed us wild animals in and around our farm, taught me how to fight and kill. I grew up a Civil War baby and the notion that the threads of society could unravel at any moment made Pap instill in me a striving for survival above all else. He fed my restless spirit, often fleeing down to California for gold, usually returning with nothing more than blackened hands, except for one time. I was awoken in the middle of the night to a light so bright shining from his palm, a golden nugget that seemed as if the entire world made sense because of it—all of our struggles: losing a sister to scarlet fever, my mother's jaundice and eventual muteness, Pap's war injuries that sometimes kept him howling into all hours of the night. This gold bullion made it all worth it. So, with frozen thumbs, he wiped the tears from my eyes and swore that we'd get to keep the farm, the very one where I'm raising my own family.

"Gold means promise," I say with a lump burning in my throat. "It means sicknesses that could be healed. It means a chance for more than food scraps. It means me making a mark on this here Earth."

"Ah," he says, swallowing a gulp of fatty milk. "You want to be revered?"

"I want to save my family," I reply, clenching my fists again.

"I believe that. But you want to have a legacy as well. All dreamers do. You want a name etched in stone."

"Is that—is that so wrong?"

"The dreamers never sleep soundly," he tells me, rubbing his astounding belly. "They are never fulfilled."

"If I find my treasure, I will be."

"Always more treasure to find, no?" He loosens some more phlegm and points with his fork at my plate. "Eating that beef, are you?"

My stomach does flips like a gymnast. The sour taste of the beef trickling up the back of my tongue.

"It's all yours."

"Fizzing, my friend. Fizzing!"

I leave Frank after we sup and make my way to the poop deck. Choppy waters cause me to finally retch, but my stomach does not feel settled even after the sickness has gone. I wonder if Frank spoke of my truth. That even after finding gold, I may still be restless enough to leave my loved ones again. That missing them will be a bigger part of my life than actually being with them. What kind of man does this make me? Heartless? Selfish? Cruel? Did the explorers of yore who discovered all the great lands think similarly? Or were they so focused on their quests that loved ones didn't engulf their woes? I resolve that since we already set sail, I must put the expedition above all else. Adalaide and Joe need to recede into the far reaches of my mind, only to be brought out when I require their comfort the most. This is how the greats achieved their trophies. And the name Barlow will become emblazoned on the biggest golden one of them all. For to return home a failure is not an option.

I'd rather not return at all.

August 13th, 1898

The ship hits a rough patch of weather in the middle of the night and I'm awakened. Teeming rains batter the windows like falling nails. The other passengers stew in their bunks, but most seem to get back to sleep while I've lost the ability to chase my dreams. The moonlight launches a blue haze over our quarters, dust mites dancing in its beam. The bunkmate to my left is a heavy snorer who will not relent. I fish out a picture of Adalaide and Joe, needing them more than ever.

At the bottom of the pocket where the picture lies, my fingers glide across a metallic object. I hold it to the blue light to discover the compact mirror given to Adalaide by her mother when we married. I certainly wouldn't have taken it with me, since her mother passed from consumption a year prior and the wound still fresh. This means that Adalaide, however angry she was because of my departure, placed the heirloom in my pocket as a good-luck souvenir. My worst fears alleviated! No doubt she was mad, but made sure I left with a good-luck charm. When I return home, I'm certain now that the two of us will overcome our dispute.

"Beautiful mirror," a voice croaks. In the near darkness, it could be coming from anywhere. To my left, the brute still plays a foghorn with his nostrils. To the right, two hazel eyes blink in my direction. "Rolling waves are keeping me up as well."

I'd forgotten about the churning ship, too wrapped up in my newfound discovery. The hazel eyes have a snake-like resemblance. In fact, his whole body does. Bald with tattoos weaving up his arms. Skin with a leathery reptilian quality. The man Frank had warned me about.

I shift in place so we aren't facing each other, so he'll understand I'm not in the mood for chatting. But the rogue has no social graces and keeps flapping his gums.

"I'm a collector. Always have been. My father owned an antique shop."

"I really must get back to sleep," I say, gritting my teeth.

The ship lurches like a dancer who had one too many. Then it dips so far that an imaginary heart leaps out of my mouth.

"Good luck at catching some winks," he says. "Piece looks to be from the old country."

"What's that?"

"Your mirror."

Somehow, he's inched close enough for me to tell that he chose fish for supper. Each breath has a wheeze at its end.

"I'm going to guess it's from Ireland or Scotland around mid-century."

"My wife came from Ireland. It's her mother's," I reply.

His whole face turns into one large grin. "Heirlooms sure are special. Connects us to history. To who we were. That's why I have such an affinity for antiques."

"The mirror's not for sale," I say, and whip it back into my pocket. I press it deep down so the photograph of my wife and son covers it for protection.

"I would never ask such a thing!" he declares, looking as if he's been spooked.

"I am closing my eyes now."

He's still talking but I've tuned him out. The rollicking waves allow me to go under and I'm submerged. When I surface in my dreams, I've reached a land of ice unlike I've ever seen before, as if the Earth has been covered with large mounds of white sugar. The air crisp like biting into a cold apple. My beard has grown. My pack heavy on my shoulders. My eyes permanently squinting from the eternal sun. I've hunted for what seems like eons but have not discovered what I seek. And then, like God's great finger points the way, the sunlight flashes against a cave. But as I peer closer, it isn't the sunlight that causes a glow, but gold itself, mounds of it, sparkling especially for me. There don't seem to be other men around, since my stubbornness has allowed me to last longer than any others in this barren expanse. I rush over, my legs creating windmills, adrenaline coursing through my body. I smell the sweet essence of my prize and I dig my hands into its warm center, but when I pull out, my right hand gets caught in a trap, a sucking void that clamps around my wrist. I yank and yank but to no avail. The cave too strong. The gold a tease. The sun sinks and night brings its fever chill. I can no longer feel my hand anymore as a blizzard brings its torturous camouflage. The snow climbs so high I cannot see anything. My world encased in dark white. My limbs crackling until they become frozen stiff. I am aware of this imminent evil death until my brain finally freezes, allowing me a sweet release, a soul never longing for the end as much as I on this tundra.

When I wake, I'm chilled to the core believing this nightmare as truth until my gaze focuses on the surrounding mattresses and bunkmates. I've never been so happy to see a bevy of dirty men. I thrust my hand with brilliant wiggling fingers into my pocket to get a quick dose of my beloved Adalaide and Joe. Not only can't I feel the photograph, but the mirror is gone too! I check my other pockets but all are empty. I check in my pack but no sign. That sneaky pickpocket with the snake eyes stole them. And he will pay dearly for his crimes.

I look around the passengers' quarters. Most of the men gone, probably having breakfast. A few missionaries huddle in a circle, their lips whispering silent prayers. I approach but they receive me with lecherous eyes.

"You seem troubled," one of them says, his voice steady unlike the ship that still beats against the waves.

"My mirror," I say, mouth dry from dehydration. "It's been stolen."

They confer with one another like they've never heard of this object before.

"Tell us about this mirror," another one says.

"My wife gave it to me before I departed." I can feel the tears creeping. "It was from her late mother."

"Where did you have it last?" a third one with a strangely boyish face asks.

"In my pocket! My bunkmate took it!"

"Did you see him do this?" the first one asks, so skinny that his cheeks cave.

"No, but he commented on it. He was eyeing it. I'm sure it was him."

"Brother," the second one says. His hand on my shoulder. "We must be careful of false accusations."

I slap his hand away. "He's the only one who could've taken it."

"Oftentimes, we misplace things," the third one says. "And then we subscribe unfair blame. Look to God as to where you may have lost your mirror."

He points to the ceiling, as if God resides there. The ceiling drips a brownish muck.

"Do you go to church?" the skinny one asks.

I went to the local church every Sunday with Adalaide. While she didn't have a religious fervor like some others, she spoke to God often, pleading to Him for Little Joe. Asking for the chills to subside. For her baby to turn warm and rosy. But I found church belaboring. I'd try to tune it out but the singing of the hymns and postulations were distracting. I would find God, or whatever He may be, while fishing. The meditative aspect of lolling on the waters, not rollicking, but simple, still. The prize not being the actual fish but a day spent in thoughtful solitude, something I often found difficult to attain. My mind always zeroing in on gold, rarely losing focus. Fishing gave me that break from the constant thrum. And if that meant God had a part in it, then I'll solely believe in Him; but if not, it's the same by me. I don't need a Bible as a guide, for that is a weakness most suspect in humankind.

I wrench away from the trio of missionaries and locate my bunkmate's pack. He has equipment for hiking in arctic conditions like I do, but I find no mirror or photograph. The missionaries watch while shaking their heads back and forth in judgment. I yell vile curses at them, then I bound up to the deck, delirious from hunger pains, nausea nipping at my belly, fearful that I'll lose the faces of my beloveds if I don't retrieve what's been taken from me.

In the mess hall, I find Frank. I tell him what has happened and we vow to make the thief pay for what he's done. We roam the room but our man is nowhere to be found. I'm weak and starting to hallucinate, so Frank gets me a plate of eggs in cream with a slab of meat as a side. I gobble it up but the meal doesn't nourish because I'm emptier than ever.

"There's nowhere for him to hide," Frank says. "We are on ship, mind you."

"If it's not in his pack, he must have it on him."

"Or he found another hiding spot."

"Why steal the photograph?" I ask. "It holds no value."

"Thieves tend not to be choosy." He blows a long gust of snot into his handkerchief. "Sometimes they commit crimes for the thrill. It's a compulsion."

"I'll kill the rogue if I find that mirror on him."

"As you should. He deserves punishment."

"I see him!"

I knock my plate over as I leap up and head to the exit. There's a mass of people with the same plan in mind and I struggle to make it through the crowd. The thief's slithery bald head shines like a freshly waxed floor and I'm determined to keep it in my sights. The crowd, however, starts to thicken and it becomes impossible to go any faster. He recedes farther and farther away. I try to reach out but it proves useless, he slips through my fingers like the slippery eel he is. When I make it out the door, he has vanished. Frank scurries up and slaps me on the back.

"Ah Wyatt, we'll get him next time. Like I said, nowhere for him to run except if he goes overboard."

Frank's laugh is more phlegmy than usual. The sound like rusty gears grinding.

I heave the creamy eggs over the side of the ship. My sickness floating, breaking up, and dissipating into the air.

August 14th, 1898

Midnight. The day has shown to be mostly fruitless. Frank and I scoured every inch of the cursed ship, but alas, no thief. We questioned other passengers, describing the rogue in full, but no one seemed to ever witness his presence. He's like a ghost that invaded and stole off with a prize. Two members of the crew, Henry and Clark, proved to be just as useless. Half drunk and slurring, they refused to produce a log of all the passengers, saying it was against regulations. Henry damn near suggested I created the whole farce for nefarious reasons. When I asked them what those could be, he eyed Clark like they were in cahoots, and told me that sometimes people make up stolen objects as a way of pilfering. Someone on the ship bound to be carrying a silver mirror, and therefore, would be subject to hand it over because of my accusation. I nearly popped him in the mouth. Frank and Clark had to hold me back, but I'm strong like a wolf, always have been. Neither could restrain me, but luckily, I calmed down. If I hit him, the captain would probably boot me off.

Speaking of the captain, I inquired about him as well. When I knocked on his cabin door, he seemed to be deep into a bottle of fine bourbon. He was nice enough to share a sniff and we sat by his lone window staring out at the waters that for once had quieted. Captain Willis Thistle, a beast of a man, with hands as big as baseball gloves and a ropey body full of muscle and sinew. He had a beard he tugged on when in deep thought and eyes that had clearly seen parts of the world I couldn't even imagine.

"After gold, are you?" he asked, smacking his lips after a heavy snort of bourbon. "We should reach Sitka by the end of the week. What do you do then?"

"Likely make my way by foot."

"Long journey. Yes. Even though it's summer, winter sneaks up before you know it."

"Unfortunately, my concern right now is about this thief you have on board."

"Took your silver mirror, say you? 'Tis a shame. Should warn passengers of bringing valuable objects on board."

"My wife snuck it in my pocket as a memento."

"Ah, women know how to please our hearts. Yes. I was married but lost her to tuberculosis. Awful way to go. Still, I spend most of the year at sea, so we rarely saw each other."

"I'm often gone too."

"After that gold?"

I nodded.

"Well, we all have our compulsions. I, for one, don't feel settled unless the ground beneath my feet is made of water. Don't like feeling steady."

He tugged at his beard and then stopped as if he was displeased with his deep thought.

"I asked your crew member for the passenger log so I could locate this thief," I said. "I know his initials. CFL. But the crew member was very disrespectful."

"Asked Henry, did ya? Well, there's a sumbitch if I ever knew one. I tell you what…"

He opened a desk drawer and pulled out a large book. Licking his finger, he opened to a page of last names that started with the letter L.

"Langford, Carl Finnegan. There's your CFL."

He snapped the dusty book shut and picked up a glass half full of bourbon.

"Although I don't know how the name will help. If this man became a ghost as you say."

"I appreciate the effort, Captain."

"Think nothing of it, my friend. Now go, find your mirror!"

I left his quarters elated. With a name plus a physical description, at least I had more to go on. Yet still no one knew of this man. People started to get angry as I accidentally asked them twice. I almost got in another fight, this time with two fishermen, which Frank had to aid me in subduing.

"Ya can't fight the world over this," Frank told me. "We'll keep trying, but we'll reach our first port soon and your man might hop off there."

"No, he's after gold. I looked through his pack. He's not a fisherman. He'll stay on like me till Sitka."

Now long past midnight, I scribble all this in my journal instead of sleeping and gearing up for my adventure like I should. Frank snores a few mattresses away. I understand his advice, but I will not heed. I will fight the world until the mirror returns because I am never one to back down.

I turn to my left. The thief's mattress stays empty but his pack remains in its place. In the alluring darkness, I go through it again searching for any kind of clue as to who this man might be. Long johns, heavy boots, a tiny hunting blade, a similar coat to mine, but nothing personal or revealing. I slide the blade out of his pack and slip it under my shirt. Eye for an eye, of sorts.

Because I am restless and sleep seems like a fantasy, I make my way up to the deck to witness the moon. The moon has always been a savior when I'm the loneliest on my quests, for Adalaide could be looking up at the same moon at the same time, bringing us nearer together.

Sure enough, the moon beams in its glory, not full but close to it and bathing the ship in illustrious blue. The sea laps dark and the waves are pointed. The sky tar-black and never-ending. The Earth seeming so grand yet so small at the same time. Limitless yet our ship feels encased in our own tiny globe. It is then I spy a man sitting by the stern. He is alone, and in the night appears like a phantasm, not quite real but more than imagination. I pursue this entity. Sleeplessness and sickness from the food aboard along with the constant rocking of the ship has caused delirium in me, and I wonder if this is a creature from my past come to pay a visit. I imagine my father's ghost willfully descending to impart advice for my upcoming jaunt. A stern man with round glasses and always a neat part in his hair, burly shoulders and palms full of cuts and grit, a life of traveling and never idling. He'd be proud to know I'm headed to Alaska to seek what alluded and eventually killed him.

But as I step closer, I see not my father, but the man I've been pursuing since yesterday. His bald head shines against the moonlight like some crystal ball. The tattoos smearing his body tell stories of his life. There's a bear I assume he killed and marked himself for glory. A couple of skulls proving he's witnessed more than one death. A sword that might indicate he was responsible for taking a life. His lizard eyes blink in my direction, regarding this battle he knows is bound to occur. I feel the blade's handle pressing against my abdomen.

"Sleepless as well?" he asks, his voice calm and surprising. I am caught off guard.

"Where is the mirror?"

A growl to my tone, purposefully threatening. He regards me with those lizard eyes, carefully blinking.

"I don't understand."

"Stand up!"

I've reached beneath my shirt, clutching the blade. My body shakes but my hand remains steady for what I may need to do.

He complies, getting his balance. It's difficult since the ship bats around in the night more than during the day. The dark sky a scourge.

"Those beds," he says, rubbing his neck. He's trying to deflect.

"Where is my mirror?"

"You've lost your mirror. What a shame."

I cannot tell if he's being facetious. His face offers a wry grin that could be apologetic or damning.

"When did you have it last?"

"When you commented on it!"

I've bared my teeth now, fangs digging in to my bottom lip.

"I do not have it, friend."

"I'm not your friend!"

He's looking over my shoulder, possibly for assistance. I swivel around quickly but there is no one. Just the two of us in this defining dance.

"I didn't steal your mirror. I am not a thief."

There exists a quiver at the end of each of his words. A palpable fear, either from being caught or the uncertainty of the lengths I will go to reclaim my treasures.

"My photograph as well. You've taken my family."

"I am not that man."

"Empty your pockets!"

His eyes go wide. I do not realize why until I see the hunter's blade has been directed at him.

"That's my—that's my knife," he says.

"I won't tell you to empty your pockets again."

He turns every one of his pockets inside out. Nothing.

"Your boots, take them off."

"Do you really think I'd hide a mirror in my boot?"

"I do not know what you are capable of."

"Nor I you, sir."

He slowly removes each boot and shakes them out.

"It could be tucked in your pants," I say, indicating him to remove them too.

"That's preposterous."

"Take them off!"

"I will not."

I jab the blade in his direction, slicing through air, showing how serious I can be.

"I did not steal anything from you!"

The two of us are yelling at each other now, hard to discern what we are saying. I've left my body, become a wild animal, the wolf within. He guides my choices. I'm tearing at the thief's clothes, patting him down to locate my mirror. He's twisting and turning and making it difficult. He reaches for the blade, grappling my wrist. We push and pull, the ship dipping and rising, and then somehow, through force of nature or plain frustration, the blade cuts into flesh. I step back to witness what I have done.

The thief staggers with the blade stuck in his stomach all the way to the handle. Blood pours forth, slicking his body in red.

"What have you done?" he asks me.

"Why did you do it?"

I'm crying now, begging for him to give me answers. But he is silent, numb. His brain shutting off, lizard eyes rolling to the back of his skull.

The ship dips again and nearly flings him over. I do what must be done and help him along. He spins over the edge with a flip and flops into the water, a dark circle forming around the body before it's swallowed entirely by the night. I cannot see him anymore, convincing myself it was all just a horrible dream. There's a little blood on the deck but I smear it with my boot until it's camouflaged into the wood.

Then I descend to the passengers' quarters, lie flat on my back, and sleep better than I have ever since I arrived on this cursed ship.

August 15th, 1898

We stop in Victoria, Nanaimo, and Tongas today. I am at peace since Carl Finnegan Langford could very well be getting off at any of the ports if he was still alive. Therefore, no one should inquire about him. When I wake in the morning, his pack has mysteriously vanished too, as if it'd been attached to the body. I slept through breakfast but Frank is nice enough to bring me down a plate of more creamy eggs. I think I have no appetite but I lap them up.

"I took care of it," he says, eyes darting to and fro.

"Took care of what?"

Those eyes land on the empty mattress next to me. A jolt runs up my spine.

"I don't know what you mean," I say, as the eggs begin to churn in my belly.

"I think you do."

His tone reads less jovial than usual. Normally Frank has a jester-like appeal, but today he is serious, foreboding.

The trio of missionaries from yesterday glide down the spiral staircase. I cannot look at them even though I feel their burning gazes.

"Last night..." Frank starts to say, but I hiss for him to quiet. "Last night..." he continues.

"Come with me."

I latch onto Frank and yank him toward the stairs. We pass by the missionaries who regard me with judgmental nods.

When we're upstairs, the air is full of rotten fish and breakfast keeps making its way back up. I must look green because Frank seems concerned.

"You should lie down," he says, directing me to a bench.

"Tell me what you meant," I say, squeezing his collar. "What did you take care of?"

"What did YOU take care of?" he asks, one eyebrow dangling at the top of his forehead. He leans in closer, then in a whisper: "I saw you last night."

The eggs come up, spraying at my feet.

"Wyatt," he says, not concerned but insistent. "Get your wits about you."

"He had the mirror."

"So you got it back?"

I shake my head. "But I am certain he had it."

"I believe you, I believe you," he says, bringing my head to his bosom and rocking me like a mother would. I feel weightless, ready to lift off and float away. "You did what needed to be done. He was a criminal."

"Yes, yes he was."

"Go back to sleep for the day. I will come down around suppertime with another plate."

"You are a true friend."

His laugh brings up phlegm, which he spits onto the deck. A wretched color. Brown mixed with red and yellow. The rot within. I wonder if I'm only imagining that.

"Come," he says, directing me back down to the thin mattress. The missionaries have thankfully gone and I am alone in the quarters. He raises the meager sheet up to my neck and tucks me in as much as possible. I almost suspect a kiss upon my forehead.

"Get some rest."

I hear his heavy feet walking away, but in an instant, I go under again. Powerless to exhaustion.

August 16th, 1898

I sleep through the rest of the day and the night and when I wake it is long past morning and two plates await me. A supper that has turned gray but I nibble on it anyway along with more eggs in cream. I hold my nose just to get it down. Frank is not there but has left this food. I drink a glass of milk, which somewhat settles my stomach, but then the thoughts start plaguing and I relive the horrid last night. I did not mean to stab the thief with the blade, but then I wonder if I'm just deluding myself. I wanted him to pay for his sins.

Luckily, the missionaries are not present so I do not have to worry about their scrutiny. I doubt I could face them without blurting out my crime. As I finish my glass of milk, I dribble some down my chin. I look for something to mop up the stain on my shirt. While I hadn't brought a handkerchief, I spy Frank's pack set on a mattress a few over from mine. Surely, a man so phlegmy as he would have one. There's only one other man in the quarters whose erupting in a coughing fit and paying no heed to me. I quickly go through the pack. No handkerchief, except to my surprise, I remove my silver mirror!

I'm in disbelief as it sits in my palm, but it is my mirror with a floral pattern etched into the back. I close my fist around it and make my way up to the deck. Struggling to maintain foothold, I pursue Frank. I am unsure what I will do when we cross paths. He isn't in the mess hall or in the lounge area where men play cards and smoke cigars. Sure enough, I find him by the deck at the exact spot where I threw Carl Finnegan Langford overboard.

"Say you," Frank says, shielding his eyes from the sun. "You're alive!"

I grab him by the collar, ready to pick his fat body up and toss him over.

"You liar," I sneer. "You are the thief."

He weasels out of my grasp, wheezing as he catches his breath. Before he can question, I thrust the mirror in his face.

"I found this in your pack!"

His countenance changes from the roly-poly jokester I had first met to a devil's visage. Reddened eyes, slick mouth, smoke practically steaming from his nostrils.

"It wasn't your right to go through my things," is all he can say.

He clears his throat and gazes at the waters. We churn more than usual because of the charcoal clouds along the horizon that spell doom.

"You are naïve, Barlow," he calmly says.

"And you are a criminal!"

"I'd be careful with using that word. For you are a worse kind."

I taste metal at the back of my mouth as I swallow.

"I did what I thought—"

He holds up his hand, silently telling me it's not worth continuing.

"I'm not sure a judge would agree."

"What would a judge think about your thieving ways?"

He yawns. "Listen, you have your mirror again. Let's not do anything you'd regret."

"Like telling Captain Thistle of your deceit."

"I could do the same. I watched you that night. Saw you remove the blade from under your shirt and gut that man like a fish."

"You told me to!" I scream, and he clamps his dirty hand over my mouth.

"Listen to me, you buffoon. Carl Finnegan Langford is one of the greatest prospectors of his time. Made a fortune in the last days of the California Rush. We would have no chance against him in Alaska."

"I thought you were headed there to be a fisherman?" I murmur through his palm.

"Wyatt, you have to be a little more aware. I hope this is a lesson learned."

"So, you duped me into killing him for you?"

"For us. For all of us to stand a fighting chance. And if it helps, he is not an innocent man. There were a bevy of crimes he committed."

"I never wanted to be an executioner," I say, a tear trickling down my cheek.

"You should be thanking me, friend," he says, his hand on my shoulder.

I knock it away. "You are no friend."

"You were wholly unprepared to enter the beast that is Alaska. Think you met heathens down in Cal-i-for-ni-a, well, they ain't nothing compared to the dregs of society that Alaska will call forth. Men who'd slit your throat for the tiniest bit of gold. Carl Finnegan would have done the same when we arrived."

"How can I face my family?"

"They are your biggest obstacle, Wyatt. Your wife and child are what's keeping you soft. I'm gonna rid you of them."

He whips out the photograph, which flaps in the wind.

"What are you doing? Give me that!"

"You are absolved," he says, tossing it overboard. I watch it spiral into the waters, the faces of Adalaide and Joe sinking. I grab Frank's collar again.

"I should kill you."

"Now you're becoming worthy," he says, and I feel the point of a knife pressing into my gut. "But if you try anything, I'll puncture your spleen."

"You are a hateful man."

"Nonsense! I am a realistic man. And you'll thank me once we get to Alaska, for I have given you a wealth of knowledge."

"I won't be speaking to you when we reach Alaska. We part ways as of now."

"That is a shame. For even if you do not trust me, at least you know where I stand. That is more than I can say for other men you'll encounter."

I spit at his boots. "I'd never align myself with a scoundrel like you."

"We'll see about that. You are better off than when you stepped on this ship, but still have much to learn."

I hear the devil's laugh rattling as I march away.

August 17th, 1898

We reach our final port of Sitka come nighttime and I make sure to tear out the pages I'd written in my journal connecting me to Carl Finnegan Langford. I've avoided Frank since our fight and kept to myself through the course of the day, mentally preparing for the upcoming leg of the journey. I've held the silver mirror close to my heart, vowing never to let it out of my sight again. As for the photograph, it was the first casualty of the adventure.

When I leave, Captain Thistle sways by the dock with a hearty hand-shake waiting.

"I wish ya all the best," he says, slapping me on the back.

"Thank you, Captain."

"Did you ever find your thief by the way?"

He doesn't mention the thief by the name, which allows me to reply that I did find him. I show him the mirror as evidence.

"Ah, good, good. And what became of the thief?"

"Judgment still needs to rain upon him," I say, as Frank strides past us—the devil knowing he's found his way inside both of us.

"Romans 3:23," Captain Thistle says. "'For all have sinned and fall short of the glory of God.'"

"Didn't take you to be a religious man, Captain."

He lets out a booming laugh reeking of bourbon. "Far from it. Guess all the missionaries on board these last few days have rubbed off on me."

"I never listened to God before," I say, "but I firmly disbelieve in Him now."

"Ah, maybe that's best. The chains are snipped then. There's no borderline as to what you can't and won't do."

These words hit me like a punch to my gut, but I take their abuse, knowing them to be ominous, but likely true.

16

Huddled on a bench as the waves bring in the fishing boats for the day, Wyatt finishes the journal entries, his hand cramping and nearly losing his grip on the pen. He'd left his body while writing, returning to a treacherous past that demonstrated his murderous ways. Since awakening in the wilderness, he knew he had primal urges—no one could've mutilated a wolf like he did who hadn't slain before—but to be responsible for a human's death shocks his sensibilities. If he killed Carl Finnegan Langford, there's no telling what else he might have done on the rest of his Alaskan expedition.

He lets this new knowledge settle. No use in lamenting. Better to know one's demons than to be surprised by them. He looks in the silver mirror to decide if his reflection appears any different, but he decides he's still the same grizzled man he's finally getting to know.

The dock soon becomes pink with the blood of gutted fish, each boat proudly displaying its catches. Dusk has arrived with its frigid chill, Alaska not listening to the notion that it's springtime yet. He blows on brittle fingers that his gloves haven't kept warm. Waiting for Trav to arrive but no sign of the boat until it slowly bobs in the dim violet light of the sinking sun.

Trav hops off and reins the boat in, and he and his partner go about gutting until they're splashed in pink and filled ice boxes with dozens of fish. They pat each other's shoulders, mirth emblazoned on their faces, satisfied with their hefty haul. Parting ways, Trav ambles toward his pickup.

Butterflies bat their wings in Wyatt's belly. He stuffs his notepad in a pocket, rises on cracking legs, and bounds toward Trav. Electricity sparks between them, or at least that's what Wyatt believes, the notion that these two souls who never should meet are being magnetically pulled into each other's orbit. Wyatt decides he will make eye contact as they pass but not say a word. He fears his mouth might betray his brain if he does.

There's no one else in the way who could distract from the inevitable happening. Sweat sops Wyatt's beard, his bowels churn, limbs noodling. They are only a few feet from each other. Wyatt can smell the sea emanating from his great-great grandson's body. And then Trav raises his head slightly but enough for them to lock gazes, for the universe to freeze this all-consuming moment enough for the two men to study their counterpart. Trav narrowing his green-gold eyes, eyebrows rising, lines on his forehead deepening, the awe that a doppelgänger can unearth. Two duplicate versions, varying somewhat in age and appearance due to Wyatt's consuming beard, but seemingly brothers, kin, eras colliding, the Earth off its regular tilt, dizzy with the wonder of no longer relying on logic to fathom the unexplainable.

They pass without lightning striking them down and upending this impossibility. Both swivel back for one final glance, but they are far enough away for it to feel like a trick of the mind. Trav shaking his head, likely dislodging the strange thoughts in his brain leading him astray. The sun has slipped away now, the surroundings colored ink black. All men who pass each other might appear as a twin due to the rolling darkness, and so Trav gets in his pickup, chugging the engine on and peeling out of the lot.

But Wyatt knows this is far from their last encounter.

The thrill of a hard day's work in Travis's bones. Something he missed, never realizing how much. What it means to feel worthy again after idling, present in his own body as opposed to being a foreigner. This is how good sore muscles can be. The adrenaline of cash in hand. Of meals bought and not hunted or taken from Callie's work. Of a man slowly piecing himself together to become whole.

He doesn't mind the stink of salt and the curdle of fish. Of fingernails lined with guts and clothes painted in shades of red. Of early mornings in the dark and driving home in the dusk. Limbs weary but firm. No more sad tunes crooning from the radio. Of a wife and child he looks forward to seeing rather than feeling shame. A promise of tomorrows rather than a hesitancy. An alarm clock a benevolent rooster, not a daily plague.

Once he finishes, he and Smitty say their goodbyes and he takes in a landscape view of the docks. Imagining his fish shack like a lighthouse calling the fishermen in after a long day on the waters. How many runs would it take to get him there? Even if it's five years from now, or ten, the idea of a goal better than nothing at all. So he keeps the vision sturdy, somehow it will materialize.

There's a man walking toward him. No chance they won't pass each other by. Likely another fisherman since he's still new and does not know everyone. The light has dimmed so squinting becomes necessary. He no longer has the perfect vision he used to but not quite ready for glasses. The man has a sprawling beard, one that has taken some time to perfect. He lifts his own gaze ready to give this man a friendly nod. Nothing could prepare him for what he was about to see.

He's heard the term bizarro before. That some alternate universe exists with a bizarre version of yourself. Seemingly alike but with a few slight differences, enough to set the two apart from being duplicates. That is this man. Equal in build: stocky and muscular but not large or imposing. Emerald eyes, like Cora used to describe his, two little jewels. And of course—that nose. Big as a doorknob but one he always thought brought character to an otherwise handsome face. A smaller nose would have made him look dainty; his made him into a gladiator. And sure, this strange man has a swirling beard and Travis kept his trim, but he's grown a giant beard before.

He thinks all this as he and the man whip by each other. By the time he spirals back to Earth, they're far enough away for it to seem like an inebriated dream. The sun has settled, darkness ablaze, and the two men stand apart as nothing more than shadows. The shadows stare at one another for one more isolated moment before parting. He swings into his pickup, shaking his head, still alive in this fantasy as it seeps from his consciousness. But he's aware it will revive again, for if he's meant to know this double, Laner is small enough that there's no way they won't collide again.

17

At night, Travis keeps the encounter with his double from Callie, not to be secretive but because he's unable to put it into words. *This man was another version of me*, he could say. Or even, *he reminded me of Bobby. Because Bobby had a great, sweeping beard the day he died. Bobby liked hiding his face as much as possible.*

Callie brings pizzas home from the Joint, making Eli ecstatic. Eli stretching the cheese as much as possible until it plops in his lap and then giggling until his face turns red. He talks of Miss Evelyn and learning how to count animal cards, being most excited when he got to the caribou card with nine of them. Nine boos in a row.

Travis reads him a picture book in bed. Immediately after finishing, Eli wants it read again. Travis's eyes are starting to close but Eli begs and he gives in. Halfway through, Eli's snoring so Travis tucks him in tight, kisses the top of his head, and shuts out the light.

Callie has a glass of red wine and listens to music on the couch with Chinook. Travis tries to worm his way between them but Chinook's decided to be a cock block.

"C'mon, Chinook, let me at my wife."

Chinook sighs and eventually moves over. Travis clinks his beer with her glass.

"How's my girl?"

"Your girl is wine flushed."

"That's how I like her."

He blows a raspberry into her neck and the two paw at each other before exhaustion sets in.

"Oh, I'm meeting Grayson at Elson's after work tomorrow. That cool?"

"I'll save you dinner," she says, tracing a finger around her glass and creating a hum. "How's he doing?"

"Lousy. Lorinda was the love of his life."

"I don't doubt that."

"She give any indication she might take him back?"

"Not really. She's embarrassed, like any woman would be."

"Put in a good word for him."

"I don't have that kind of power."

She leans against his shoulder and soon she's asleep, so he picks her up and carries her to bed. Takes off her socks and her jeans, tucks her in tight too. Crawls into bed as well and thinks of how much luckier he is than that duplicate man—no way does he sleep next to someone as wonderful as Callie. During the night, they stay locked together, both twisted into the shape of a question mark.

Little do Trav and California know that Wyatt has watched them from outside all night. Heard every word they said through thin walls. After getting the information he needs about Trav's plan for after work tomorrow, Wyatt makes the long trek back to where he's been sleeping. Five miles through the woods wouldn't be easy in the dark for anyone, let alone someone as emaciated as him. He'd nibbled on the chum the fishermen left on the dock. Fish heads with filmy eyes, guts, and digestive tracks, tails he could scrape against his teeth. Far from nourishing. The temperature has surely dropped to single digits and he ponders giving up halfway, except that would mean death. He's not ready to die, at least until the mystery of how he made it to 2019 gets solved.

As the wind tears through his coat and icicles map his beard, he imagines Trav and California on their couch with a fire cooking. He's easily able to supplement himself for Trav and once she's in his arms, a thawing follows. He kisses the freckles down her neck. Luxuriates in the scent of flowery perfume. Makes love quietly, just the sound of his weeping audible. She consoles rather than chides.

It's dawn when he steps through the broken glass into his new home. He's found bags to cover the hole but inside remains frosty. He curls up next to the picture of Adalaide and Joe, his nose against hers, desperate for sleep to come. When he wakes, he has no sense of time or how long he's been under. He's seasick so he imagines he's back on the steamboat, reliving the same horror, possibly forever.

Outside in the gray afternoon, he begs for money. The town quiet but he sticks to the main street and kindly asks outside of Elson's and Pizza Joint, the grocery store and the feed shop, until his pockets jingle jangle with coins. In 1898 this could've fed him for a week but he's smart enough to know that won't be the case now. Just before sunset, he heads into Elson's.

He's not as disheveled and stinky as he was the last time. Aylen had cleaned him up some before she let him fall asleep in her bed. Brushed his teeth, washed his skin with a cloth and soap. Combed the knots from his hair. Not entirely presentable yet but in the wilds of a town like Laner, not obviously a hobo. He situates himself at the bar and orders an ale, discovers that it costs half of the coins he received for the day once he spills them out on the counter.

"What food can I get with what's left?" he asks Elson, a burly man whose body has to shift to make room for him behind the bar. He has muttonchops that would have been in style in Wyatt's time and a similar eye that has closed over, although Elson's seems like it will never open. Maybe that's why he takes pity.

"How about a baked potato with the works?" Elson asks, scooping the coins into his dirty apron.

"The...works?" Wyatt questions.

"All the good stuff." Elson winks with his good eye. "I ain't gonna let you leave here hungry."

"Thank you, kind sir."

A pint of ale gets placed under his nose, the hops smelling delightful. He takes a long swig but then cautions himself to ration the rest. The bells above the front door clink and Trav enters with Grayson. The two sit at the end of the bar, far enough away for Wyatt to remain unnoticed but close enough that his trained ears can hear their conversation.

"You could've showered before," Grayson says, waving his hand in front of his nose.

"You could've too. Least I was up to my neck in fish and have an excuse."

"Usual, boys?" Elson asks, and begins pouring suds.

"So, did you ask Callie about Lorinda?"

"I'm gonna stop you there, Gray."

"No dice?"

"You've dug your ditch."

"It was always the same girl at Raye's."

"I don't think that makes it any better."

"Try and see if you can arrange a meeting. Or, or…have Lorinda over and I'll show up that night too."

"Yeah, that won't look suspicious."

"C'mon, buddy, I'd do it for you."

"All right, all right. I'll make it happen."

Grayson pulls Trav into him and leaves a sloppy kiss on his cheek. Wyatt's definitely not seen friends behave like that before.

His baked potato arrives covered in cheese, loose meat, and sour cream. It's heavenly, his cold furnace of a body radiating with each bite. He proceeds to lick the plate clean.

"Guessing you hated it," Elson says, taking away the plate.

Wyatt smacks his lips. "Quite the opposite."

"I know, that's called sarcasm."

Once Elson leaves, there's nothing blocking Wyatt from Trav's view. So he takes a sip of ale and lets out a satisfactory, "Ahhhhhhhhh," ready to catch his great-great grandson's attention. Looking over, his eyes meet Trav's. Trav cocks his head to the side and Wyatt swallows his heart as Trav pushes his stool out and makes his way over.

He's numb when a hand is thrust in his direction, ready for destiny to ignite.

Over a century has passed to bring the two men to this defining moment. But only if one believes in magic and the ability to suspend a body and mind for that long. Logic dictates, what exactly? That they might be distantly related, accounting for any similarities, and Wyatt in the throes of amnesia has latched onto the most fantastical explanation.

Travis feels drawn to his doppelgänger as well. And when they finally shake hands, experiences a familiarity that seems to demolish logic, even for a second.

"Travis Barlow," he says, unable to break from the handshake. This man with cold palms and poor circulation like himself, something that runs in the family with all Barlow men.

"Wyatt."

"I saw you over at the bar and…I think we passed each other on the docks yesterday," Travis says, still fused to his double.

"That was I."

"You look," Travis stops himself, nervously laughs. Cutting through the mystical aura that surrounds and moving back to realistic notions. "You look like me. Is that weird to say? That must sound weird."

"No, we do. We do."

Finally, they let go of each other but a wave of energy festers between them. Each can sense it crackling. This tricking of the universe.

"Are you from around here?" Travis asks, his legs turning to mush. A woozy sensation forces him to take a stool. Elson's got a cold beer waiting. He sips it like it's his lifeline.

"Washington State," Wyatt replies confidently.

"I'm from here. Laner. We don't see too many outsiders. Are you headed to Nome?"

"No. This is where I'm meant to be."

Wyatt rubs his beard in a hypnotic fashion, and Travis gets lost in the repeated motion. He wants to reach out and touch this grizzled man's features, to size them up against his own.

"Without the beard, we have the same face," Travis says. "Doesn't it seem like that? I thought so when I passed you on the docks. Like I was looking at—no, that's insane."

"We could be related," Wyatt says. "Although, I do not know much about my family, so I doubt I'd be much help."

"Let me buy you a beer," Travis says, since Wyatt's almost tapped his dry. He calls over Elson who pours another.

"That's very kind of you."

"What brings you to Laner?" Travis asks, his face sparkling and engaged. A fire lit within.

"You'd think I'm crazy if I told you," Wyatt replies, with suds collecting in his beard.

"I'm giving in to crazy right now."

Wyatt winks his good eye. "Gold."

Travis nearly spits out his drink. "Wasn't expecting you to say that. In these parts? Really?"

"I'm a believer."

"I mean, a gold rush passed through here some hundred years back. Maybe there's scraps left?"

Grayson joins them with a powerful hand on Travis's shoulder.

"And who's this talkin' your ear off?" Grayson asks, already wobbling.

Grayson with the ability to pound three beers in the time most take to finish one.

"This is Wyatt," Travis says, indicating him with a bottle.

"I know you, rider," Grayson says, pointing. "The man with the golden nugget."

"I'll take that as a description," Wyatt says, with an exaggerated bow.

"He was just telling me about gold," Travis says.

"Yep, had a little piece the size of a stone," Grayson says.

Wyatt smiles. "And I'm hoping to get more."

Travis steps outside of himself to really view this man beyond their likenesses. Wyatt's clothes tattered, not only worn but truly lived in, like they might be his only home. There's dirt in pockets a quick bath won't scrub clean. Trapped behind his ears and ground in wrinkles. A second skin, a drifter's shell.

"You recently came up from Washington?"

"Took a boat," Wyatt says, mimicking the rocking waves he experienced by rising and dipping in his seat.

"You at Killbessey's Inn, or the Motel 6 off the route?"

"'Fraid not. Just handed over my last bit of money." He nods to his empty plate.

"If you're sleeping on the street," Grayson begins, pulling up his belt, "can't have that. Got a no vagrants policy in Laner."

"Don't listen to him," Travis says. "Do you really have nowhere to stay?"

"I'm all right," Wyatt says. "Found a semi-warm spot and trust me I've slept far longer in colder conditions."

"If money's what you need."

"No, I don't want a handout."

"Hey, Elson," Travis whistles. Elson shuffles over, spit-cleaning a glass. "Elson, this here's Wyatt. You still looking for a dishwasher like I heard?"

"Sure am."

"I've heard Wyatt's the best dishwasher out of the lower forty-eight."

"I can put him through a run."

Travis claps. "See there, should keep you afloat until the gold pours in."

It seems as if Wyatt's heart booms, not expecting this kind of goodwill from a stranger. But they aren't complete strangers, at least it doesn't feel that way.

"Can start you tomorrow morning?" Elson says, inspecting his semi-cleaned glass. "Got one of them Oxendine boys working tonight's shift, but if you ask me, he's high as a UFO in the sky. You into drugs, man?"

Elson widens his one giant eye.

"No sir," Wyatt says. "Never."

"I'll see you for the breakfast rush then. Town's got our very own sun-up boozers."

Elson tips his head toward Grayson in jest before tending to another customer.

"Fuck you, old man," Grayson says. "I never start the well goin' till after my shift ends."

"Thank you, Trav…Travis," Wyatt says. "That was very kind. You're a good man."

"Tell my wife that. I usually even out as decent at best."

Wyatt tugs on his lip with his fang tooth.

"You married?" Travis asks.

"Was."

"I'll leave it at that, man."

"It's a big trap," Grayson says, spilling a fifth of his tall beer on the floor. "Minute I saw my girl setting it up, I ran for the hills."

"Right into a prostitute," Travis says, before Grayson pounds him in the shoulder. "Don't make Elson cut you off."

"I'm grabbing a smoke!" Grayson howls, and is out the door.

"Forgive my best friend," Travis says. "He's really a cool guy at heart."

Wyatt finishes the swill at the bottom of his glass and stands. "I should be getting back."

"Back to where? I can give you a lift."

"It's not far."

"Come on, I'm parked outside."

Wyatt shrugs and follows Travis into his pickup. They wave at Grayson, who's struggling with lighting a broken cigarette. It's warm in the pickup with the heater. Wyatt seems like he'd be happy to sleep on the seats.

"So where to?" Travis asks.

"It's that abandoned store," Wyatt says, hanging his head in shame. "The window's broken and I can slip in."

He directs Travis to his pseudo-home, which in the nighttime appears more pathetic than usual. Travis gives an audible sigh.

"You won't freeze?"

It's as if he wants Wyatt to ask to go home with him. But he can tell that Wyatt would be too proud. It'd be an insult to offer.

"I've got blankets, and I'm cold-blooded," Wyatt says. "Really, I'm fine. You got me work today. You've been a friend."

"I wanna hear about this gold in our area," Travis says. "Maybe we can hunt for it together? I'm a very good hunter."

Wyatt nods. "I think that might be swell."

He extends his hand so they can shake again. This time when they do, a brotherhood is established. Travis understanding deep down that neither realizes how much the other will impact their life, that nothing will ever be the same.

Wyatt pops out of the pickup and eases his way through the broken window until he fades into the darkness like a ghost that may have never been there at all.

Travis stays with the motor idling. Not ready to leave. Afraid to shatter this uncanny introduction.

18

Travis wants to share with Callie about his double, the mysterious prospector who's come to the edge of the Earth for gold. But how to put it into words? He tries in front of a mirror, but it sounds insane. So better to keep quiet. She's putting lotion on her cracked hands, Alaska a scourge on her already dry skin. They've set up a humidifier that seems to do little.

"You want to take a picture?" she asks, because he's been staring.

"Just zoned out."

"You're getting good at that."

She has to be aware that he's been different these past two days, more withdrawn. For a while he'd been opening up. Working on Smitty's boat a boon to his personality.

"It's the long days on the water."

"Is it?" She's hesitant but snuggles up close. "You know you can tell me anything. If it's about Bobby..."

"Nothing to do with Bobby," he says, a lie. Because to lose one's brother like that, even if they fought most of their lives, causes you to lose faith in whatever you once held true.

"How's Gray?" she asks, after a challenging lull.

"Oh yeah, something I wanted to run by you," he says. Callie raises her eyebrows. "Think we could set up a meeting between him and Lorinda?"

"This one of his brilliant schemes?"

"Have her over, and I'll bring Gray. And we see what happens."

"A disaster of biblical proportions."

"Or maybe they work through their issues?"

She closes the lotion cap and turns over on her side. "Okay, but you'll take the heat from the bomb if it's set off."

He runs his hand down her shoulder to her waist, but she's already snapped off the light, and it's hard to visualize her in the dark.

Morning with a purpose, a night without a fitful sleep for once. Wyatt uses the snow outside in lieu of running water, removing surface dirt from his face. Whistling as he walks the few blocks to work. Elson the only one there before the sun rises, pleased he showed up early. He learns how to work the machine that cleans the dishes. Each needs a scrubbing first before being placed inside. He's mystified by the smell of the dish soap, floral and inviting. Locals fill in as the hours pass, wolfing down their breakfasts, their black coffees, some adding a swill of liquor. The dishes pile up, but he gets into a groove, a system working eventually. Elson pops in around midday with an A-okay.

He has to slightly alter his system for the dinner rush boom, but he manages. He peeks out every so often for a sign of Trav, eager to continue their talk. Once he's ready to set off to find his gold—if he could remember where it'd been left—he'll need an extra hand. A great way for the men to really bond. As the dirty plates slow down, Elson sticks his head in the kitchen to say "last customer." Wyatt's tired from standing, but he senses his powers returning, more of a fully realized human than when the day began. Elson asks if he wants to be paid daily in cash, to avoid any IRS "sticking their noses in," and Wyatt agrees, also knowing it'd be impossible for him to pay taxes since he doesn't exist in this century. Elson gives him two twenty-dollar bills, worth about a thousand in his time, and he thinks that he's never had this much money in his hands before.

After eating another baked potato with the works, Wyatt makes his way to Raye's. He's sad that Trav didn't come by Elson's, hoping their encounter hadn't been a fluke and Trav's interested in forging a friendship. Raye's is rowdy when he gets there, music coming from a phonograph, a jaunty tune. A girl sits atop the bar in stockings kicking her toes to the ceiling. Two fishermen clap below, smiles stretched wide. Raye slinks over, her nest of black hair pinned in a tower, a nightgown hugging her body. Her eyes betray her age, older than she appears.

"Can I help you with anything in particular?" she asks, her voice with a Southern twang. Her mouth painted with dark red lipstick, the whitest teeth ever beneath.

"Aylen?" he asks, hopeful. Raye takes out a pack of cigarettes and pats it against her palm until one comes out.

"With a client right now, but if you wait?" She loosens another cigarette for him. "On the house." Lighting it for him, they smoke in silence. He's smoked pipes before but nothing like this, the tobacco singeing his throat. When he's nearly finished, Aylen steps down the staircase.

She notices him, pretending she doesn't. Raye catches her at the bottom of the stairs.

"Sweetie, I believe one of your regulars." She guides Aylen over to Wyatt who puts out his cigarette and removes his hat.

"You look exquisite tonight," he says.

"Come with me," Aylen says, a hint of a smile surfacing. Raye leaves to relight some candles that have extinguished, and Wyatt follows Aylen up the stairs, to her room with the muted yellow light and sweet smell of lavender, to sheets warm from her last romp.

"Let me just tidy up," she says, but he stops her.

"This is all I have." He holds out the two twenties. "I made it at my new job."

She puts a hand on her hip. "That won't get you much."

"How about a story?"

"I could blow you."

"I don't know what that is. A story will suffice."

"Any story?"

"About you, your history...I saw part of my history the other day, and it was magical. Where do you come from?"

She exhales deeply, tugs the knots out of her long curtain hair.

"There's a Native American reservation on the outskirts. Born there. Parents died so young that I was raised by whoever felt like it. Aunties and uncles, cousins. It could have been a sad childhood, insular, lonely, but I was loved by many. The reservation is not the same now."

He takes off his boots and lets his feet air. "How so?"

"Taken a hard hit due to drink and drugs like a lot of them throughout the country. And then with the layoffs at the oil refinery over the last two years, there's little opportunity in Laner. That's why I'm doing this kind of work."

"You shouldn't be ashamed."

"Who said I was ashamed?"

"I'm sorry, I didn't mean to upset."

"You haven't. You're kind, I guess. Most don't want to know anything about me."

"I want to know everything."

"That's a little creepy." This time she exhales a slight laugh. "So you said you saw a part of your history?"

"Yes, my progeny."

She scrunches up her face.

"My great-great grandson, he's alive. Lives here. Travis Barlow."

"Unless he's come through these doors, I don't know too many people outside the reservation."

"We look exactly alike." He tugs at his beard. "Except for this old thing."

"I could trim that for you."

His eyes light up, but he is not ready to be an exact duplicate of Trav yet. So he shakes his head.

"That story I told you is not worth forty bucks," she says. "Let me do something else for you."

She gets on her hands and knees, crawling and unzipping his pants, pulling him out. Massaging his penis, he instantly grows hard.

"You don't have to—"

"I want to."

She takes all of him inside her mouth, something Adalaide had never done, at least he doesn't believe she ever did. The sensation like rolling waves, a delicious ocean, rocking him soundly. He leans back, hands tucked behind his head, Aylen bobbing up and down. When he's ready to release, he goes to pull away but she stays glued, swallowing him whole. She stands and spits him into a garbage bin, dabs her lips with a tissue. His own tongue salty from tears.

"You are so kind," he says, twiddling his thumbs.

She lifts up her head, tickling his chin with her fingernail.

"I'm here if you need me. Do not hesitate. I can listen. I can perform. I can bring you back from whatever hell you've been to."

His eyes go wide. "How did you know I've been there?"

"Because this is heaven," she says, as if she's told other men this before. "Most come to us after they've been to the other side. Because we're good at putting out the flames."

She lies on the bed, directing him to come to her. He slips inside, burrowing his nose in her chest.

"Just a few minutes, baby," she coos, stroking his chaotic hair. "Just till I feel your heart is ready to go back out into the wild."

The heater spits a chorus of steam, his bones no longer brittle and cold. The ice man melted, a new form waiting to emerge once all the frigid crystals get shaken away.

19

Travis tries to finish up work early on Smitty's the day prior so he could stop by Elson's, but it's night when the boat pulls in, and the fish need to be sorted, and by that time Elson has already let Wyatt go. He drives past the abandoned goods store. The hole in the window boarded up with bags and no sign of his lookalike. He heads home, swearing to get off earlier the next day so the two won't miss each other again.

That night he dreams of fishing from an ice hole with his newfound friend. The two sharing frozen brews, talking of their wives, their sons, waxing philosophical. A tug on his line forces him to peer inside the hole, a swell of dark water and nothing else. But he finds there are no fish unless he wants to dive in to claim his prize, so he does. The water like knives cutting through flesh. A scream muffled. He can visualize the ice sheet above him, a way to freedom, but he's sinking too low. His breaths stop but he can still feel a tiny beat of his heart, unwilling to let go.

He wakes with a start, sweat pouring, enough to rile Callie who puts a hand to his forehead to check for fever. He tells her he's all right, then disappears into the bathroom. Runs the shower but doesn't step inside. Waits until he stops shivering and is ready for the day to begin. The air moist on Smitty's boat, the fish biting unlike in his dream. They finish up earlier than usual and he skins and scoops out the guts with a mad dedication, so fast that Smitty's eyes bug. Travis is in his pickup and headed to Elson's before the sun even sets.

Chewing on a Mondo Burger, shooting the shit with Tuck and Jesse, he's eyeing the kitchen door. It swings open and he sees Wyatt by the dishwasher. He goes to wave but the doors swing shut before Wyatt can see. He sips beer after beer until Tuck and Jesse ask if he figured out how he and Wyatt are related yet. Then they head home and there's only a few regulars left slumped at the bar. Wyatt emerges from the doors with a dishrag over his shoulder.

"Trav," he says, a genuine smile creeping up his face. "You staying? Lemme wash up and join you."

Travis orders another round for them and remarks to Elson about his double. But Elson's watching a hockey game and cursing at the tube. Elson brings over two brews without taking his eye off the puck. Wyatt pulls over a chair, his hand on Travis's arm.

"Wondering when I'd see you again," Wyatt says. "This for me?"

He scoops up the beer and chugs half of it down.

"I couldn't get off work yesterday. You had already gone."

He's about to say he swung by the abandoned goods store but doesn't want to come off like a stalker.

"I was hoping you'd stop by tonight," Wyatt says, and raises his half-empty beer stein.

"To my brother from another mother," Travis says, but Wyatt looks confused. "Just a saying."

"Well, okay." They clink and sip, each with a million things to ask the other, but nothing comes out. Finally, Travis begins.

"I'm curious. What makes you think there's gold in this area?"

"It's complicated, but it's here. Just a question of where. That something you'd be interested in?"

"Money has sure been tight. Hell, though, gold, it's probably a fantasy, right?"

"Let's say you find a windfall, Trav. What would you do with it?"

Travis rubs his chin in the exact same way Wyatt rubs his beard, the two synchronized. Both stop at the same time, share a laugh.

"So I got this dream. I wanna open a fish shack right on the docks. I know it would do well."

"What's stopping you?"

"Pretty much everything. No savings. No bank that would give me a loan. So it stays a dream."

"For now, but that doesn't mean forever."

Wyatt gulps the beer until the suds outline his beard. Travis feels like he's speaking to an prophet, eager to tap into more answers.

"And I assume your dream is to find your gold?"

"Part of it. But there's more. I lost two people close to me. Don't know where they are."

"This your wife?"

Wyatt lowers his eyes. "And my son."

"Oh, man. Oh, wow, I'm sorry. Really, Wyatt. That's horrible. She took your kid?"

"No, I...I left them. And now I don't know where they are."

"Ever just Googled?"

"What?"

"Looked them up online. People move all the time, but everyone could be found. Do you not understand what I mean?"

Wyatt shakes his head.

"The internet, like, you can find anyone." Travis pulls out his phone. "Here, type in her name, see what comes up."

Wyatt stares at the phone looking completely overwhelmed.

"What's her first name?" Travis asks.

"Adalaide."

Travis shows Wyatt how to type, then he hands over the phone for Wyatt to fill in the rest. With shaking fingers, Wyatt conceals the screen and types. He thrusts back the device.

"Didn't work."

"Yeah, I guess not everyone's in Google. Actually, I'm not either. You gotta really do something to have your name there."

This is a lie, since Travis's name would come up in relation to Bobby. A quick byline, connecting them as brothers after Bobby's death. His only claim to fame excruciating.

"Could it be that you don't really want to find her?" Travis asks. "Like, you're afraid of the outcome if you do? How much things might've changed?"

Wyatt nods, his eyes glazed over, delving back into the past.

"She'd be ashamed of the things I've done."

"Gotta give her more credit than that, Wyatt. Sometimes I can't believe what Callie, my wife, puts up with."

"Is that true?" Wyatt asks. "Tell me about her."

"Callie? She's amazing. She's from California, she's a waitress at Pizza Joint a couple of stores over. She's an awesome mom, really patient with Eli and everything. I'm not, I get upset with him when he's not behaving. And she likes crystals a lot, that's her new thing. Says they have certain energies. That our entire planet has good and bad energies and it's important to go after the good and stay away from the bad. I used to think it was rubbish, but I dunno, who's to say?"

"All of us are capable of good and evil," Wyatt says, and something about the way this man utters those words sends a liquid chill down Travis's spine, as if the devil goosed his flesh. The lights have dimmed at the bar, the swish of the hockey game the only numbing sound, and this stranger at the stool beside him. "Another?" Wyatt asks.

"What?"

Wyatt calls over Elson. "Two more for me and my friend, my good friend."

The liquid chill has dissipated as Wyatt kneads Travis's shoulder. The beers arrive and the men sink in, sobriety long gone. After they finish, Travis walks Wyatt back to where he's sleeping while he sobers up. Flakes of snow spiral down, even though it's nearing May, Alaska too stubborn to relent.

"When are you setting out to search for this gold?" Travis asks, the two walking in step.

"Still have some work to do to find out where it is," Wyatt says, and taps his mind. "But you want in?"

"What have I got to lose?"

"This is me," Wyatt says, as they stand in front of the abandoned store. The bags taped to the window flapping from the rough breeze.

"What do you make of this?" Travis asks, tasting snow on his tongue. "Of us?"

"You mean our likeness?"

Hesitantly, Travis nods.

"Another time, Trav," he says.

"Do you know something—" Travis begins, but stops himself. Shakes his head in disbelief, the uncanniness morphing into incredulity.

"Another time, Trav," Wyatt says, his prophet's voice more in full effect. This man knows beyond what is tangible; he has access to the unexplainable. Travis too frightened and exhilarated to peel back more layers. They are meant to have met, he decides. This is no coincidence.

Travis closes his eyes to settle his nerves. "When?" he asks. After he opens his eyes, Wyatt has already disappeared inside like he was never there, an apparition mimicked by the strong wind.

20

Callie's hesitant about this forced meeting between Lorinda and Grayson. Knowing Lorinda, she'll get pissed at Callie for setting it up. But Travis seems certain it could work so Callie picks up a bottle of citron vodka after her shift finishes and convinces Lorinda to end hers early.

"You work too hard anyway," Callie says, pulling the bottle out of a paper bag. "C'mon, place is dead tonight."

Lorinda gives Pizza Joint a once-over, counts two tables left. She goes to Roy and asks if he can cover. Roy, a man of few words, shrugs with the same hang-dog expression he always has. Julia, who picks up shifts after school lets out, should be fine to clean up.

"You two got something fun planned?" Julia asks. Callie thinks how the girl is nothing like Callie was as a teen. Callie usually came home, packed a bowl, did a little homework and then went to clubs with friends. She guesses that Alaska forces you to be more responsible, since there's little distraction compared to L.A.

"Drinks at my place?" Callie says. "Miss Evelyn's gonna be watching Eli till late."

"You had this all figured out?" Lorinda asks, bumping Callie's waist with her butt.

"You got me."

Back at Callie's, they get right to the vodka. Lorinda known to drink anyone under the table, maybe why she'd gotten along with Grayson so well.

"Are you dating again?" Callie asks, pouring the tiniest dollop of orange juice into her vodka.

"I think I've been through most of the men in Laner," Lorinda says. "What happens when you're single in tiny-town Alaska in your thirties.

I should go to Nome."

"Don't leave me here," Callie says, desperate. She even takes Lorinda's hand.

"Girl, I'll be running the Joint until I'm in adult diapers. I ain't going nowhere. Some Nome guy better come to me."

She cackles and Callie's loves her uninhibited laugh, already feeling guilty for the setup about to occur. And with perfect timing, the door swings open to her husband and an as-sober-as-possible Grayson, kicking snow from their boots.

"Oh, no," Lorinda says, jumping up. She cuts Callie with her eyes, but Callie just plays dumb.

"Lor," Grayson says, going in way too soon for a hug.

"What did you all think this would accomplish?" Lorinda asks, pointing at each of them. "It's dunzo between us. Ain't nothing could bring it back."

"He just wants to talk to you," Travis says.

"Hear me out," Grayson says, hands locked together in prayer.

"Fine," Lorinda says, plopping back in a chair and pouring another massive drink.

"Let's leave the two of you to..." Callie begins to say, but Lorinda grabs her wrist.

"No way, sister. You all are in this with me. Sit."

They take a seat and wait for someone else to be the one to speak first. When no one does, Travis jabs Grayson.

"Okay, to start, I owe you an apology, Lor."

She crosses her arms and turns so she doesn't have to look at him. "It's too late."

"I love you, I really do. But I got scared. We fight a lot."

Lorinda blows her bangs away from her eyes. "That's true."

"Raye's was just a way for me to blow off steam. The girl there meant nothing."

"That supposed to make it better?"

"No, but you need to see that I was always thinking of you when I was there."

"Shit, Gray," Travis says, as the women shake their heads in embarrassment.

"So, you fucked whores but pictured me the whole time?" Lorinda asks.

"No, what I meant was I knew we were solid even when I was there. I wasn't trying to replace you."

"Gray, I put up with your police bullshit, strange hours and such, and hell, I dealt with your drinking too. I shut up about it all. But Laner's so small you had to know I'd find out, which means you did it to be cruel."

"I told you I was scared. I want to marry you, but the thought of forever…"

"I would've been a great wife and a great mother, but that will never be."

She hops up and knocks over her chair before running off to the bathroom as Callie follows.

Travis squirms. The last thing he wants is to be here right now. After last night, he feels like a drug addict without his fix—needing a hit of Wyatt. All day on Smitty's boat, he fantasized about trekking into the wilderness for gold, returning with a bounty, and starting life anew by doing what he loves.

"I really fucked up," Grayson says, taking a swig right from the bottle.

Travis grabs the vodka from him. "Yep."

"Don't tell me you weren't scared shitless to marry Callie, to never stick your dick in anyone else?"

"Jesus, Gray, why do you have to be so crude?"

"Ah, I'm sorry. I'm an asshole because I hate myself. I really do."

Grayson begins crying, wipes his nose on Travis's sleeve.

"You're the only one who never leaves me," Grayson wails. "Everyone else finds a reason to walk away."

"I ain't going anywhere," Travis says, but he's stilted as if he had to wrench those words out.

"No way she'll take me back?"

"Don't think so, buddy."

Callie and Lorinda return. Lorinda's eyes surprisingly dry.

"I think you should go, Gray," she says. "Callie and I are having our girls' night, and I don't want it ruined."

Grayson stands, a shriveled version of himself. "I understand."

Callie's rubbing Lorinda's back as Grayson makes for the door. Travis doesn't want to drive him home, but he thinks that maybe Wyatt's still at Elson's so he'll take him there.

"Don't wait up," he tells Callie, and kisses her on the cheek. She seems disgusted, blaming him by association. They turn on the road into town, but Grayson shakes his head.

"No, drive me home."

"Can't leave you like this."

"I'll sleep it off. I'll be fine."

"A round is on me."

They get to Elson's and it's quiet, just Tuck at the bar tearing into a steak with gravy. With a full mouth, he salutes them. They pull up and Grayson commiserates with Tuck about lost love. Tuck speaks of a girl-friend down in Anchorage that he never saw so they called it quits. They cheers to being old bachelors.

Elson's watching the hockey game, doling out drinks without taking his eyes off the TV.

"Hey, is Wyatt still here?"

Elson raises one thick eyebrow. "Just left."

"How's it working with him?"

"He shows up, does his job, so I'm pleased as punch."

Travis throws his arms around Grayson. "Hey, buddy, I'm gonna step out for a bit. You okay with Tuck?"

"I'll be fine," Grayson says into his glass.

Travis hurries out of the bar over to the abandoned goods store, but Wyatt isn't there. *Where does he go?* he wonders, feeling a twinge of jealousy. That this drifter has others to rely on in town. He walks the barren streets covered in a thin film of white over the permafrost, hands brittle because he hasn't brought gloves, teeth chattering. Turning down a side street, he passes by Raye's, a possibility of finding Wyatt there. Inside glows warm, the air full of perfume and music. Jesse's at the spider-webbed bar with a woman twice his size. They're giggling and then she yanks him by the collar, leading him up the stairs. Travis unsure if Jesse spotted him. Raye leaps upon him like a cat ready to mark its territory.

"Hi, new handsome face," she purrs, her dark red lips formed into a kiss. "What's your fancy?"

"I'm looking for someone," he says, coughing nervously.

"Blonde, brunette? I peg you as a red."

He gulps, thinking of Callie and the hot water he'd be in if she knew where he was.

"No, I'm looking for a friend of mine. We look quite similar although he has a big beard. Name is Wyatt."

She lights a long cigarette and holds it between two sharp fingernails.

"I'm not about to reveal my clientele. Wouldn't be professional."

He takes out his wallet, removes the money Smitty gave him today. "That change your mind?"

She eyes the bills, licking her teeth with her tongue.

"Sure, he comes in here. Even saw him tonight, except his fancy called in sick so he marched right out, no interest in anyone else."

"What time was that?"

"About an hour ago."

"But he wasn't where he's been staying."

"Sweetie, I'm sure he'll turn up. Doubt it's all that serious. Now, while you're here…"

The sleeve of her nightgown tickles his cheek as she fingers his chin. He recoils, which only makes her want to pounce more.

"Sweetie, lots come in here proclaiming ulterior motives, but I've found that pussy usually reigns."

"I have a wife," he says, inching toward the door.

"You tell yourself that, but my music will trickle over to where you live some night and you'll find yourself floating to me, unable to resist."

He turns the doorknob, a rush of cold air blowing in. "I doubt it."

When he's outside, he wonders why he feels the need to find Wyatt after only twenty-four hours apart. It's like a piece of himself is missing, although that makes little sense since up until a few days ago, he'd never met the man before. But every other relationship of his seems to pale in comparison to his double, his gleaming mirror. So he waits by the abandoned goods store, almost taking a chance and going inside the broken window, but deciding against it. He waits with the gale-force winds, and the crackling of ice on the branches, and the dark, dark street for Wyatt to show. He doesn't know how long he keeps watch, only that he won't allow himself to go. Midnight ticks by, then two in the morning, his fingers blue, his toes numb in his boots. His doppelgänger has found somewhere else to sleep, and since he's got to wake up to fish in a few hours, he must sleep as well.

Back at Elson's, his car is the only one in the back lot. The drive home is eerily quiet, so he turns on the radio, an old, jaunty tune like he heard at Raye's, a long-gone era invading. He listens for a while, but then feels like he shouldn't, so he snaps it off and continues in silence. At home, he checks on Eli who's fully in dreamland and Callie who's likely faking. He peels off his shirt and jeans, hoping she won't stir but when he sinks into the covers, she rustles awake.

"Where were you?" she murmurs, in and out of consciousness.

"With Gray."

"Elson's closed a long time ago, I called there."

A jolt wreaks havoc on his insides, the few drinks he had bubbling.

"We were driving around," he says, praying that she hadn't called Grayson as well when the clock hit three in the morning.

"Hmmm," she replies, into the groove her arm. Either disbelieving or too tired to care, saving any accusations for morning. He can't keep his double a secret much longer. But he truly worries that if he tells someone else, the whole miracle might vanish.

Along with the promise of gold.

21

Wyatt had already found out from Elson where the Native American reservation was located so when Aylen didn't show up at Raye's, he knows where to go. Technically, it isn't an actual reservation since it's unrecognized by the federal government. It resembles more of a settlement: a string of trailers, a few homes tucked away in various stages of disrepair. It'd been about a three-mile walk to the area, and his limbs are frozen solid, so he welcomes a bonfire where a couple of teenagers pass around a tin cup, their eyes as red as the sun.

"Mind if I get warm?" he asks. One with floppy hair shrugs.

Wyatt lets the flames almost touch his paralyzed fingers. Slowly, circulation begins.

"I'm here for Aylen," he says. "Although that might not be her name here."

A girl leaning on Floppy Hair's arm looks directly at a trailer. "What you want with her?"

"She's someone I care about," he says, surprised by that response. "I was told she's sick. I came to see if she needed anything."

"A good fuckin'," Floppy Hair's friend says, and the two slap hands.

Wyatt has the urge to grab this boy's throat, choke him good. But he maintains.

"Which of these is hers?" he asks, indicating the trailers.

The girl points at the one she was staring at, then she removes a corroded glass pipe from her pocket and takes a putrid puff.

"What is that?" His nose rejecting the smell.

The girl starts laughing, a weird and uncomfortable cackle. She passes over the pipe.

"Go on. Try."

Her voice has an otherworldly quality and he almost complies, but guesses that the red in their eyes is due to whatever's in this pipe. He tried opium in a Chinatown in California and it kept him sedated for days, his limbs like they were made of mud. So he hands the glass pipe back.

"We're always here if you ever want some," the girl says.

"Don't you go to school?"

The teens laugh more until it seems like he's being assaulted, so he goes over to Aylen's trailer. On one end, instrumental music spills out of the window. At the other, the violent sounds of a gun being fired except it doesn't sound real, as if someone captured the sound and replayed it.

He knocks on the trailer. The gunfire becomes muted as a man opens the door.

"What the fuck do you want?"

He's lean, almost disturbingly so, tall enough to have to stoop to fit in the doorway. His shirt soiled and he's not wearing pants, only undergarments. A tic in his eye that a scratching finger won't fix.

"I'm here to see Aylen," Wyatt says, lowering his voice to assert dominance.

The man spits in response, an orange-brown glob against the stark white snow.

"Aylen!" he yells.

"What?" comes a murmured voice.

"Some bum's here to see you."

Because of the way he eyes Wyatt, they both turn into animals. Wyatt knowing a tussle in store for their future. He'll keep coming to Aylen and this man won't like it. Wyatt watches him disappear into his side of the trailer as the gunfire resumes.

Aylen's door creaks, her eye in the crack. Unsure what stranger has come to her home.

"It's you," she says, her throat hoarse. "I'm sick."

He takes out a jar of honey and a lemon from his pocket. "Got these from where I work when I heard you're sick. A remedy from my time."

"We still do that," she says, opening the door fully. She's in a lavender nightgown and covered by a hand-stitched blanket where a detailed bison chase plays out across her body. "I'll add some whiskey and make two."

Afterwards, in her cramped room with a record player and a loom, they toast mugs of hot toddys.

"Are you, like, trying to be with me or something?" she asks him.

"Am I courting you? Why, yes, I do believe I am." He goes to the record player. "Think I worked one of these things once. Or at least, it sort of looked like it." He observes the large black plastic disc. "What's a Fleetwood Mac?"

Aylen laughs into her hand. "It's an old band. My mother, she used to listen. It's the first music I remember hearing. Do you not know how to use a record player? After your time?"

"We called them phonographs."

"Raye has a pretend version in the main room. Looks like it's old, but it's really playing CDs, which actually is old too."

Wyatt puts on the record.

"*Gypsy*," she sings.

"What's that?"

"That's the beautiful song."

They see a spinning of red lights outside her iced window.

"Police," she says. "Shit, fifty percent of the time it's for Tohopka."

"That's the man you live with?"

"It ain't like that. He's my cousin. He's my only family left so we're connected, always will be."

Wyatt peers out the window. A sheriff stands at the bonfire, talking with the teenagers.

"What kind of criminal things does your cousin do?" he asks.

"Drug stuff mostly. Hell, that's pretty much why the police come. There's an underbelly in these parts, right outside this town, but it's close and we feel it. Wayward kids getting lost to these parasites."

"Who?"

"Let's just say my cousin's involved with people he shouldn't be. I pretend to know nothing."

Wyatt sees the girl that tried to give him drugs point right at the trailer.

Aylen's bedroom door flings open, Tohopka panting.

"I'm not here!" he yells.

"What did you do now?" Aylen whines.

Tohopka's sweating profusely. He slaps his own face.

"Fuck if I know. I'm out the back window."

"What should I tell him?"

"Figure it out."

Tohopka goes to the desk with the loom, flings out a drawer causing stuff to spill everywhere.

"Get out of my shit, Tohopka."

She hits him on the back, but he turns around, smacking her on the head. The blow looking like she'd walked into a wall. She regains composure, but Wyatt steps in, their inevitable tussle happening earlier than he imagined. He doesn't raise a fist; he only speaks calmly.

"You touch her again and I'll end you."

"And who the fuck are you again?"

Wyatt slams him into the wall, his hand on the man's throat.

"I am *Death*."

He lets go as Tohopka coughs. Rushing over to the desk drawer, Tohopka grabs some bills. "I just need some cash, I'll pay you back."

"Get outta here!" Aylen yells, holding her head. A knock at the door. They watch Tohopka hop up on the sink in the kitchen and slither through a small window, then a *plop* of him falling into the snow and scurrying away.

Another knock.

Aylen smooths down her thick hair, fixes her disheveled blanket, and opens the door, making her cough more pronounced. Wyatt observing from the darkness of the bedroom.

"Yes, Sheriff. Can I help you?"

The sheriff, a squat older man with a buzz cut and ropey arms.

"Your roommate here?" He's rubbing his hands together since it's cold outside.

"Haven't seen him around all day. Think he's in Nome on business."

"Business," the sheriff says, in a huff. "The kind of business you both do..."

"Plenty of your officers come to see me, so you can leave your judgement at the door. We done?"

She goes to close the door on him, but he stops her, takes off his hat.

"I want to ask your roommate some things. I believe he knows a lot of people, people who might have answers. I'll stop by again in a few days. You make sure to tell him because I can just as easily come into your trailer and find enough junk to arrest you both."

"I'm not a part of anything he does."

Wyatt steps out of the doorframe now, his shadow cloaking Aylen. "I think you should go now, Sheriff. She was mighty compliant."

Right away, the sheriff squints, as if he's trying to read him. "Sheriff Barlow." He extends his hand.

"Wyatt," he says, lighting up upon touching his great-grandson. He witnesses shades of himself in the sheriff's visage: the Barlow nose, the solid and defined shoulders, the twinkle in each of their eyes like they all know a secret everyone else in the universe doesn't.

"He's a friend of mine in town," Aylen says. "Staying with me."

Wyatt looks at her startled, then catches on. "Yup, yup she's been very kind."

"Well," the sheriff says, sucking in a deep breath, "enjoy Laner. It's a special place."

"I plan on it," Wyatt says, and the sheriff reiterates for Aylen to tell her cousin about him stopping by.

"I will, Sheriff."

The sheriff's taking his sweet time leaving, saying, "I wouldn't want to have to bring you into your cousin's messes. You don't want to be guilty by association. You're better than this."

He chews on the last words. "You take care, Ms. Oxendine."

She mumbles under her breath as she closes the door on him.

"I'm staying with you?" Wyatt asks, but she shakes her head.

"Just for tonight, barely room for two in this shit can. I'm going to bed."

She folds under the covers, wrapping herself tight. Wyatt gets in beside her, eager for a warm night. Outside, his great-grandson walks up to the next trailer, ready to give the same speech. But then Aylen pulls the curtain shut and he sleeps more soundly than he has in years.

22

By the time Callie wakes, Travis has already gone. Sometimes she gets a moment with him in the morning: sharing the mirror while they brush their teeth, early coffees in silence before she has to get Eli up. Today she didn't want to face him until she can get her thoughts together.

When he hadn't returned until three in the morning, she called Elson's finding out he had left prior to midnight. Then when she woke up an inebriated Grayson, he verified the same thing. The two of them had not been driving around, which meant whatever Travis was doing, he was keeping it a secret from her.

She confirms the worst. Much like what happened to Lorinda, she believes Travis was cheating on her. He'd been withdrawn, barely even acknowledging Eli after they'd spent so much time together when Travis had been out of work. Even Eli questioned, "What's wrong with Daddy?" Usually, her answer had been his unemployment, but now she feared a more sinister explanation.

At Pizza Joint, Lorinda acts chilly from last night, and Callie's fine with that since she doesn't really want to talk to anyone. She switches off during the breakfast rush, pouring coffees, but not registering who she's serving. Until Tuck and Jesse sweep in around lunch.

"Jesse convinced me to do lunch off the boat," Tuck tells her.

"Waves were choppy and I thought I might hurl," Jesse says.

"You need food that'll stick to the walls then. We got a gumbo as the special today."

"Gumbos all around," Tuck says.

After she puts in the order, she can sense someone standing right behind her. Cool breath on her neck. Sweat that smells like the boys she used to fool around with in California.

"Callie?"

She turns around and has to peer up to see Jesse who stands at six-six. He's all angles, sharp elbows and bony shoulders.

"Is everything all right?" he asks, in his sweet way. Unable to look her in the eye.

She's caught off guard, the waitress pad falling to the floor. He picks it up and static sparks between them.

"Yeah. Thanks. Yeah it is." And then, with more curiosity. "Why do you ask?"

"You seem melancholy," he says, as if he's proud of using vocabulary like that. "Wanted to make sure."

"That's nice of you." Now she's suspicious and wants to flee his gaze. "I got orders."

"Just that...well, I saw your husband."

"Okay, Jesse."

"I mean, I saw him at a place he shouldn't be. That I shouldn't have been either. But I haven't met someone I liked in some time, and..."

"Spit it out," she says.

"It was at Raye's."

The rest of the day in a timeless blur. Callie can remember being at Pizza Joint until her shift ended, but what she said to Jesse, or anyone else, a mystery. She knows she picked Eli up from Huskie Day Care, since he's home with her now watching some cartoons and drinking apple juice, but how she made it there is beyond her comprehension. For Travis to set himself apart from Grayson when he was doing the exact same thing is disgusting. She's seen the girls at Raye's too, nothing special. In Laner, Alaska, she's as good as it's gonna get for a guy like Travis. When her cruise ship pulled into this nothing town, she added a spark to his life—while now she realizes, he mostly dulled hers.

Since infidelity is a sickness, she decides over an overflowing glass of red wine that this won't get any better. She'll bring Eli back to her parents in California while she figures out the next step. Travis won't let her go easily, and while it'd be nasty to take Eli from his father, Travis hasn't been holding his own as a parent these last few weeks anyway.

She boils as the clock ticks away, the sun sets, and she forgoes giving Eli a bath because she wants to pounce on Travis when the door unlocks.

After an hour of simmering and staring, she hears his car churn through the packed snow.

"Go play in your room," she tells Eli, the circles around her eyes reddening.

"But Daddy's home."

"Go play!" she roars, a lion rumbling, and Eli's wise enough to saunter away.

Travis gets halfway through the door when she's upon him with a slap, a white handprint forming on his jaw.

"What in the hell?"

She hits with a fury, saying everything she wanted at once, too much for him to decipher. The word "cheater" floating between curses.

"Whoa, whoa," he says, backing away and scooting around the couch. "Cheating?"

"You were at Raye's, that filthy place."

She gives up now, collapsing into the couch and removing a sopping tissue from her sleeve. She hates to act so vulnerable but doesn't know how else to behave.

"Callie, I was just looking for—"

"If you say Grayson, I swear to God I'll hit you with a pan."

"No, not Gray."

"You were *not* driving around with him last night either. I called his place and he'd been in bed for hours. You were fucking some brainless whore while your wife was at home worried sick."

"I know I was there, but…"

"Honesty," she says, flinging her hands. "Finally. And for how long has this been going on?"

"I met someone."

"Oh God, Travis." She's shaking and he wants to hug her close but he's too afraid to move.

"It's not like you think. His name is Wyatt."

"*What?* A man?"

"No, no, no. Not like you think. He's homeless. Jeez, I don't even know where to begin. Will you just let me explain?"

She sits up and swipes her glass of wine for comfort, then gestures for him to begin.

"So a few days ago I pass by this guy and, this is crazy, Cal, but he looks exactly like me, a dead ringer. 'Cept he's got a big bushy beard."

"Really, Travis, this is gonna be your excuse?"

"C'mon now, just wait. So we pass each other, and I dunno. Have you ever had an out-of-body experience? That's what it was like. I watched from above as these two identical men passed by each other, and I have to say the moment stuck in my mind, like I couldn't shake it. And then we met again at Elson's and he's this prospector, a genuine modern prospector come here looking for gold, he's convinced it's here, and we talked about the fish shack, and I dunno, he's listened to me, like working on Smitty's is fine and all, but you know my dream. So it got me thinking, what if he's in the know about gold in these parts and I could find some too?"

Callie dips her nose into the glass as she sucks out the rest of the red wine.

"What the fuck are you talking about, Travis? What does this have to do with that whorehouse?"

"So this guy, Wyatt, he's been going there. He's staying in the abandoned goods store, but it's cold, like it's been unseasonably cold so it's warmer there I guess. I got him a job at Elson's, you can even ask Elson, and I stopped by to see if he was there. You always talk about your crystals and energies and things that can't be logically explained, right? A current of energy is drawing me to him and I need to see it all through."

"Well," she says, her mind spinning. His explanation so outlandish, it couldn't have been made up on the spot. Yet still, she's wary. It could be true, but so could his cheating ways.

"Baby, you could ask down at that place. I spent five minutes talking to the owner and that's it."

"I'm not going there."

"I need you to believe me!"

"All right, I believe you. Don't get hysterical." She grabs the bottle and sees it's empty. "Shit."

He moves in for a hug. For a second, she fights it but then gives in.

"I'm sorry I didn't tell you before. It's all hard to put into words."

"So you're gonna follow some homeless guy into the wilderness for gold?"

Callie's speaking but really thinking of California receding further and further away. All day, she'd been making plans. Needing its beaches, its closer sun, and even her chilly parents' embrace. They'd call her a fool, but only for a little. She'd have her old room back and Eli in the guest room until she got work and could move out. It'd only be for a while, then she'd ease back into an L.A. lifestyle, reconnecting with friends, even joining Tinder, a solid reason to leave Travis, when now, in a span of seconds, the fantasy has shattered. The walls in her Alaskan home with traces of water damage, the mallard painting over the mantle she hates, the insulation covering the window that began to peel forcing her to wear sweaters inside, the fact that beyond Lorinda she has no one else to confide in. In all her time here, she's never felt more trapped.

But Travis seems so excited. He's babbling about this fucking gold he's sure exists. And the conversation veers to his wants and needs, leaving hers at bay. Okay, he wasn't cheating on her, but since she thought he had, it's hard to completely extinguish that notion. She hates that she might've been more relieved to know that he had. The door closed now.

"Bring him for dinner tomorrow," she says, hand on her hip. "Your new friend."

"Okay, I'll ask him. Thank you, Callie. I know this is a lot to absorb."

"You're a lot to absorb," she says, under her breath but it's audible. She's finds another bottle of whatever and wanders down the hall toward the bathroom.

"You deal with dinner for Eli," she says. "I'm getting in a bath and I don't want to emerge till I'm pruned good."

"Of course, baby."

"I ain't your fuckin' baby," she says, louder this time so it bounces off the walls and sinks into his skull. "I ain't your fuckin' anything right now."

In the bath, she bobs underwater, a layer of suds coating the surface. All she can see—whiteness, like a tundra, like the story of her life.

23

Wyatt's surprised to find Trav pop his head into the kitchen before the morning rush even arrives. He's spent the night at Aylen's since her cousin never returned home, cramped in her twin bed with his feet dangling off the edge, yet he's slept more deeply than he had in some time. He was doing a double-clean on the dishes from last night, which Elson liked, when his great-great grandson gave a booming, "Hello."

"Wasn't expecting no one," Wyatt says, starting the noisy dish machine.

"Thought I'd catch you before I headed on the water. My wife wants to invite you for dinner when your shift ends."

"That's mighty kind."

"We're on Elk Road." He hands Wyatt a slip of paper. "Address plus directions."

"Should I bring anything?"

"Just yourself, man."

The rest of the day passes with a hummingbird fluttering in Wyatt's chest, a rapid beat of excitement. All night with Aylen, he hadn't thought of Trav's wife, or even his own. They made love and she didn't charge him nothing. He was content. But now, with the idea of Trav's wife on the horizon, Aylen gets shuttled to the back of his mind, forced to wait in purgatory until she's needed again.

Elson lets him off early and donates a bottle of wine to bring to the Barlows. He offers to call him a cab, since the walk is far, and Wyatt pretends like he doesn't know. The cab costs a quarter of his day's wages, but it's worth it to not show up all disheveled and sweaty.

California opens the door, a smile so wide he can see her molars.

"Welcome," she says, with a hug and kiss on his cheek. "I've heard a lot about you."

The sensation of her touch—incandescent. He's soothed and swaddled and mystified by her charm. She's wearing dungarees, a sweater that looks made of snow, her red hair pulled back into a ponytail. He wonders if Adalaide ever did that, but decides it wasn't the style at the time.

He steps inside and the home has a beefy smell like they're living in a great pot of stew. He thrusts the wine at her to give his hands something to do.

"This red will go perfect with the meat," she says. "Come, let me take your coat."

She kicks aside some scattered toys and hangs up his coat. He tugs on his beard, a ball of nervous energy.

"Travis is chopping wood for the fire." She indicates the fireplace, a bed of soot, ash, and crumpled newspapers. "I heard by the end of the week the weather's supposed to take a turn for the better. We might even be able to have an outdoor barbeque."

He has no idea what a bar-be-que might be, but nods as if he's familiar.

"Wyatt," Trav says, as he comes through the back door with an armful of logs and dumps them in the fireplace. "I see you've met Callie."

"Actually, I didn't introduce myself." She extends her hand, and it's like silk when he shakes it. He doesn't want to let go. "Callie."

"Wyatt," he says, and then with a laugh: "Well, thank you both for hosting. Looking forward to a home-cooked meal."

"Been some time for you?" she asks.

"Longer than you can imagine."

"The little one just went down for sleep so I'm afraid you missed him," she says. "But this way we can have a night of adult conversations. So rare."

"How old?"

"He recently turned three."

He's about to speak of Little Joe, but clamps his mouth shut. He's not ready. And he doesn't know how he'll react.

"Let's pour this wine," Callie says, disappearing into the kitchen and coming back with three glasses. She pops the cork and fills each one, passing them over.

"To new friendships," Trav says, and Callie looks between him and Wyatt, assessing how closely they resemble each other.

"It's uncanny," she says, like she just realized. "The two of you. Have you ever had family in these parts?"

"I don't know," Wyatt says. "Only know of my father's origin, but he was from Washington State. No one in Alaska."

"Travis's family goes back for generations in Alaska," she says. "Your great-grandfather came here, right?"

"Yup, although Papa Clifford rarely talks about him. He was so young when he died, I don't think he has any memories."

"And you?" Wyatt asks her.

In mid-gulp, she responds, "California. I'm the first, and nuttiest in my family, to come all the way to Alaska."

"They say Alaska is a place for new beginnings," Wyatt replies.

"Who says that?"

"I don't know, but I've certainly heard it."

"It *was* a new beginning for you, Cal," Trav says.

With lips stained wine-red, she nods. "What's your last name?" she asks.

"Langford," he quickly says, before he might blurt out *Barlow* by accident and cause them to think he's insane. Langford was the name on his tongue because it had been locked in his mind. The man he killed never truly died, only became preserved.

"Wyatt Langford," Callie says. "Sounds like a character out of the Wild West." She fires a round of shots at him with her fingers.

"Smells delicious in here," Wyatt says, wanting any discussions about his name to end.

"Are you hungry? We can eat now."

"I'm always hungry, ma'am."

In the dining room, Callie serves a stew from a giant pot and seats herself across from the two men, these twins separated by a beard.

"When Travis told me," she begins, pouring Wyatt another glass of wine, "I didn't believe. But the resemblance is remarkable. Maybe Cora had twins and gave one up?"

"Cora would've had quadruplets and been delighted," Trav says.

"Okay, I have a theory. Read something similar somewhere." She clears her throat. "Everyone has a duplicate on this planet and our whole lives are about coming into contact with this double."

"Success!" Trav says, holding his hand up for a high-five. Wyatt doesn't know what to do so Trav picks up Wyatt's hand and slaps it. Wyatt looks at Callie, confounded.

"Maybe that's what's taken me to Alaska?" Callie asks, already slurring. "To meet my own twin?"

"No, I see what you mean," Trav says. "Like it was destiny for us to meet."

Wyatt's enraptured by her, his double nary a thought. "What's that?"

"You spoke of gold, man. I want to find it with you."

"Gold?" Wyatt asks, spiraling back down to Earth. "Yeah, of course. I just need to remember where it is."

"Remember?" Trav asks.

"I mean, remember where I was told it might be. You know the wilderness around here well?"

"Been trekking out there since I was kid. The meat you're eating is from caribou I hunted."

"Finally, the last of it," Callie says, crossing her eyes.

"That boo fed us real well for a month."

"Yeah, we ate everything down to the lips and asshole."

She lets out a gush of a laugh. And Wyatt laughs as well, tears blurring the edges of his eyes. Adalaide would make him guffaw like this, too. When she wasn't worried about Little Joe running too cold. They had good times around a table with spirits like he was doing now.

"So it's set then?" Trav asks, more serious now. "We go on this adventure together?"

"What's that?"

"The gold, bro. We attack that gold."

"Of course, Trav. We're partners."

"Trav?" Callie asks, scrunching up her face. "Never really heard you called that."

Trav shrugs. "Never had a twin before. And Gray's called me that before."

"This food is mighty fine," Wyatt says, shoveling it in his mouth until the plate shines white again.

Trav takes her hand from across the table and the two hold onto each other, a locked unit. It makes Wyatt bubble with jealousy.

"My girl's an amazing cook."

She's an amazing everything, Wyatt wants to say.

"Mommy?" In walks a little child in footed pajamas rubbing the sleep from his eyes.

"Hey, buddy, did we wake you?" Trav asks, scooping him up. The child twists into Trav's chest, a string of drool connecting them.

"I smelled food," Eli says, turning to the stew now.

"But you had dinner."

"Not dinner like that!" he yelps, and then giggles.

His giggles like glass shards to Wyatt, the mirth of a child stabbing his soul. The room goes in and out of focus, his chair tilts and he nearly falls back, but he manages to maintain.

"Eli, can you say hi to Mr. Langford?"

Eli gives a tired wave. "Hi, mister."

"Hi, child," Wyatt says, the lump in his throat bulging like a tumor. The tears well up, his face blanches, and he gets faint again.

"Are you all right?" Callie asks, concerned.

"I'm not feeling so well." He rises on shaky knees.

Callie leaps up, ready to catch, but Wyatt squares himself.

"Possibly too much to drink," Wyatt says, heading toward his coat. But that's a lie, since it's from the sight of the boy, a direct and cruel link to his own. He cannot even look at him anymore. "I must go."

"No, maybe just lie down," Callie says, jumping over to the couch and fluffing a pillow.

"Very kind of you again, ma'am, but I'm not right."

He pulls on his coat, the sickness lurching into his mouth like acid.

"Can we..." He blinks his tearing eye. "Do this another time? You are so kind, but I really must go."

"Of course, of course, Wyatt." She goes to rub his back, but he doesn't want that either. Every sight of them, every possible touch, an implosion in his heart. Better to shut his eye to only darkness.

Trav puts down Eli. "Lemme drive you back at least."

Wyatt's already at the door. "No, no, Trav."

"It'll mean five minutes as opposed to hours walking. And it's still so cold."

Wyatt has his fingers on the doorknob that radiates an icy chill. "Okay."

"Lemme get my coat."

Trav shoots out of the room, Wyatt left alone with the very people he was dying to meet but now can't bear.

"I'm sorry," he says, about to start weeping.

"No," Callie replies. "Can't tell you the amount of times I've drank too much for my body."

"It's not the drink, it's..." He catches sight of Eli, peering around from behind his mother.

Trav rushes back before Wyatt can respond. "C'mon, man."

Wyatt's out the door without looking back at either of them, the snow an assault on his senses. In the pickup, Trav speeds, the winding roads of the woods sloshing everything around in Wyatt's stomach.

"It was from seeing your son," Wyatt says.

"Yeah, I figured."

"I miss mine."

That's all the two men say because silence trumps an attempt at comfort. Trav allows Wyatt to truly weep, the tears collecting in his bushy beard. And when he reaches the abandoned goods store, Wyatt doesn't say goodbye, wanting only the deafening roar of all the demons inside his head, the last moments of his family he's held onto and nothing else. He keeps them rattling as he assumes the fetal position indoors, but this time, he takes down the picture of Callie and Eli that he stole. Maybe soon he'll be able to be in a room with them again. For now, the darkness of closed eyelids is all he can handle.

24

It's late when Wyatt unravels himself and makes his way toward Aylen's. He'd rocked with his knees tucked up to his chin and shed enough tears for a lifetime. He doesn't want her in particular but a warm body will suffice. Without even thinking of checking at Raye's, he makes the long trek to the settlement, assuming she's still sick.

The trailer's dark when he arrives, no amount of knocking could conjure her. The four teenagers are smoking and wrestling around the wonky bonfire. He remembers the girl the most so he speaks directly to her.

"Have you seen Aylen?"

The girl sips from a can of Coke, a film covering her eyes. Her other hand holds a pipe made from tinfoil.

"Who do ya think I am, the hostess of this place?" the girl says. "That bitch comes and goes at all hours of the night."

"She's not a female dog," Wyatt says, and the four teenagers double over while holding their stomachs.

"Take a chill pill," one says. "Or more like a drag."

This one's pipe gleams in the moonlight, creating a light show in his palm.

"What is that?" Wyatt asks.

"Meth," another one burps, his teeth browned.

Wyatt takes a sniff, decides it smells evil. "Opium? Do you have any of that?"

Three of the teenagers laugh at this, but the girl removes a bag of powder from one pocket and a lighter and a spoon from another.

"How much have you got on you?" she asks, and when he shrugs she rubs her fingers together and mumbles, "Money?"

He procures balled-up twenties from the last two days of work.

"That should do it," she says, swiping the cash before he can change his mind. He stares at the bag of powder and the corroded spoon. She squirts a needle. "One last thing. Here, I'll show you."

"This is opium?"

"Heroin."

She mimes for him to pour some of the powder on the spoon, then cooks it with the lighter until it hisses and bubbles. She stabs the needle into the potion and fills up a hit.

"You inject," she says. "Do you want me to do it?"

He doesn't respond so she takes it upon herself and rolls up his sleeve.

"Ya gotta find a good vein, that's the trick." Her fingers glide down his arm. "Ah, here's a juicy one."

The prick of the needle entering flesh. A dollop of blood surfacing. Skin flushes, body heavy, mouth dry. It rushes up in tingles. Then it hits. Explosion of pure pleasure. The sadness due to Adalaide and Little Joe eliminated. He loves everything. The teenagers watch with spooky fascination. He loves that he has a body, that he's an actual being. The girl touches his arm and feels like fire ants rushing across, all of it delicious.

"Sit down," they tell him. "Nod off. It's okay. Lie back, gaze at the stars."

Even though the ground is cold, it's the warmest bed he's ever experienced. Dozing in a stoned dream, but lucid, like the dream is real, like he can control every facet.

"Take me to them," he says, drooling until the twinkling stars grant his wish.

Returning from his first golden jaunt, wallowing away sorrows in an opium den in San Francisco when the search came up empty. Stoned and sluggish, he meanders up the coast, taking boats and trains until he spends every last dime to get home. Once there, he finds a chilled Little Joe a shade of blue in his bassinet, flames from a fireplace licking, and Adalaide with a thousand kisses awaiting his return. He scoops her up, carries her to the bed, peels off her long floral dress, her tight undergarments, leaving her boots on as they dig into his back. His tongue burns but hers is sweet with sugary love.

"You were gone longer than you said you'd be." She lets her wild hair out of a bun as it tumbles across the pillow.

"I didn't find it," he replies, shooting himself in the heart for failing. "I have nothing."

She laces her fingers in his. "You have us."

"Little Joe grew so much since I left."

"That's what babies do."

"And his pallor?"

"Dr. Greeson says not to be concerned. Just keep him close to the fire during winters."

"They are whispering about Alaska."

"Who's whispering?"

"Gold," he says, in his own lilting whisper.

"When I think of gold, I think of poison."

"Why?"

"Because it takes you away from us and even when you're here, you're not really here."

"Where am I?"

And in her lovely Irish brogue, she replies, "In its lure."

"It's nowhere near as pretty as you."

"That's a lie and you know it."

He rolls over, rises, and cracks his back. Her boot dances down his spine.

"Look at me, Wyatt."

"Anytime, love." He stares into the worried dent between her eyes.

"We can sustain. The farm. My wares. I'll knit till I bleed if that keeps you home."

"I'm going to check on Little Joe."

The dancing boot morphs into a hard kick. Like a shock to his system. When he turns around, she's capsized into a ball armored by a swirl of red hair. He pets its delicate silk, but she only curls up smaller.

"I could've stayed in Ireland if I wanted to feel empty," she says.

He kisses her fire-red locks. "You'll see one day when you're showered in gilt. You'll see what kind of man your husband truly is."

"The only kind of man for me is one I know will be around."

"Guilt won't keep me here."

"I know. But let me have that. Because it's all I have."

Tears collect on the pillow and he uses them as a cue to leave. In the far room, Little Joe stirs in his bassinet, blue cheeks puffed out. Wyatt rocks the baby in his arms as its black marble eyes open to the world.

The baby lets out a cool yawn.

The Wyatt from the future tells him to hold onto his child longer, endlessly, because once the spell breaks, he'll never be able to embrace him again. Heroin's magic touch and own telling whisper. So he listens. He spends eternity with his child tucked into his chest, then brings the baby over to his and Adalaide's bed, placing Little Joe between their heated bodies as he speaks of lies he knows he won't follow. He'll leave behind his golden dreams, live for the farm and them, find happiness in stasis. And while in reality she never heard this, heroin's dust allows for whatever manipulation he wants. So he gives her ghost a thrill of a lie causing her to uncurl with a smile of relief, as Joe's cheeks turn from blue to red, and they all stay paused in their floating bed of hope. Until it becomes unmoored and crashes into a tall buoy, going under and descending into the black of the ocean.

The raindrops patter against Wyatt's face in the early morning. The teenagers gone to sleep off their drug binges. He emerges from his cocooned shell with a shriek at the heavens for interrupting his fantasy.

But reaching into his pocket and pulling out the powdered baggie, he knows he holds the ability to return to whenever he fancies with a mere prick of the skin.

25

Upon hearing that the weekend will be unseasonably warm, Cora buzzes about getting plans for an outdoor gathering. It had been a rough winter due to Papa Clifford's deteriorating health, which in the last week had gotten worse. Stu was more detached than usual spending most of his time home in the basement. She'd gone down to tidy up the area, making sure not to touch any of his newspaper clippings or files. Each time made her sadder to know that nothing had moved forward with Bobby's case, and Stu was veering closer toward a breakdown. Early on, she'd tried to get him to talk about it, but Stu was never a man for words, usually responding in grunts, and he'd always had a closer relationship with Bobby than she. Bobby scared her, even as a child, even though she pretended there was nothing to worry about. He was secretive and vindictive, untamed and moody, some of the same traits she saw in Stu.

As for Papa Clifford, Stu had been distancing himself from his father as of late. She understood, having lost a mother to grueling rounds of chemo that would give glimmers of hope only for things to get worse. During the last round, she and her mother spoke in rudimentary questions and answers, nothing deep or that required thought and concern. Cora would go over but focus on keeping the house in order, the bills stacking up, rather than trying to stretch out the last few moments to be as memorable as possible. She'd lost the mother she knew a long time ago and had already been through mourning.

With Papa Clifford, it was different. She loved the man because he was one-of-a-kind, a relic of a far-gone more brutally honest era. But he wasn't her father, or even a replacement father. He was an old man who needed a nurse at times and that was a role she could play. Recently, however, he'd taken to sleeping more. She'd attempt to get him up in the morning only for him to crawl back to bed a few hours later after nibbling on toast for breakfast. The afternoons followed a similar pattern. He'd wake for lunch only to require a nap that would bleed into dinner. And when he was awake, he wasn't much company, the house rocking with an unsettling silence.

She convinced herself it was all due to the winter that wouldn't end. Usually by May, there are visible buds on the branches, springtime thirsting to bloom. Not the pervasive death she sees out of her window everyday: browns and whites but no green, no vibrancy. Certainly, that's affecting Papa Clifford too.

But news of fifty degrees! That would be cause for celebration. She'd plan an outdoor event with all of his favorite people. Travis, Callie and Eli of course. Miss Evelyn, who Papa always likes to flirt with. Grayson and his girlfriend Lorinda…wait, maybe not Lorinda since she seems to remember Callie saying they called it quits. Elson, who served Papa Clifford for years. Smitty, who'd been a family friend. A few of the girls from her book club who always ask kindly about Papa. And Dr. Emmanuel, who'd been Papa's doctor for decades. She checked in with Stu whether he thought it a good idea, to which Stu replied with his signature shrug. He had police business and was putting on his coat when she brought it up. She could've asked him for a ride to the moon and he would've barely blinked. She calls Travis first, speaking to Callie, and they settle on Saturday rather than Sunday, since by Sunday the weather would drop to below-freezing again. Callie suggests a barbeque, and Cora becomes tickled with trying a new spice rub she picked up at the market that made Stu frown. At least she'd put it to good use now. After calling everyone else and getting mostly yesses with a few maybes, she goes into Papa's room. The heater on full blast, the windows locked shut, she could hardly breathe. She watches the rise and fall of his chest, his mouth wide open in a never-ending snore. She hates to wake him, but he must have slept fifteen hours already that day.

"Papa," she says, shaking his shoulder. Bones protruding more than ever before, he's becoming a skeleton. His skin so cold for a second she worries he might've died, but then she realizes her theory was debunked due to the snoring. "Papa!"

She shakes him hard enough to rouse the soundest sleeper and he chokes on a snore, his milky eyelids unsticking.

"What's that?" he asks, a frog in his throat.

"Papa," she said, in the tone she reserves for speaking to a child. "Papa, I'm planning a party for you."

"Lemme break out my kazoo."

"Oh Papa, it's gonna be nice weather on Saturday, and I thought a barbeque."

"Can't eat that stuff anymore."

"Nonsense, I could make ribs."

"Too messy."

"Well, a steak then."

"Only things in little bites work."

"I'll cut it up for you."

He turned back into his pillow. "Too much trouble."

"Now Papa," she says, her voice shrill. "We've been cooped up in this house all winter and it's enough."

"I just wanna sleep."

"And I wanna be with George Clooney on a lake in Italy. We don't always get what we want!"

Either he senses what this means to her, or he simply wants her to go away. "Fine."

She claps her hands. "Oh goody. You'll see. I'm gonna make an Angel food cake too."

She leaps up and dances out of the room. This would be the end of winter and doom and gloom. This would be what the whole Barlow family needed.

Wyatt had just left when Cora calls and Callie picks up the phone. She's not in the mood to have a long conversation like Cora tends to do. She agrees with whatever her mother-in-law says to get her off, puts Eli to bed, and finds Travis washing the dishes.

"Your mother is throwing an outdoor party for Papa on Saturday."

With the faucet on full blast, she's unsure if Travis heard.

"I said—"

"No, I heard ya." He turns off the water, lets the dishes soak, and dries his hands on a towel flipped over his shoulder.

"You drove Wyatt home?" she asks.

"He doesn't have a home. He sleeps in the abandoned goods store that has a hole in the window."

"He seemed nice," she says, because she doesn't quite know how else to describe him.

"He lost his son. I don't know the story, but that's why he got so upset when he saw Eli."

"His son died?"

"I think the wife, or ex-wife took him away. And he has no idea where."

"Invite him to Cora's party."

"You think? You saw how he acted with just the three of us."

"That man's in a lot of pain. Clear as day I saw that. He needs to be around people. We don't get homeless up here, I guess cause of the cold. But back in California, I volunteered at a soup kitchen. In L.A., it's heartbreaking to see them on the streets, but at least they aren't freezing."

They hug, her nose pressed into the dish towel.

"Makes you appreciate the family you have."

"We're lucky, Travis. Even when we're struggling, we're blessed."

"I'll swing by his place tomorrow."

In the morning, Travis can't find Wyatt in the abandoned goods store, or at Elson's. He doesn't have time to wait around since he has to get to the *Cutthroat*, but afterwards he convinces Smitty to call it an early day and swings back to Elson's, who tells him that Wyatt never showed. He tries the goods store and finds a rheumy-eyed Wyatt mumbling incoherently in his sleep. Trying to wake him proves fruitless, and when a needle falls out of the man's pocket, Travis chooses to ignore it.

We all have demons, Travis thinks.

He carries Wyatt out to his pickup, heading home and knowing Eli will still be at daycare. Wyatt rouses a bit from the bumps in the road, but not enough to fully emerge from his webbed slumber. Back at his place, Callie's gone too, likely picking up Eli, so Travis gets Wyatt in the shower, turning the water on full blast.

"Wha...what's going on?" Wyatt cries, swinging his arms.

"You were passed out. Just trying to clean you up."

"No one asked you!"

"Get your shit together, man," Travis yells, not wanting to go there but unable to quell his frustration. He throws Wyatt a towel and leaves the room.

About twenty minutes later, Wyatt steps out with the towel around his waist. If the men are identical in their face and their builds, even scars that they've obtained, Wyatt's closed-over eye betrays their differences.

"I ain't one to judge another man's vices," Travis says.

Wyatt digs a finger into his ear. "Yet I feel like you have more to say about it."

"Anything you need a needle for is gonna bring problems."

"I'll deal with them as they come along."

"Lemme give you a change of clothes."

Travis heads into his bedroom. When he returns with a flannel shirt, boxers, and jeans, Wyatt is observing the picture over the mantle of Callie and Eli. He turns away while Wyatt changes.

"Thank you."

"We're here for you, man. Callie and I. We want you to know that."

"Appreciate it."

"Tomorrow's gonna be a really nice day. My mother is throwing a party for my grandfather. He's old and I don't know how many parties he has left in him. Callie made it clear she wants you there."

"Your wife is too kind."

"But you can't come high. Can't have you around Eli like that. Gotta make me a promise."

Wyatt chews on a fingernail, as if debating. "It's a deal."

He spits into his hand and offers to shake. Travis looks baffled but spits into his hand and shakes back.

"We'll pick you up around noon and take you over. Lemme drive you home before Callie and Eli get here."

"I can walk."

"Wyatt..."

"Let me clear my head, Travis. Let me return from the places my mind has gone."

Watching Wyatt leave, Travis knows he's entering an unwinnable test. He's done it before with Bobby and maybe enjoys the masochism, or believes that with Wyatt he can right the wrongs that befell Bobby. He can rewind time and make a difference. The lighthouse as opposed to the anchor.

Or Wyatt's demise will pull him under too, limbs caught under a rock, unable to squirm free as his lungs fill with water, suffocation inevitable.

26

Through the woods, Wyatt stumbles. The warm front hasn't hit yet, everything on ice. He knows he should be cold but doesn't feel the shock. It's what allowed him to freeze for a century, blood in veins different than other humans', a heart that could withstand. He's seen kin of his with this same ability before, a clue to their immortality.

Digging in his pockets, the needle's been left behind, but the baggie remains. He scoops some on his index finger, takes a snort. Decides that's not enough and does it again. Jolt to his brain and then everything goes numb. Eye sparkling with crystals. Stars reflected in his gaze. He's all-powerful, all-seeing, poring through layers of the past until he reaches the memory he desires. The coldest day of the year, 1897. Little Joe's first winter. And a window remaining open all night.

Barefoot in the morning, the chill spills over his toes through the crack in the door. The doorknob like a snowball. His heart punches as he bursts inside and finds Little Joe in his bassinet right against the windowsill, blizzard flakes covering the child's purpling face. He grabs him, rushing to the fireplace in the living room. Brushes the packed snow from the baby's eyes. Listens to his chest for a heartbeat, relieved to hear a steady purr. Cooks him over the fire until limbs begin to magically uncrack. A wail that causes his own tears to fall, as the child's face turns beet red.

Joe surely should be dead. But a heart still beats. He can visualize the child while back in the woods, tucked in a snowbank, pale blue and flirting with death. This is how he must've looked all those decades in suspension too. But his own heart still beats. It had to.

"What unites you and me?" he asks his zombie child. "What makes us able to withstand such temperatures?"

On Saturday, he'll be meeting his other kin: a great-grandson he was informally introduced to at Aylen's, and even more, his grandson, a direct link to Joe. Joe's child would have insight into what kind of man his son became.

"We're closer now than we've been in a long time," he tells the baby, an ice block in his hands but alive and writhing.

A giant hand sweeps down from the sky, not connected to any body. It scoops him up, forcing the child to fall from his grasp. As he's carried away, the baby's framed by snow. A bleating dot amongst the stark white. What could be heaven, but he cannot stay there for long. Doesn't deserve absolution. He'll descend to an opposite destination. The giant hand plunging down now with Wyatt locked in its fist. Smell of smoke until his nostrils are on fire. A pit of flames awaits, ready to char his sins.

While the cries of Little Joe never cease, a constant ringing in his melting ears.

27

When Travis picks Wyatt up, Callie moves in the back seat with Eli. Wyatt seems a version of himself, more whittled, as if he'd been carved over the past few days. Despite the beard, his cheeks sink in like the *Scream* painting.

"Are you eating okay?" Callie asks, touching his arm.

"Was a bit ill," Wyatt says, into his lap. "I want to apologize for the other night. You were so hospitable."

"I hope you're doing better."

"Hi, mister!" Eli chirps. "I have a butt."

All three adults let out various stages of a laugh, Wyatt's the quietest.

"You better have brought your hungry," Travis says. "Because my mom's been preparing all winter for this."

The snow turns to mush once they arrive, the sun doing extra work to clear any signs of frost. Boots splash through puddles, but it's the first time everyone has seen each other outdoors this winter without giant coats swallowing their bodies. Cora's done her hair in a perm, curly with a bounce. Stu's at the grill, likely manning the fort for the entire party. Papa Clifford sits in a wheelchair, a heavy blanket draped across his broomstick legs.

"You're early," Cora says, embracing Travis and Callie and then leaving a big lipstick smear on Eli's cheek.

"Gramma," he whines, wiping it off.

"I could eat you whole, little one," Cora says.

Wyatt steps out of the car, all of them having a different reaction. For Cora, it's between a gasp and the feeling of being completely at peace, like seeing a ghost you've been waiting for. He's an image of her dead son, but only fleetingly. He's his own person once she gets her bearings.

"This is my buddy, Wyatt," Travis says. "Wyatt. Mom."

"Ma'am, you have a lovely home."

He gives a type of bow, clenching her palm, and leaving a kiss on the back of her hand.

Flustered, she bounces her hair. "Well…"

"This is my pop. Stu, Wyatt."

Stu's got his focus on the grill so any introduction would come second. While Bobby doesn't come to mind because he's tucked Bobby deep down for today—a rare break—there's a recognition he can't quite place. He's seen this man before. This man has etched into his brain.

"Stu," he says, shaking hands, using someone's grip as a window into their personality. This soul has been through a lot, he decides. He's worn like an old shoe.

"And here's the honoree of the hour," Travis says, sweeping his arm over to Papa who wakes up with a snort.

Upon seeing Wyatt's face, Papa Clifford immediately thinks of those lost too soon. He has one photo of his father, grainy and whitewashed, curling from age, on a hill when he arrived to Alaska, backdrop of white-tipped mountains, face full of a beard. Younger than this man, barely more than a teenager, but that's what his mind goes to, this photo that sits in a cigar box filled with his father's keepsakes.

For Wyatt, he's overwhelmed with the love of family, the energies firing around their orbits, how they interact sweetly with one another. Cora checking to make sure Papa's not cold. Eli hugging Stu's leg as Stu plays a game of *what's on my leg?* Travis with his arm around Callie, picking a ball of lint from her hair. And Wyatt alone, in the middle of it all.

He's relieved when another car pulls up, and Elson and his wife step out.

Soon enough, other guests arrive. The women in Cora's book club: Minnie, Jane, Ro, and Barbara, two of them with husbands, one with a Great Dane to play with Chinook. Elson falls into bar duties, making sure everyone has their beers. Eli runs around with two other children, their pants soaked from the slush. Elson's wife Sammi talks with Smitty and his wife about pickling. Smitty never knew she made the jarred radishes and artichokes sold at the store on Main. Smitty's wife Nancy balancing a plate with a burger in one hand and her other in a cast after a fall on ice. *We've all been there*, each one says. Travis and Grayson are figuring out a good time to go hunting next, since they haven't been since shooting the caribous. Grayson tells Travis that it hasn't been easy to lock down plans with him as of late. He wonders if it has to do with Lorinda. Travis brushes it off. He won Grayson in the divorce and Callie gets Lorinda, that's just how it'll have to be. Papa Clifford's attempting to get potato salad into his mouth but the fork keeps trembling, causing the potatoes to ooze back on the plate.

"Lemme help you," Wyatt says, sitting down beside him on a bench.

"It's like I've become a baby again," Papa Clifford says. "I have no control anymore."

Papa's tongue the color of liver, broken with grooves. A puff of hair sticking up from his skull the largest sign of life. Skin blanched and bad shakes, not from cold, from wear and tear. A body at its end.

Wyatt spears a slab of potato coated in mayo, brings it to Papa Clifford's mouth. Papa bats around the potato between his cheeks, working to chew it down, making sure it's as gummy as possible so he doesn't cough it back up.

"Again," Papa says, almost a minute later once it's traveled down his throat.

Wyatt complies and they take their time until a few bites have been eaten.

"My wife used to make a version of this," Wyatt says. "Vinegary with grain mustard seeds. I don't know this white sauce."

"It's fucking mayo," Papa says. "Tastes like a garbage disposal. I remember potato salad like you said. Mayo was a thing that got big in the 1950s, the worst era of food. Everything sealed in gelatin."

"I wouldn't know."

"Right, too young."

"More like I missed it."

"You didn't miss much. Yeah, we were glad the war was over, but try bringing that back with you. And then my sister carted off to some nut house. But I got married in the 1950s, right in this town at a lodge that was torn down when they built the refineries. Frannie wore white and we joked that she really shouldn't, since we'd been together in the biblical sense. My father had long passed but my mother came. She danced the whole night, never seen her so happy. Most of my childhood she was working multiple jobs, trying to make it through the Depression without a husband. One of the last memories I have of her. Eh, I'm babbling, shut me up."

"I want to hear more," Wyatt says. "What do you remember of your father?"

Papa's scrunches up his face. "My father? Why do you ask?"

"Because you talked of him. Because I had a father who was rarely around. I know what it means to grow up without guidance. To have to teach yourself."

"We're dealt the cards we're dealt, son."

"What's your father's name?"

"Why it was Joseph," Papa says. "Joseph Barlow."

"*Little Joe*," Wyatt whispers, an ice cube running through his veins. A reaffirmation of how they are all connected, his true family.

A hand pats his shoulder. He's unaware if he's repeated "*Little Joe*" over and over like a benediction.

"Who's Little Joe?" Trav asks, thrusting a cold beer into Wyatt's hand.

"Oh, my…" Wyatt shuts his eyes for a moment, forces himself not to breakdown. "My son. Your grandfather was speaking of his father named Joseph and that was my son's name."

"It's a popular name," Papa shrugs, not seeing the big deal.

"Yes, I guess it is. If you would excuse me for a moment? The bathroom?" he asks, recalling what these people of the future call their in-houses.

"Right through the back door, first room on your left," Trav says.

Wyatt weaves through the guests to reach the bathroom. Smitty and his wife try to start a conversation, but he apologizes that he has to tinkle and the two of them laugh. Two kids run by, slowing his pace. Before he's about to go inside, Stu steps in the way.

"You were in the trailer," Stu says, picking at the label on his bottle, his head down but his eyes locked.

"I need to use the bathroom."

"The one that whore shares with her druggie cousin." Stu wipes the spit from his mouth. "You were in the bedroom. I remember your face."

"She's a good woman," Wyatt says.

"I bet there's three new bumps on your pecker that would tell you otherwise." He leans in close, breath full of suds. "How do you know my son?"

"From Elson's."

"And that druggie cousin of hers? Where is he?"

"I never met him before that night."

Stu scratches his stubble, assessing this stranger, locating his cracks.

"What about your girl? Tell me about her."

"She works at Raye's, that's how I know her."

Stu kicks his boot, causing a splash. "You think I'm not aware of that? That settlement out there, the drugs killing 'em in spades, infecting us too."

Wyatt jams his hand in his pocket, squeezing his stash.

"I wanna know who's feeding them. Someone has to supply, and I'm guessing their range goes way beyond Laner."

"I-I have no idea, Sheriff."

"Do you see sheriff's clothes on me today? I'm just flipping burgers. But you ask your girl. You ask her where that root of evil sprouts from. I have a good mind to think that's where her fuck-up cousin is right now. He's the middleman, but I ain't interested in him."

"Are we finished?" Wyatt asks, because he's struggling to hang on. Memories of Little Joe swirl. The surreal pummeling of being surrounded by this backyard of kin. His stomach gnaws, vomit rising.

Stu spits at the ground, a show of authority, hooks his thumbs in his jeans pockets and saunters away, one eye left trained on Wyatt.

Wyatt jolts to the bathroom, flipping up the toilet lid but unable to regurgitate. A dry heave that scratches his throat. He runs the water, pumps some soap that smells of flowers. He splashes his face, tugs on his beard, and stares in the mirror, a hollowed-out core watching back.

A knock at the door.

"Are you all right?" a voice asks, and he recognizes it as California. Soft yet demanding.

"I'm fine."

"Don't mind Stu," she says. "He can be gruff with new folks. It's the kind of town this is. They were the same with me."

She tries the door and it's not locked. "Is it okay if I come inside?"

"Sure," he says, too exhausted to tell her no.

She enters brushing her hair back behind her tiny ears. He sits on the toilet and she hops up on the sink.

"Travis told me about your son," she says. "That you don't know where he is."

"Yep, that's true."

"I can't imagine."

"Hopefully, you never have to."

"Is there anything we can do? Help you locate where he may be?"

"There's no way for me to travel there. It's too far."

"Everything is just a plane ride away."

"Not where he may be."

She's staring at his eye that has closed over, since it's gnarly and off-putting. He's aware he must appear monstrous, recalling Mary Shelley's *Frankenstein*, a creature he now resembles. He tells her that.

"No, no," she says. "Not at all. Maybe there's something I can do."

She opens the mirror to his astonishment. Behind it lies shelves full of small bottles. She takes out one along with a puff of cotton.

"Witch hazel," she says, and he shrugs. She dabs the potion on the cotton and then presses it against his bad eye. "It's one of those cure-alls. I had a grandmother who was obsessed with it as a disinfectant. Even used it as bug spray."

He winces as she dabs harder, unsticking years of his lids sealing.

"It hurts…a little."

"I can feel it working. Just be patient."

She pours some more, and like a miracle, his bad eye parts, a tired pupil peeking out. The world becomes three-dimensional instead of flat and he could kiss her. He almost does.

"You are magnificent." He leaps up, observing the brand-new sight of himself in the mirror.

"Just handy."

He won't cry because he's cried enough, but inside of him the saltwater churns.

"Thank you."

There's shouting from outside of the bathroom. Someone screaming for Papa Clifford. Someone yelling for Callie as well. The chaos getting closer. It's Trav, the sound of his footsteps harsh. The bathroom door opens and he stands there panting.

"It's Papa," he tells them. "He…he had a stroke."

Cora took a moment from the party. She'd steered clear of Wyatt, not entirely sure why. But Bobby was in her thoughts as much as she wanted to keep him away. An excuse to refill a tray of fish cakes led her past the piano, which displayed pictures of the family over the years. She'd curbed the amount of Bobby, retiring most to photo albums. A picture of him in his twenties with a thick beard remained, his lumberjack phase. The time they were the closest. Travis had moved out and Bobby finished high school at nineteen. He worked some odd jobs Stu wrangled for him, but mostly stayed at home. It had been an exceptionally brutal winter and they fell in a pattern. Bobby didn't talk much, but his presence was felt. Cooking for him, watching seasons of *24* on DVD. Before he started using, or at least he'd been better at hiding it then. She liked to think he did that for her. After he moved out a year or so later, things were never the same. He'd vanish for days at a time, sometimes weeks. He'd pop in and out of their lives, never explaining where he'd been, assuming they didn't need to know. Maybe it was safer that way. Stu gave up. He refused to understand Bobby's problem was a disease. So the sickness wasn't properly treated. There are years she chooses to block out, for her own sanity, her mind's defense. She cannot relive them again. Even though she's aware that Stu pores over every detail, all the wretched moments, poking for clues, what he missed back then. He and Bobby kept their emotions bottled, more alike than either thought. They were hard to read so how could anyone have known how bad things were, how deep Bobby descended.

The fish cakes turned cold. She's about to shoot them back in the microwave when Travis barrels through the back door, face flushed, panic in his voice—Papa had a stroke and the ambulance is on its way.

28

Every Barlow in the back lawn outside forming a circle around Papa Clifford. The ambulance had been called, but the nearest hospital five miles and a town over and would take at least ten minutes due to slick roads. The left side of Papa's face droops as if it were made of putty. He's trying to speak but Cora's telling him not to, tucking the blanket up to his chin that he proceeds to throw off. Stu watching the scene but not actively participating, removed or in shock; Grayson with his hand on Stu's back. Trav ushering Cora away, Cora flinging up her hands, Callie rubbing her crystal necklace. Friends and neighbors on the sidelines observing, with Wyatt wanting to rush over to his grandson and help perform a miracle. They just met and now he's about to lose him.

An ambulance bleeps as it grinds through the slush. EMTs jumping out, getting Papa on a stretcher, and whisking him inside the vehicle.

"Got room for one more," one of them says.

"Pop," Trav calls out. "Go."

Stu seems hesitant but then scurries into the ambulance. The siren turns on as it shoots away.

"Mom, you'll ride with us," Trav says, fingers shaking as he tries to get the car keys from his pocket. Callie holds his hand steady, guides it to where it needs to be.

"I'll take anyone else," Grayson says, wiping beer off his chin and any evidence of drunkenness.

"I'd like to go," Wyatt says, calmer than anyone else.

"And who are you again?" Grayson asks.

He wants to yell that this is his goddamn grandson and they need to show respect, but it's not the right time to make them believers.

"A good friend," Wyatt says, meekly.

"Well, I don't know who the fuck you are. Elson, you and Sammi take the back seat."

"I want to help," Wyatt tells Trav, who stares back as if he doesn't recognize him for a moment.

"Wyatt, just…thanks, but we need to go." Trav heads for the car, but Wyatt grabs him by the sleeve.

"I was talking to your grandfather," Wyatt mumbles. "I was learning about who he was."

Callie picks up Eli and rushes him into the car. Cora stands at the side door, waving over Trav.

"C'mon, let's go," Cora screeches.

"You all are family, like family and…"

"Wyatt, let go, man. We don't have time for this."

"What's the name of the hospital?" Wyatt pleads.

"Jefferson over in Killey." Trav yanks his arm out of Wyatt's grasp, gives a foreboding look, one full of curiosity and concern.

Wyatt stutters to form words. "I-I'm sorry, I wish his health to be okay."

A car horn beeps, Cora pressed against the wheel. "Travis, what's wrong with you?"

"Coming!"

Trav gives a hop and books it toward the car without properly ending the conversation in Wyatt's eyes. He longs for reassurance and the desire to be needed, for the family to include him and crave his wisdom at this pressing time. But Trav hadn't thought of him at all. Trav is in his car with those he actually considers his family, leaving Wyatt to pasture.

Wyatt gets pushed from behind, but the attack doesn't register at first.

"What the fuck is wrong with you?" Grayson yells, a threatening finger thrust in Wyatt's nose.

"I mean to help."

"You have a fucking screw loose. I've seen you hanging around Travis too much. I don't know what your game is."

"Game?"

"Your MO, man. Whatever you want from him."

"We are connected, he and I, in more ways than you can imagine."

Grayson gives another push. "You're batshit."

"A bat's shit?"

"Means you're crazy, loco. You want me to bring you in for disturbing the peace?" Grayson flashes his badge, and Wyatt goes silent. "I thought so. Stay away from the Barlows."

"I am a Barlow," he says, so softly but Grayson hears, his ear twitching. Instead of fighting anymore, Grayson gets in his car and drives away.

When all the other guests have gone, Wyatt kneels and picks up Papa's discarded blanket. A thick wool with a scratchy feel. He brings it to his nose, takes in a whiff, smell of leather and cabbage. He covers himself with the wooly scent as he makes the long trek to the next town over.

Rotation of doctors and nurses in an out of the room. Drips and oxygen. CT scan, MRI, carotid ultrasound, cerebral angiogram, echocardiogram, TPA injection in Papa's arm. It's hours before the family is spoken to: ischemic stroke, hard to tell if they got him here in time, the next twenty-four hours being key. Papa Clifford resting from medication but can be seen. Grayson leaves with Elson and his wife while the Barlows push inside.

Papa looks mummified in bed with the blankets tucked tight. Mouth open in shock, eyes fluttering, half of his face still like putty. Bare feet exposed, the toes horny with nails sharp and yellow. He seems to have lost weight since the party. Cora a mess of tears. Callie taking Eli outside when he gets afraid. Travis with his hand on Papa's exposed shoulder, the flesh pale. Stu limps over.

"Son of a bitch can survive anything," Stu says, his voice sounding like a croak. The fear apparent. "Right, Papa?"

"Honey, it's okay," Cora says, hugging him at the waist. "Let yourself be vulnerable."

When Stu doesn't respond, she goes to Travis.

"Your grandfather loved you very much."

"He's still alive, Ma."

"We need to prepare," she whispers, as if she doesn't want Papa to hear. She hugs Travis at the waist, who's more inclined to comfort her.

A nurse comes in: stocky, no-nonsense, gray hair pulled into a bun. "You can talk to him," she says. "He's listening." And then she gets closer to Stu. "This may be the last time to tell him anything you need to."

Stu's angry gaze sends her away fast.

"Tell him a story you remember," Cora says, nodding until Stu finally nods as well.

Stu crouches down, his bum leg trembling. He thinks how tiny Papa's tongue looks, shriveled up and receded into his mouth, a sign that he doesn't have long. He's seen enough deaths to guesstimate. Hours? Days? What ninety-three-year-old man gets sent to the hospital and makes it out alive?

There's a memory that shines. When Stu decided on his calling for law enforcement sometime around high school. And Papa took him into the wilderness, not to hunt, but to comb through the land for the gnarliest sight they could witness. He wanted to put him to the test, see how much he'd squirm. There was a carcass, hard to tell what it once was, possibly elk. Maggots devoured until a cave of a body remained, organs turned black.

"You wanna be a sheriff, this is the kind of thing you'll see. 'Cept it might be a human."

Stu waited for the acid in his stomach to become a violent spew. But he wasn't grossed out. He poked the carcass with a stick as the maggots erupted into a frenzy. Animal, human, it didn't matter. Once we're dead, only a vessel remains. But how this animal met its fate, that rocked his brain. The steps leading to a death, the mystery to our ends if we're suddenly cut short. That's what mystified him, caused the gears in his mind to keep him up at night.

"Yep, you're cut out for it," Papa Clifford had said. He had massive hands like they should be holding an axe at all times. His hand rough against Stu's chin but calming, always calming. His father from another era when people took their time to say what they needed to. "You have my blessing, son."

"And on the way back," Stu says, the saliva heavy in his mouth, "we stopped at Ambee's for a beer and fried fish, that tiny little outpost by the docks that used to serve the fish in newspaper. And you didn't just let me drink your beer, you got me my own, and toasted me like I was a man in your eyes for the first time. I wasn't a little kid no more. I had exceeded your expectations."

"That's lovely," Cora says. "I know he can hear you."

"Would you get me a coffee, Cor?" Stu asks. "Hot as can be."

"Of course, honey. Of course."

She scuttles out of the room, and Stu closes the door behind her.

"We need to talk, son."

Travis blinks in confusion. "Of course."

"Papa's insurance won't cover the entire hospital visit. That's why we've been keeping him at home. He should've been in a facility."

"Stu, you can't blame yourself. He's old, this could have happened just as easily at some place."

"Will you listen? Now I'm tapped, in debt."

"Debt like how?"

"Debt like I'm in the shitter. These poker games I've been going to. And don't get on your high horse about them being illegal."

"I wasn't gonna say nothing."

"Anyway, so yeah, your mother doesn't know. It's been my, well, my escape. God knows I deserve an escape after the last few years."

"Why are you telling me this right now?"

"Because we don't have the funds to pay for Papa's care here. The stroke could clean us out."

The air in the room gets prickly. "What are you saying?"

Stu puts his face his hands, emerging a different man. "I don't know. I don't goddamn know." And then, as if he realizes, "What have you got saved?"

"I don't have anything. Since the refinery let me go, I haven't been able to save dick."

"That fish shack you've gone on about, like the one I mentioned Papa took me to, what about funds for that?"

"Emptied those accounts. Went to diapers."

Stu eyes him closely, one tiny black pupil zeroing in. "I don't believe you."

"*What?* I've been out of work for two years and only recently started on the *Cutthroat*."

"What about Callie?"

"Waitressing tips?"

"Her parents have money," Stu says, his lips wet. "What if you asked them?"

"Asked them to help Papa, or for your gambling debts?"

"I go to that underground site we play at for reasons beyond which you can understand."

"Yeah to get away from Bobby."

"To what? No, son. No. To get closer to him. Don't you see? That was his world. I'm trying to find breadcrumbs."

"I don't want to talk about this here."

Travis observes his father, and Stu can tell what he sees: smaller in stature than usual, braying and desperate when normally larger than life, so Travis gives him a hug.

"Get offa me," Stu says, pushing away and heading out of the room.

"The fuck…" Travis says, as Cora comes in with two coffees.

"Where's your father going?" she asks, innocent like a child.

"I'll take his coffee," Travis says. "Let him be for now."

Stu doesn't buy cigarette packs but always keeps a solitary rolled tobacco joint in his inner coat pocket for emergencies. He sucks hard, enjoying the burn and heavy cough. He winces, wanting to rewind time because of what he unloaded on Travis, but at some point, Travis would need to know the state of the family's affairs. He has until the end of the month to pay off any poker debts, the ringleader of the game not threatening to chop off his fingers, but worse, expose his leniency to certain illegal trades in town. And with a reelection coming up soon, he can't go into it with dipping numbers.

"Can I have a drag?" a voice asks, Callie creeping up behind.

He coughs. "You smoke?"

"When it's necessary."

He passes over the rolled cigarette. "Drag away."

"Cora's right, you don't always have to be the steady one."

"Trust me, I'm not."

"I heard you and Travis fighting," she says, her eyes darting every which way.

"Not my proudest moment."

"We really don't have any savings."

"I shouldn't have asked. I'll take a second on the house. We'll give Papa a little more time. I was just venting."

"I would ask my parents, but they aren't generous with money. They would want it paid back with interest."

Stu shoos the thought. "Don't need to get into more debt than I already am."

She steps closer, fingering the lavender crystal around her neck. "I admire you."

Stu lets out a gruff laugh.

"I do. You've devoted yourself to finding out what happened to Bobby."

He looks at her like she's not allowed to say his son's name.

"But you have family here, Stu. They love you. Give them your focus too."

She passes back the cigarette, a hint of lipstick on the nub. He takes a final hit, the smoke roiling throughout his body, exhaled in a streaming cloud. Then he pivots back inside like a solider returning to war.

29

"He's out of the woods," the doctor says, but then adds, "for now." The doctor, a slender man with a severe part in his hair and barely any lips, who speaks in a monotone. "Injured brain tissue mimics healthy tissue on the scanner so possible infarction strokes can be deceiving. We'll monitor closely overnight."

"Should we stay?" Cora asks, both to the doctor and Stu and Travis. Callie had already taken Eli home. Everyone tired, ready for bed.

"I can't make that decision for you," the doctor says. "But there is nothing you can do here. He might wake up at some point to talk, but likely he'll stay sedated."

"I can't feel my legs," Cora says, embarrassed. "I'd do well to lie down."

"I'll stay," Travis says, turning to Stu. "We'll stay."

"There's a waiting area with couches," the doctor says. "The nurse can get you blankets."

"That would be fine," Stu says, surprising them both because he hasn't spoken at all during this exchange.

They kiss Cora goodbye and call her a taxi. A nurse brings them thick soups for a late dinner along with pillows and blankets. The lights click off in the hospital's hallways, only a few rooms betraying the darkness with thin florescent lights. The sound of whirring machines, the occasional squeak of clogs against the floor, the murmur of a phone ringing. They're facing each other on separate couches.

"Forget what I told you," Stu says, fluffing his pillow. "Money is money, who cares if we owe more of it?"

Travis uncertain how much he believes that but doesn't want to argue.

"Night, Stu," he says, but Stu is already snoring.

* * *

Wyatt waits until the hallway lights snap off. He'd stayed close enough to hear Papa Clifford's prognosis and watched Trav and Stu retire to the waiting area. He'd timed how often the nurse checked on Papa, every hour on the half hour. He makes sure Travis and Stu are sound asleep, and once the nurse goes to check on another patient, he tiptoes inside Papa's room and closes the door.

His grandson a more depleted version from when he talked to him at the party. The decay that just twelve hours can bring. He scoots a chair up to the bedside, takes Papa's wrinkled hand. It's cold but still has some life: a twitch, the fingernails pale pink. The face turns to him, a phantom's mask. Eyes unglue, peer out through a layer of mucous, teeth develop into a lopsided smile.

"You came," Papa says, throat full of nails, the words gargled.

"Yes. Do you know who I am?"

The oxygen mask makes Papa's nod difficult.

"I'm your grandfather," Wyatt says.

Papa's eyes go wide, the mucous flaking away. Now that Wyatt has said it out loud, he is at peace. At least one person knows the truth. He's no longer carrying the burden of the secret alone.

"Yes," Papa says, like he had to take a second to decide whether to believe.

"You never met me before. I left your father Joe when he was a very little boy to find gold."

He's still holding Papa's hand, stunned when Papa slides it out of his grasp. He could have held on forever.

"I don't understand." Papa rotates so he's facing the crescent moon out of the window, as if it could provide answers. "Am I dreaming?" he croaks. "Have I died?"

"Neither. You are here and I am as well. Can you tell me about your father? Anything you can remember. It all would be such a gift to me."

Papa gums his lip, mouth dry. Wyatt brings a plastic cup of water to his mouth but Papa declines.

"How old were you when he died?"

"He was killed."

The cup trembles in Wyatt's hand as some water spills. "Killed, you say?"

"I was very young, maybe six years old. Times were tough. We had nothing. Mother and father would forgo a meal at times but they always made sure I ate. Common during the thirties."

"What did your father do for work?"

Papa scratches at the droopy side of his face, realizing the futility since there's no sensation. "He…we had a small farm in Alaska."

"I raised him on a farm."

Papa scrunches up his nose. "I don't know of that. I don't recall him speaking much about his upbringing. He came to Alaska before I was born."

"What about his mother? Your grandmother?" Wyatt wants to say *my wife*, but chooses not to confuse Papa any more.

"I remember her once," Papa says. "Lovely red hair."

"Yes, yes."

"I must have been three or so, but I can recall being in her lap. She gave me a sucker, what we called candy at the time. I finished it by biting and she gave me another. She had a very sweet voice that sounded like music."

"How come you only have that one memory?"

"She died around when the Depression began. Sickness. I don't remember what. I have an image of my father crying on my mother's shoulder when he got the news and them bringing me into their huddle. Crying with them because it seemed like the right thing to do. But I didn't understand."

Papa looks over at the beeping machine, mouth open in awe. "What is going on?"

"You're in the hospital."

"Is that what this is? I'm so very tired."

"I have a few more questions."

"And who are you again?" he wheezes, the words more spaced out than before.

"I am your grandfather."

"I am *your* grandfather." Papa taps his chin, then shakes his head. "No, you are not Travis."

"Correct. I am your grandfather."

"But how is that possible?"

"Because not everything can be logically explained. We are surrounded by unanswered questions that might never be fulfilled. I awoke suspended in ice, but for a *reason*, there has to be for a reason. You are my closest link!"

"To what?"

"To who I was, to Adalaide, Little Joe, everything I once held dear. I am in foreign territory here. A century swept by without me and I'm trying to catch up."

Papa lets out a cough laced with a thick substance that he spits into the cup of water. He checks his arm and sees the drip.

"They have me hooked up to some good stuff, don't they?"

"Hospitals were very different in my time so I can't tell you what."

Papa gives a sad laugh, resigning himself to what's occurring.

"How did my son die?" Wyatt asks. "Little Joe, your father?"

"Ah," Papa says, his eyelids fluttering. "My father came and went a lot. The farm was never for him and too little to make a living off of. He always had a scheme."

"Gold?" Wyatt asks, wondering how much of him had transferred to his son.

"I don't know, just that he spent more time away than at home. And he and my mother fought a lot. He was sick since he was a child."

"With what? Was he cold all the time?"

Wyatt takes Papa's hand again as if to test, an ice block gripping back.

"You are cold too," Wyatt says, in astonishment. "Have you always been?"

Papa's eyes loop around. "I'm not long for this world. My father had a sickness, I don't recall what. But he was stabbed coming from town. This killed him. The thief wanted his groceries. That's what witnesses said."

"Did they catch the man responsible?"

"He was a drifter, or at least that's what the police assumed, since no one could recall him. Wrong place, wrong time, I presume. My mother often talked about it through my childhood, played the what-if scenarios. But I wasn't interested." Papa gives another cough of brown gook into the cup. "She passed soon after I returned from the war and married."

Wyatt bites his bottom lip, a flood of tears building. His wife's early end and his son's too. How come *he* got to live for so long? What's different about *him*?

"Haven't thought about this all in some time," Papa says. "It's when we come to the very end that we think of when we began. The early people who shaped us. They are barely memories since it's been so long. I've had to rebuild and recreate who they are."

"So have I." The tears come in hiccup form, firing from Wyatt's sockets.

"There, there, son," Papa says, patting Wyatt's palm. "Don't cry for me. I will get to see my lovely Frannie soon. She's been waiting."

"None of this is fair. I should've gotten to be there, for Adalaide and Little Joe, for you too. I should've been able to hold you in my arms when you were born, given you a nickname..."

"Tut, tut. The game of coulda, woulda, shoulda never turns out well. Take it from a man who's lived longer than most. Regret is not a worthwhile emotion because there is nothing that can be done. We have to move on."

"I'm trying, I am. Meeting you all, feeling the love of your family, my family. How they look out for one another."

"See, so there may have been some bad, but good too."

Wyatt dries his tears. "Thank you."

"I assume I will not remember much of this," Papa says, nodding at the IV. "And maybe that is best. But I'll give you a last egg of advice." He curls a finger for Wyatt to lean in close. "Chase for whatever it is you truly want and don't stop until you have it firmly in your grasp."

The oracle closes his mouth, pleased with his divine wisdom.

"You mean the gold?"

The oracle sighs, ready to end this conversation, to let sleep sweep away this wild vision.

"You mean Callie and Eli?"

The oracle's drooped face tilts to the left.

"Or do you mean..."

The oracle holds up a pallid hand, palm out.

"Listen. Don't speak anymore," he says. "*Whatever* it is you truly want. Understand?"

The air in the room becomes filled with a sparkling glow. God's finger poking in, making sure this moment gets intensified.

The oracle's eyes snap shut. A loud snore erupts enough for Wyatt to scooch his chair back. The glow reflects in the window, a fluorescent shine. The door to the room has opened, the hallway light streaming in, along with Stu.

"What the fuck are you doing in my father's room?" Stu shouts, as Wyatt turns to Papa Clifford to explain, then sadly realizes that none of this could ever be properly put into words.

30

Stu attacks Wyatt, since it's in his nature. As a sheriff, he's never allowed himself to hesitate. Especially after his injury in a dank cabin in the middle of the woods. The moon had been blocked by fog. A tip led him there foolishly without backup. He could barely see his hand in front of his face, let alone the shadow of a man reaching for his gun. He shot at the dark, the bullet captured by a mattress on the floor. He heard the man fire twice, the first bullet lost in the wooden wall, the second piercing his thigh. He fell over, which saved his life, since the other bullets all shattered the glass window above. Crouching on the floor, he tried to see his assailant, nothing more than a hovering phantom dashing for the door, not entirely human, massive like a sasquatch. He thinks of its gait every time he limps, even now as he lunges at Wyatt, visualizing the sasquatch in his place.

"What are you after?" he thunders, getting Wyatt in a headlock and bringing him down to the ground. They ram into the table on wheels holding Papa's untouched supper, which careens across the room.

"I wanted to talk to him," Wyatt struggles to say.

"Why? Tell me why? *Tell* me."

Stu's face turning bright red, the veins throbbing, saliva dripping from his lips like a bear.

A nurse steps inside, witnesses the melee, and throws her arms to the ceiling before running out.

"I...had questions," Wyatt slurs.

Stu has his hands around Wyatt's throat now. He's squeezing but not enough to harm, only to subdue. Although he could easily press harder into the man's windpipe, could end things quickly.

"Grigory, does that name ring a bell?" Stu asks. "Did he send you to watch us?"

There's a chart somewhere in the madness of Stu's basement that attempts to link a few of the undesirables in the Native American settlement, to the underground gambling ring run by a man named Grigory, the underboss of a vile human he's been trying to locate, an unnamed ghost he believes to be the nucleus of all the crime in the area, who must've ensnared Bobby in his web and then sacrificed his boy for knowing too much.

Wyatt's eyes float up, his neck turning gray. He swings his arms in an attempt to connect with Stu's face.

"Who does he work with at the settlement?" Stu roars.

"I don't know who you speak of—"

"That's bullshit. You're cozying up to Travis, now to my father. Keep enemies close, right? You're sick."

Finally, Wyatt's fist meets Stu's cheek. It's a hard blow, since Wyatt's swing's full of muscles. Stu's stunned for long enough for Wyatt to push him off. Travis rushes in.

"What the hell's going on?" Travis asks, surveying the scene. Wyatt hacking up a lung, Stu rubbing the lump developing on his cheekbone, Papa snoring away.

"He's no good!" Stu cries, pointing at Wyatt as if Travis wouldn't understand who he meant.

"Your father attacked me." Wyatt affects his voice so it sounds helpless, a fawn in distress. "I was visiting Papa. We had gotten along so well at the party."

Travis goes to help up Wyatt and brings him a plastic cup of fresh water. Wyatt greedily gulps it down.

"You're gonna tend to that man first while your father lies here from being struck in the face?" Stu whines.

"Stu, you attacked him!"

"Well, why is he here?"

"He just said he came to visit Papa."

Stu stands and wets a paper towel at the sink that he presses to his cheek. "That man has ulterior motives."

The nurse comes back inside, a thin woman with a brittle face and tiny eyes. "So you know, I've called the police."

"I am the police," Stu says, waving her away. "The situation is under control."

The nurse heads over to Papa to check all his connected tubes.

"Wyatt is a friend," Travis says. "I got him a job at Elson's."

"He was with that Oxendine whore."

"Then that's his business, what's it to you?"

"Because illicit things happen at that settlement. Drugs and…"

Travis quickly looks over at Wyatt, a telling glance.

"You're into drugs, aren't you?" Stu asks, charging over to Wyatt. "That's why you're with that woman?"

"No," Wyatt peeps.

"Leave him alone, Stu."

A show of red lights clears across the window. A deputy's car pulling up to the hospital parking lot.

"Ah shit," Travis says, as Grayson steps out and heads inside. "Don't egg Gray on."

"This man knows something about Bobby," Stu says, not roaring anymore, meek now. The charged bravado covering a wounded child. That's what he returns to, what the death of a son can do.

"I don't know a Bobby," Wyatt says, and then he repeats it again to Stu. "The woman, Aylen, she makes me feel good is all I know. That's why I go there. I don't care if she's with other men. That's her business. And when she's with me, she's only with me."

"See?" Travis says, massaging Stu's collar bone.

"Nah, her cousin's involved. I'm certain. And if you're involved with her, you're involved with him."

Grayson swings into the room, gun ready.

"Jesus, Gray, put that thing away!" Travis yells.

Grayson blinks to take in the scene.

"Oh no, not him," Grayson says, an accusatory finger thrust toward Wyatt. "I thought I told you to stay away."

Travis jumps between them. "Gray, he's just here to see Papa. It's all a misunderstanding."

Wyatt has his hands up. He nods in defense.

The nurse pipes up. "All right, all of you out."

She shoos until they leave the room. Unsatisfied with them being in the hallway, she pushes the posse toward the waiting area where the four men reconvene.

"I'm sorry," Stu says to Wyatt, cutting the silence. "For the choking. That was uncalled for."

"Ain't nothing," Wyatt says, but Grayson's giving him an evil eye.

"Don't trust this one for shit," Grayson says. "He's got a stinger. He's just waiting for a target."

"Gray," Travis chides. "Let's not make it worse."

"Shows up out the blue," Grayson whines, "and highjacks you as a friend. That's right, I said it. You've been MIA, off God knows where with this one."

"Gray, I can have more than one friend."

"My life is in the shitter, and have you once offered to go hunting?" Grayson asks.

"Son, have you had some sips?" Stu asks.

"No," he says, but Stu smells his breath. "All right, but night patrol can be dull as fuck in this town."

"I'm gonna pretend I didn't hear that," Stu says.

"Gray," Travis says, like an older, wiser brother would. "We'll go hunting as soon as possible. You can unload all your Lorinda woes."

Grayson sniffs. "Promise?"

"First chance I can," Travis says. "I love you, buddy. We'll get you through this."

"I apologize as well, sir," Wyatt tells Stu. "For hitting your cheek. Looks like it smarts."

"Been hit worse."

"I am new in town if Trav didn't tell you. And he's been so kind to me. I wanted to be there for the family too," Wyatt says.

"As a sheriff, always got my antennae up," Stu says.

"Don't know what that means exactly, but I believe I understand." Wyatt backs out of the room. "I've bothered you all enough. My condolences to Papa Clifford. I will have him in my heart."

Grayson holds his nose as if the man stinks.

"He's weird, Trav," Grayson says. "That's a given."

"He's sad, like both of you."

Stu rubs his fist, the knuckles turning purple.

After Travis leaves the hospital room, Stu remains dumbstruck so Grayson stays with him.

"What do you think he meant by both of us being sad?" Stu asks.

"Ah, he's right," Grayson says. "It's this town, this edge of the world, we're all in different stages of despair. How's Papa?"

Stu's sighs have the weight of torpedoes. "First twenty-four hours are key to a recovery. But all I see is the end."

"C'mere, old man," Grayson says, pulling Stu into his chest. "He's a fighter like every other Barlow. He'll outlive us all."

Stu wipes his nose against Grayson's shirt. "I'm gonna hold you to those words."

"You Barlows are cut from a different cloth. Can withstand whatever calamity is thrown at them."

"That's so?"

"Yep, I've decided it. *Superhuman*, that's what you all are."

Grayson cups the back of Stu's neck, cold to the touch like an ice brick, so frozen that Grayson removes his fingers in shock.

"Superhuman?" Grayson wonders.

31

Outside of the hospital, the weather's already turning. Branches melting hours ago form ice crystals again. Wyatt's breath a thick smoke. He rubs his hands together to create warmth but doesn't really need to since the cold affects him differently. Always has. He can recall Adalaide bundled up in wool sweaters and heavy blankets while she sat glued to the fireplace with Little Joe in her arms. Wyatt could waltz in naked and still not be chilled. It's not as if he never feels cold, more that it simply doesn't bother him.

He digs in his pockets as his saliva intensifies. He could use a hit, but the baggie of heroin is only filled with white dust. He licks his index finger and dabs the remnants, snorts whatever's left up his nose but it does not sate.

There's an anger bubbling he's trying to contain. Here he went out of his way to be there for Papa and the family treated him with contempt. Things may have ended okay with Stu, but Wyatt's aware it's bound to get worse with a man of that nature. He's met similar before in life and can't imagine that a century changes that kind of temperament. Stubborn, persistent, rude, and foolhardy. Grayson too. Like most lawmen are.

Trav, however, stood up for him. It was expected, but Wyatt would be lost without him in his corner. Tricky to decipher how long their connection might last. He thinks to how excited Trav got when he mentioned the gold. A clear way to solidify their relationship would be to hunt for that prize. Problem being, he still can't remember where he left his treasure. He wonders what might be his end goal. Obviously, the gold, but if both Adalaide and Little Joe are long dead, what does he want in terms of family? Would he be content to be a part of Trav's world but not the center of California and Eli's? Is the only chance at happiness to

164

somehow take Trav's place? He hates to ponder this but can't help it.

Out of the corner of his eye, another cloud breath puffs. Trav stands there, hands jammed in his pockets, no clue what to say. The two men stay simply breathing for some time.

"Thanks for sticking up for me," Wyatt finally says, so Trav will understand there's no hard feelings.

"You didn't do anything wrong."

"I don't believe your father and friend thinks the same."

Trav steps closer like he's about to reveal a secret. "They're cut from the same cloth. Fiercely protective. Highly suspicious. My brother... You don't know this, but my brother Bobby died about two years ago."

"I'm sorry."

"He was found at sea. Don't know if it was self-imposed or if someone drowned him. He was involved with some shady people. Laner's a good town. Hard working people, families, but on the outskirts there's a stain. People who likely got to Bobby."

"And Grayson and Stu are determined to see who messed with him?"

"Yep, precisely."

"That might explain their reaction. Losing a child, a brother, anyone close. No one deserves that. Take it from me."

The saliva ramps up in Wyatt's mouth and he'd beg anyone to oblige with a hit. Talking of death and loss does this, strips his core.

"And my father's dealing with debt along with hospital bills for Papa," Trav says. "We're all being challenged now is what it is."

Wyatt places his palms on his great-great grandson's shoulders. He'd love to solve the family's problems, become their hero.

"*Gold*, Trav."

"You remember where it is?"

Wyatt gives a snort, tiny heroin particles traveling up into his brain, opening up a pathway to remembrance. It's his best chance of traveling back in the wilderness to the spot he left the gold. It's more than worth a shot. He taps his skull.

"It's all here," Wyatt says. "I just have to access it."

"How will ya do that?"

"Lemme try. And when I do, I'll take you with me. We can split the gold fifty-fifty, I won't need any more."

"That's mighty generous."

"I want to do this for your family. I haven't had kindness in some time. Your grandfather..." He wants to shout, *my grandson*, but maintains his composure. "Please, I want to do this for you all. I only have to pry it from my brain. It shouldn't be hard. I have ways of accessing."

Trav scrunches up his face. "Drugs ain't worth it, dude."

"I haven't told you this, but I lost a lot of my memory due to an unfortunate incident." Wyatt gums his bottom lip, debating how honest to be, deciding only to give out minimal information. "My wife, my child, it's all slowly coming back." He pulls out the baggie with the white powder stains. "But yes, this helps."

"That shit's real bad for you."

Wyatt holds up a hand in protest. "I can handle it. I must. Let me do it once more to access the part of my mind that's been blocked. One last chance. But I need to do enough to really go there."

Trav kicks at the dirty snow. "Shit, man, I really don't like this."

"I'm a wolf," Wyatt says, a blossom of truth he's able to reveal. "I'm bred tough, you see? The drug won't be my end."

"You have to go to the settlement to get more?"

"I'll go right now."

"Let me at least drive. It's like a five-mile walk."

"Only to drop me off. I do not want you involved."

"Okay, man."

They get Trav's pickup, ride in silence. Trav flips on the radio as a quiet song croons, Bob Dylan's "Song to Woody." At the break of morning, they are the only car on the white-capped road, the sun a line of orange on the horizon, the sky a violet explosion.

"You don't have to do this," Trav says, because it needs to be repeated one more time. But Wyatt chides that he does. Nothing has ever been more essential. "Is there something else you aren't telling me?" Trav asks.

More silence, the air clogged with unasked questions. Wyatt could reveal the entire truth right here: who he is, how they really are united. But that would slow down getting to the settlement and having more heroin to inject in his veins. There will be a time and place for Wyatt to come clean. The Dylan song nears an end as they arrive at the settlement.

Here's to the hearts and the hands of men
That come with the dust and leave with the wind

Trav snaps off the radio and puts the pickup in neutral as it idles. Around a bonfire, sleeps the group of teenagers, each in a sleeping bag. From a grainy window in Aylen's trailer, a yellow light beams.

"You must leave now," Wyatt says, stepping out.

Trav puts the car in drive. "I'm coming back here this time tomorrow to make sure you're okay."

Wyatt grips the side of pickup, leaning in through Travis's window. "Here's something I didn't tell you." He wipes a sweat ball from his forehead. "I can't die. From most things that is. Rather immortal. So, there's no need to worry."

And then Wyatt whisks away, shuffling over to the teenagers and nudging their sleeping bags. They wake, blinking their eyes to a drug-induced morning. Trav turns the radio back on. The end of the Dylan song.

I'm a-leaving tomorrow, but I could leave today
Somewhere down the road someday
The very last thing I'd want to do
Is to say I've been hittin' some hard-travelin' too

32

The teenagers don't have any heroin on them so Wyatt follows one back to their trailer. Upon reaching it, he understands why they sleep outside. A dead drunk elder lies sprawled on the floor with a moonshine bottle clamped in his hand. Cigarette burns as artwork along the reed-thin walls. Stains along the floor, mix of water damage and dried blood. The teenager in his sleeping bag steps over the passed-out relative, disappears behind a curtain, and returns with a baggie.

"And a needle?" Wyatt asks.

The teenager vanishes again, returning with the request. Wyatt pays with crumpled-up bills as the teenager shuffles outside still cocooned by his sleeping bag.

"Do you stay out here all nights?"

The teenager narrows his eyes, agog that a stranger could care. "If it's not below freezing," he says.

"Who was that in your trailer?"

"Uncle." Spit. "He's a fuck."

The teenager flops back between the two teen girls. Through sleeping bags, their limbs enclose him and he nestles.

"Thank you," Wyatt says, heading to Aylen's trailer.

Across from it, an elderly man steps out of his own. He grips a cane with intricate carvings, but he's too far away for Wyatt to make out the details. The elderly man stabs the cane into the solid snow, chews at his gums since he doesn't have many teeth, observing this new visitor, this white man. The elder would have been imposing in his younger years. Thick shoulders, a powerful torso that has sunken in due to age, beak of a nose and eyebrows like caterpillars. A sweet smoke pours from his trailer, honey-like and reaffirming. He points his cane at Wyatt, calling out in a language Wyatt can't understand. He dubs the elder as insane, then knocks on Aylen's door.

It takes a minute of knocking before Aylen arrives. She opens the door in a pink bathrobe and fuzzy slippers, hair in shock mode, a mug of hot coffee steaming from her hands.

"What do you want?" She coughs as she moves away from the door but leaves it open. He takes it as a sign to go inside. In the morning, the trailer looks sadder. Old magazines fill up tables. A sink overflows with dirty dishes. She sits on the counter with her knees up to her chin, lights a cigarette.

"You caught me on my day off," she says, not excited, nor angry, simply letting him know.

"I have a favor to ask."

He tells her as much of the story as her brain might handle. That gold exists in the wilderness, which he hid for some reason, and he needs to find out why and where. Her eyes dance at the mention of gold, but dull when heroin gets brought up.

"I need you to inject me," he says. "Again and again so I don't come out of it too soon. And to monitor me so it doesn't kill me neither. Is that something you can do?"

She stubs out her cigarette, sick of it. "Tohopka came back. Tore through this place last night looking for something, swearing like hell. Not sure if it was because he found whatever it was, or because he didn't."

"If you want my opinion, you shouldn't live with him."

"No, I don't *want* your junkie-ass opinion. What gives you the right? But he was high like the devil. That was plain to see. And he wasn't himself, or maybe that's who he actually is. So, you want me to inject you?"

"All I want is my past. You have that. Most do. Only fair I find a way to get mine too."

"The *past*," she says, with a thumbs down. "You can have mine. A million dicks I didn't need. Starting from when I was as high as your knee."

She bites a knuckle, pops another cigarette out of the pack. "The illusion of Raye's is gone, isn't it?"

"What you mean?"

"This is me, nothing to be idolized like the men do there. We have no souls, just bodies." She lights another cigarette, the cherry glowing.

"Being sick these last days and having time off has got me thinking."

"You don't have to do anything you don't want to do."

"Really? I have your permission?"

"You're smart. You can excel at whatever you choose."

"Do you see where I'm from?" She indicates her surroundings, yanking on dirty curtains and giving a view of the apocalyptic settlement, an area that time has ravaged. "No one gets out of a place like this. We only get older."

"No one has to stay stuck," he says, lip quivering, recalling his own hundred-year stasis.

"Why, because you melted like the fantasy you are? You're just a parlor trick. Your whole story nothing more than that. And no amount of heroin will make it any more real."

"It is *real*," he thunders, towering over her, letting her smoke coat his face. "Adalaide, Little Joe, our farm, the steamboat, the Gold Rush and landing in Alaska. I set forth a chain of events by coming here. My son followed soon after when I never returned. It can't all be for naught."

She flips her hair between her fingers. "Just cause you want something to be true doesn't make it any less false. You've told your heart this is how things were and your heart has believed. But men cannot survive a hundred years trapped in ice. That's the tale of a fool. And that's what you are."

He clenches the needle, raising it like a weapon. "Are you gonna stab me or what?" he asks.

She chews on the cigarette as she gets a spoon and a lighter from the drawer. Bringing him over to a crowded table, she searches his arm for a ripe vein.

"And what are you gonna give me?" she asks.

He swallows, digs for an answer. "I'd like to be someone to you."

She laughs a sad laugh. "Lies. More lies. You don't want me. I'm a placeholder."

"I don't know what that is."

"A stopgap. A moment. You come when you need things. You'll never stay. You'll use and abuse because that's how I'm destined to be treated."

"You should stop feeling sorry for yourself."

She exhales. "Got no one else to feel sorry for me. Why can't you at least let me have that?"

"I do care," he says, but his voice strains. He knows she's right.

"You're sweet enough to at least try. And for that I'll hold your hand like I'm your mama while you go under. I've certainly been around enough heroin comas to know what to do. In each of these trailers a needle is entering someone's blood right now. We were delivered an escape some years ago and we all like it enough to keep it around."

"This is my last high."

She taps a vein she decides she likes. "Is that so? Well, congradu-fuckin-lations." After pouring a scoop of heroin onto the spoon, she lights under the base. The sizzle cutting the silence. Needle sucks it in.

"And what if it kills you?" she asks. "What if I can't bring you back?"

"I don't die easily," he says, for the second time that day.

"Right, the whole hundred years thing. But sweetie, you know what that means?" With her tongue, she moves her cigarette from one side of her teeth to the other. "It means that you've stolen from Death. And that son-of-a-bitch is gonna come one day with his scythe and want what's owed to him."

"So be it then."

"So be it."

Aylen stabs the needle into Wyatt's arm. Draws out some blood to mix with the heroin. A curl of a smile plastered on her face. She releases the drug slowly into his vein as the world goes warm. He's dipped in honey, recalling the sweet smell of smoke that oozed from that elder's trailer. The needle is removed and the ritual resumed. Spoon heated again. Another vein searched and found. The ease of the tip breaking skin. The ethereal pleasure of giving oneself over to its power. Aylen becomes hazy and then she's gone, along with the trailer and the settlement too. He passes over snow-capped mountains until Laner recedes as well. Now he's a soaring bird exploring the wilds of Alaska's isolated frontier. The wilderness where he fell asleep and awoke in a brand-new century. But he hasn't reached that place of embalmment yet. He's gotten off the boat after killing Carl Finnegan Langford, flecks of the man's blood still staining his shirt. He's passed by his nemesis and former friend Frank who seeks the same shine that he does, the brilliant gold that has turned others inside out, wrung out all that is good and left bodies filled with discarded rot. The root of evil in a nub. He's killed to get to it and understands he might have to kill again. For there are no laws here in the wilderness, in the rush for treasure, no lawmen, no jail time, only victory and hardened defeats. While it may seem like he'd been defeated, he's outlasted all his contemporaries, none of them given a second chance like him.

So when he's placed down one hundred and twenty years ago in an ice town called Sitka where his journey will begin, he's as hopeful as he was back then, when success seemed inevitable and failure far from his vocabulary. What perilous adventures await? What high-stakes challenges must he face? Whatever they may be, at least he knows he survives.

This allows Wyatt to take the first step.

Back in the trailer, Aylen wets a cloth she drapes over his forehead. He's twitching and his eyes have escaped into his skull. He murmurs something about a *cave*, a future his mind travels to where his body has already been. He's so cold it seems to her like he's been injected with ice water. At first, she's scared and debates not sticking him with another needle. But as she feels his extremities, hands and feet, ears and the top of his head, she understands he exists not like anyone else, the coldness he exudes warming and safe. So she gets him on the floor, tucking him beneath her legs, guiding his journey as best she can, this frozen man at her whim.

And then he moves suddenly, reaching down his shirt and pulling out a notebook attached by a string around his neck. A pen gripped. Words furiously erupting. And not just chicken scratch. Beginning with a date.

August 18th, 1898

33

I glow like a freshly scrubbed piece of gold upon my arrival in Sitka. The journey aboard the steamboat has been difficult, but I learned early on in life that the past must remain in the past. No use in letting it damper the wonder of my present. This will be the entry to my destiny.

Many millennia ago, gold was formed in the earth's core and then traveled upward toward the surface into nooks and crannies as the planet shifted. Abrasion caused the rocks to loosen the gold and the waters carried it to valleys and riverbeds, down streams and creeks, of which Alaska had plenty. One could get it by mining, but us prospectors call it "placer gold" and we get it through panning. Stick a tin pan in the water, give it a good shake, hope for golden colors.

Sitka is a harbor town, a commercial and trading center of the Alaska Territory, the entryway of thirty thousand some-odd folks who lived in a state of lawlessness roughly a third the size of the US. But it holds a promise, this new and uncivilized land. The Wild West has ended, an era to be remembered on trading cards, and I know I'll be joined by cowboys, wayfarers, journeymen, trappers, and Indian savages in my quest for dreams. I have little money in my pockets and must rely on trade and charm to get me up the Yukon where the true gold lies.

The freezing air packs a wallop, even in mid-August, a foreboding sense of what will come. Sitka Harbor overlooks ominous mountains capped with black ice that walls in the small town. Other prospectors seem to welcome one another's arrival: shaking hands, slapping each other on the backs, showing off their gear, but I pay them no mind. A key to success in the unchartered land is to partner with an Indian guide that can take me into the crevices which haven't been tapped yet. For the white men attempting this on their own, death will likely be their fate.

After walking some while off the main strip, I see a Tlingit settlement. Whale blubber mixed with dried salmon hangs in the air like foul cheese. They have cabins made from cedar logs scattered about, some touching each other, a few almost hidden. Soon I am surrounded by a circle of brown faces with flat noses and sunken eyes. I do my best to smile while I reach into my pocket and remove some of the money I have left. Unimpressed, they grunt at each other. One slaps the money from my palm as it falls to the muddy ground. I scramble to pick it up while they laugh and puff out their chests at this foolish white man.

"I need a guide to go up the Yukon," I say, acting out rowing in a boat so they might understand. But they don't care. These are not savages. The jewelry they wear intricate, their campsite filled with well-built wares like an artist's colony. They do not need my money or anything to do with me at all. Even the children are brought over to make fun, aping the way I walk and talk. I leave disillusioned.

Back on the main strip, I debate going into an inn for a drink but then I hear a cannon announcing the arrival of a passenger ship called the *Ancon* with a picture of a side-wheeler. Rushing over to the dock, I ask a gentleman with a smushed face where the boat will go. He tells me Juneau and I ask him the price. It will be fifteen dollars. I only have about fifty dollars on me and figure I can't bear to part with fifteen, but then another cannon fires and a freight ship pulls in. It docks to unload some goods and I overhear two men discussing the next stop at Juneau. The *Ancon* takes off distracting them and I swing onto the freight, wedging between two crates. I wait, expecting to be discovered, but soon I'm in motion. We sail past green glaciers shining in the harsh light and thickets of forests that lead to dark worlds, glimmering valleys with flowers, and oozing marshes along with dark slabs of rock.

The sun wanes as we sail into Juneau, the air fresh with the tang of fish. In the late 1890s, I knew Juneau would be a prosperous place, but I'm astounded to see its boom. I hop off the freight ship on the wharf surrounded by one-smokestack steamers tied up to the dock. A light rain pours. Men in hip-length coats head down the wooden wharf to Front Street. Some with packs while others have valises, their hats pulled low over their heads. Buildings are raised on stilts with makeshift ladders leading to the front doors because of flooding or muddy streets. Hundreds of workers spill out of hard rock mines after being done for the day, the town coated in a gray mist from the smelting furnaces that seem to stretch toward the rain-forest country in a labyrinth of trees. I'm famished and thirsting for alcohol, but as the sun sinks, the artificial lights from the mines turn on, blazing the area. On my farm, I have no electricity but here the future rages. And I'm saddened. We got along fine with the sun as a guide and there would be no preventing machines and electric lights from taking over. A frontier land soon to be buried in the past and here I am getting a taste of the brand-new world. That's progress! So my spirits become slightly uplifted.

Since so many workers are streaming out of the Treadwell mine, it's easy to worm my way inside without anyone questioning. The place is filled with stamps that are heavy metal rods powered by a hydraulic engine. They slam down on tiny boxes like hammers. Rocks are being smashed to pieces in the hunt for gold. The floor vibrates and the continual slamming sounds so loud I think my head is going to explode. Without realizing, I whirl backward and the sleeve of my mackinaw coat gets stuck in the hydraulic mechanism in the belt of the rollers that carry the rocks. I try to wiggle out, but it's like being in the grip of a bear. Any second the heavy metal stamp will come crashing down on my hand.

I attempt to remove my coat, but it's impossible due to the way I'm trapped. My right arm in range of being crushed. I debate closing my fist to receive the brunt better and avoid getting my fingers severed. The stamps smash into the metal box, obliterating the rocks inside, surely about to turn every bone in my hand into a fine silt.

And then, a magic gift! An arm reaches in, grabs the sleeve of my coat, and yanks it free. I spin back as the stamp slams down. I turn to see an Injun walking away. I rush after him, figuring he doesn't speak English, needing to thank him for saving my life. But when I catch up, I see he has a drooping mustache like the Tlingit's at the last settlement, along with a string of green beads around his neck and a grimy hat with a salutary feather in the brim. But this is not an Injun. His eyes not sunken, his nose protruding rather than flat, his skin color pale save for the grime.

"Who do I have the pleasure of thanking for saving my skin?" I ask, extending my hand.

"George," he says, with a devilish wink. "George Cook."

* * *

To celebrate my escape from death, George Cook takes me to a rowdy watering hole replete with singing miners, their fingertips flush with a golden gleam. A jaunty tune sounds from a player piano and a barmaid sweeps around collecting empty glasses and refilling all those who stay. George and I find a table in the corner away from the din.

"A prospector, huh?" George asks, pulling at his drooping mustache. He's unlike any man I've ever met before, almost like he was raised by animals. His pants seem sewed together by a patchwork of lesser pants and his slouchy hat refuses to stay upright. He exudes a stink that's a mix of fish and wood and mountain, but it's oddly alluring—like he's had adventures I couldn't even dream of. "First time to Alaska?"

"Yep, come from a farm in Washington State. My wife and child are there."

"Yet you were drawn to the wild," he says, nodding as if we're one in the same. "I have a wife and child as well. She's an Indian and my daughter a half breed. Most like to sneer. I love them just the same. Their tribe holds wisdom that white men would be lucky to come across. They are richer than all of us combined."

"With gold?"

"No, with love, respect for the land, with things that matter."

"Yet you search for gold, George."

"I am not from there so material possessions still delight me. And gold brings promise."

"You aiming to head up the Yukon?"

"Sure am," he says, knocking back his ale and wiping the foam from his mouth with his sleeve. "Looking to rouse a gang together with some Indians as well. Figure my knowledge of their ways can help me get the best guides to join."

"That's what I'm after too. 'Cept I don't have much money."

"They won't want your money." He stands and beckons. "Come, follow my lead."

We head toward the bar and when the barmaid bends over to retrieve a dropped washcloth, George reaches his long arms down and procures two bottles of whiskey. He sticks them under his coat, his eyes dancing.

"Your turn," he says. I don't know what to do until George—while concealing the bottles he already stole—tells the barmaid that he thinks she's lost a button from her blouse, and when she bends over again, he nudges me and I reach down and grab two more whiskey bottles. By the time she raises her head, we're out the door with the booty.

Juneau at night seems different than during the day, more remote, less populated. Any other prospectors either getting a sound sleep or finding ways up the mouth of the Taiya River one hundred twenty miles north so they can begin their expedition through the Yukon. George leads me to another Tlingit settlement and I worry about duplicating my same fate. The way those savages laughed and made fun of me back in Sitka still stings. George explains he'll handle everything since he speaks their language.

A campfire blazes at the settlement. A dozen Tlingits turn from the fire, wary of the white men approaching.

"This is their *kwan*," George says.

"The last *kwan* I was in was not so welcoming."

"Tlingits have different units. And besides, you have me as a tagalong this time. They are at odds with Juneau, the mines conflicting with their lifestyle."

"How do they feel about gold?"

"Gold is universal. They just don't believe in machines as a way of obtaining it."

"Neither do I."

Two little girls observe us warily, both with rings through their noses and necklaces made of beads and shells. They take George's hand but not mine and lead him over to the fire where the elders sit. George waves me over too.

"I've been here before," George says. "They know me. Some prospectors try to pan around their settlement, but I come for the company."

George starts talking in Chinook to the man I believe to be the chief. The chief speaks in a low gruff while George gets animated, gesturing with his hands. Another man passes George a long pipe and he complies with a puff. The man points at me and George says something in response, which I assume to be an introduction. One of the little girls sits close, placing her cheek against my leg. She sticks out her tongue.

"She likes you," George says. And then I see him get down to business. He loses his jokey persona and becomes very serious, pointing in various directions and acting out rowing a boat. I want to tell him that won't work, but then the chief nods as if it's all been decided. The chief points to two men and orders them to stand. Then he looks at George with eyebrows raised, asking: *What will you give me in return?*

George whips out the two whiskey bottles from under his coat and motions for me to do the same. The Injuns' eyes all go wide, they couldn't be more pleased! George opens the cap, takes a small sip, then passes it to the Injun on his right. The Injun sticks his eye into the bottle, then places his lips over it and chugs. After finishing, he howls at the moon, then passes it along as each Injun does the same.

We sit around sipping whiskey as one of the Injuns tells a story. He's acting out a lot of it so I can understand some. It involves some type of animal, possibly a wolf, and the journey this wolf goes on. It's an arduous trip filled with sacrifice and at the end I'm not sure if the wolf died because the Injun just stops moving but his eyes are wide open in shock. A lot of the Injuns are drunk, and I'm drunk too, so I tuck my coat under my head to make a pillow. But this little girl with the ring in her nose shakes her head. She leads me to a plankhouse with totem poles erected at the sides where a makeshift bed has been set up. She grunts and closes the door behind me, vanishing before I can thank her. I'm so sleepy from my trek that once I lay my head down, it's already morning.

August 19th, 1898

I wake up to a beautiful Tlingit girl with long hair and button eyes. She beckons me to join the campfire where the tribe eats a breakfast of fish with Indian potatoes, along with greens, seeds, and berries. George has already finished and plays games with the Injun kids. When he sees me, he hurries over.

"Enjoy breakfast? When the tide goes out, the table is set. It's an old Tlingit saying." He indicates the fish bone on my plate, all that remains.

"It was delicious."

"So, we have two options. One, we can have them build us a canoe, but that will take some time and we'll have to leave the canoe at the Chilkoot Pass, since it will be too much to carry."

"What's the other?"

"I've learned that a gang of Indian braves has passed through Chilkoot and a US Navy gunboat was dispatched to apprehend them. One of the tribe members speaks decent English, better than myself. I didn't tell you this but I'm former Navy. I think I can convince the ship to take us up the Taiya."

"The ship is still there?"

"We'll find out."

We leave with foodstuffs: jerky bacon, flour, beans, and some tools to build a boat once we cross the Chilkoot Pass: a two-man whipsaw, sturdy axes, iron nails, along with pitch and oakum. In addition to the whiskey bottles, the two guides loaned are paid in gold and silver from George's pocket with the promise of many more riches. George was right that they didn't care about white man's paper money.

The little girl with the ring in her nose runs up, pinching my palm to say goodbye. She's about the same age as Little Joe seems but so much wiser, like she's lived a dozen lives already where all he's experienced is our farm. I plan on taking him on an expedition sometime so I can watch his eyes dance. I miss him so already.

As we head back into Juneau I'm introduced to the two Injun guides, a man named Kaawishté, who was the Injun who knew some English, and one other whose name is a blur and speaks nil English.

We reach the dock off Front Street. The streets have muddied due to a sleety rain, and sure enough, the USS *Pinta* galley's stovepipe rises from the harbor. George boards with me and the guides in tow and marches right for the captain. With a glint in his eye, George the showman pleads his case, tells of his military background, and how if we can get a lift to the Taiya, it would position us to begin our adventure up the Yukon. The captain, Commander Henry Nichols, USN, seems to have a wanderlust bone in his body and agrees that they could take a detour and deliver us and our supplies to the Taiya.

I'm in disbelief but George seems nonplussed. I get the sense that lucky things like this happen to him all the time. He simply has that kind of easy charm. Until he tells me, "I'm AWOL, just so you know."

"What do you mean by that?"

"I deserted the military so if I'm caught my goose is cooked. But I enjoy living on the edge of danger."

We eye two sailors passing by as my stomach churns. About halfway to our destination, the captain comes down from his quarters to check on us. The Injuns sit across from each other sharpening their knives in case there's trouble with the captain. The captain holds two Springfield rifles, and I think he's about to shoot us for George's deserting, but then he hands over the rifles along with rounds of ball cartridges.

"When ya make it back to Juneau, just return 'em," the captain says, and walks away before we can object.

As I hold the rifle in my hands, I'm aware of the many shots I will take. The animals I will slay for sustenance, and those I will kill in lieu of them killing me. The rifle is heavy with history, alive with a sense of its future. When I look up, hours have passed and we've arrived at the rapid, glacier-driven waters of the Taiya River, into the wilderness now, civilization a memory.

34

Chilkoot Pass and a Tagish Village
August 20th, 1898

George warned about the perilous Chilkoot Trail, but I didn't believe until I actually faced the thirty-five-hundred-yard climb up its steep white slope. Prior to reaching its base, the greatest difficulty was the fifty-pound rucksack on my back. But the breathtaking country makes up for its weight. Snow-capped peaks and proud evergreens, fields of green-jeweled grass, the pine aroma outside of Dyea and the calm blue waters with etchings of mountains reflected. One of them being the Chilkoot. Despite its outward beauty, it stands before us harsh and unremitting. George and the two guides woke bright-eyed and bushy-tailed, already ahead of me toward its base. There is no way I can turn back.

Even in the summer season, the snow is packed thick with layers of iced boulders. The wind cuts like knives. The glacier majestic yet seeming like it might dislodge at any second and come crashing down. My mackinaw coat rimmed with sweat. My rucksack digging into my back. Two miles up, we reach a flat area where we can rest. I can vaguely spy the summit, yet my legs betray my excited brain. No longer able to stand, I take to crawling, inching over boulder by boulder. I can't feel my hands and there are pools of ice water in my boots. I reach the summit on all fours as an animal, no longer entirely human.

August 21st, 1898

The ice on Lake Lindeman has broken up enough that a boat could pass through. After a breakfast over a fire of beans and jerky bacon, we set to work with the guides on a canoe. First, we make a saw pit, take the bark off logs, then place them on top. George holds one handle of the jag-toothed six-foot whipsaw, while one of the guides clasps it from below. Then they switch and me and the other guide take over. We finish come nighttime and paddle across, the lake still, barely lapping, the surrounding world ours alone. No sign of man, but we know that'll change once we close in on the Klondike. For now, we'll travel and pan in spots we think might produce gold. From everything I've been through to get here, I'm thrilled to no end!

August 22nd to September 3rd, 1898

The next few weeks prove to be a blur of disappointment. The gold we find no more than dust. The loneliness settling in. The guides speak to each other and George occasionally but not much to me. I miss Adalaide and Little Joe terribly, having left them for well over a month now. I wonder if Little Joe has gotten over his chills. If Adalaide waits for a letter that I am unable to send. I swear once we hit a town that will be the first thing I do. I think of mornings spent in bed cuddling with them both, a fire roaring. George tries to keep my spirits up, but he is unsuccessful. Once the grip of depression has you in its vice, it won't dare let go.

Having always been a good rifle shot, I spend the time honing my skills. I can hit a bobbing duck or a goose that we can roast over a spruce fire. Salmon are caught with netting, and clams and bottomfish just from digging. So we eat okay, trying not to cut into our preserves too much. As we near September, the weather takes a turn. Our tents barely keeping out the chilled rush of winds that howl throughout the nights. My dreams even cool, icy realms devoid of sun, a blue-cheeked Little Joe shivering, my bones brittle enough to snap. What a fool I am to think I could strike it rich in the Yukon. The only thing I'll bring back home is frostbite, if I survive. One morning we wake and the Injun guide who spoke no English is dead. We put pennies over his shut eyes and drift him out on one of the lakes, holding our hats to our hearts.

"He had a sickness in him," Kaawishté says. It's the first he's spoken to me in days. He has jet-black hair that sweeps down to his shoulders, his mouth in a permanent frown the shape of an umbrella, broad shoulders with hands the size of pans. He could break my neck with barely a twist.

"What was the sickness?" I ask.

He looks at me like I'm a dunce for not knowing. "He was never a believer. That's why the chief chose him to go. He wanted him out of our tribe."

"And you?" I ask, as the question hangs in the air. I'm nervous to hear the answer.

"I am our future."

He pivots so he is no longer looking directly at me, the conversation ended. George shrugs and I think about how I represent my family's future as well. Each day I wonder if I should turn around and head back. I know George does as well. I've heard him murmuring in his sleep. But not Kaawishté, even the death of his tribemate doesn't hasten his determination. Rather noble.

September 4th to September 30th, 1898

The next day, Kaawishté decides we must find a settlement in the area to replenish our supplies. Without realizing, we've come low on beans and flour and simply eating fish or game does not reward enough sustenance. My belly has sunken in, ribs poking through, my tongue flush from dehydration. George and I agree.

After floating upstream for days, we come across a Tagish village. George replies that he only knows Chinook and won't be able to understand, but Kaawishté reassures us. He's spent some time with the Tagish, knows of their ways. We've no other choice but to have him lead. As we plunge into the ice waters of Nares Lake, we hear a cannon that makes me think of when I first arrived in Sitka and the steamboats were setting off. At first, I wonder if we're being attacked, since the boundaries between American Alaska and the Dominion of Canada are fuzzy at best, but the noise keeps mutating, drawing closer, headed straight for us. Across the channel, the thunder from a herd of pounding caribou, thousands of them, roaring through the earth, their fur shimmering, galloping a fierce beat as they charge as a united front. The raw mystique of their power brings tears to my eyes, not from sadness like I've felt so far, but at the awe that nature inspires. I had only destinations in mind from the start of my journey, but I must breathe in the entirety of this adventure, for we only live one life.

About fifty miles from the herd lies the Tagish settlement, which hugs the banks of a channel that curls around two lakes. A small clan, no more than twenty or so families with two large community houses and a strip of tiny log cabins in a crescent shape. A woman as old as the hills greets us, barely able to stand, yet her voice throbbing with authority. Kaawishté tells us the Tagish women make the decisions for the tribe while the men are off hunting.

With slight difficulty, Kaawishté explains our situation and the elder tribe woman receives us sweetly. Kaawishté says that they will house and replenish us but we must work for the trade. First, we are joined by the men finished with their hunt and are served caribou tongue. They laugh as I spit out its sharp hairs. Over the next week, I hunt with the braves and they are impressed by my rifle skills. When we kill an animal, the carcass is given to the entire village as the women work to dry and smoke the meat. I feel like I'm part of a family for the first time since I've left my own.

"Their way of life," George says, gnawing at a dried piece of Caribou skin. "It has its benefits, yes?"

"When was the last time you really spent among white men?"

George shakes his finger. "Not since I was young. I'll head into Juneau, partake of alcohol and a few modern luxuries, but all I need is a taste. I'm entirely full."

"Yet you leave your family?" I ask, wanting him to justify me deserting my own.

"Kaawishté spoke of being the future of his tribe. I am the same. We've fallen on hard times. Even though we do not require much, the land has changed and does not provide like it used to. The gold will help us settle somewhere more prosperous."

"My son is sick," I say, because I've barely spoken of Little Joe since we began our trek.

"What does he have?"

I shrug. "He's always cold."

George tosses away a sour piece of caribou. He tugs at his mustache. "Maybe that's actually the secret to longevity."

"What do you mean, George?"

"Our bodies are all very different. What might kill one causes another to survive. I am saying he may not be as sick as you think. Have faith."

"I don't have faith."

"No God?"

"No."

"Well, I don't subscribe to God like you may think. But I do believe in my own gods, in the teachings elders have passed down. You should let the Tagish do a ritual to you. You may come out of it enlightened."

The next day I follow a moose on my own, a wickedly fast animal that the hunting party has been after all week. It has been teasing us but could feed the village for a month, so I'm determined to be victorious. I shoot from a far distance, while the Tagish people cry at its defeat. They dance around the collapsed moose with a high-pitched chant that their ancestors have sung to bless noble warriors. It's then I'm allowed into the men-only tribal dances where we dress in wooden masks and painted caribou robes, telling of the ancient myths. Kaawishté explains that George and I will be initiated. We are surrounded by Tagish braves, draped with caribou cloaks and yellow raven's beaks placed over our heads. The shaman dances and chants around us, then we are handed a dark potion that tastes of blood and tart berries. We migrate into the woods.

"You will stay here," the shaman says in broken English. "But you must not eat or light a fire. An animal spirit will speak to you. Every Tagish has an animal as a guide in their life. You need to discover which is the animal that watches over you."

"How long does that take?" I ask, but George and Kaawishté shake their heads. You do not question a shaman. The shaman walks off in silence, and George and Kaawishté disperse from my sight. I am alone.

A light snow begins to fall. My mackinaw coat keeps me warm along with gloves made from rabbit skin and a rabbit-fur hat that covers my ears. For what feels like two days and nights, I wait for the raven to speak, the most esteemed of all spirits, or even the eagle. Sweat pours from my face and armpits despite the cold. I assume this is from the potion I drank. A storm pushes through, snow falling in dizzying flakes. I'm unable to walk, a sitting target for the blizzard. The snow piles on, covering me with its icy quilt. I fall into a deep and dark sleep, wade through a dream. It's the realest dream I've ever encountered. A wolf with glacier-blue eyes locks me in its gaze. It speaks with a powerful, calm voice, the words in Tagish but I'm able to comprehend.

"I am your protector," the wolf declares. "My spirit will guide you to your future."

I awake and dust off my snow blanket. The Tagish spoke of their reverence of the raven and the eagle, so I'm disappointed to be visited by a wolf. When I return from the village, George and Kaawishté are there.

"You've been gone long time," Kaawishté says.

"A couple of days."

"No, eight nights," Kaawishté corrects.

I'm baffled and reply, "A wolf came to me in my dream."

"No dream," the Injun guide says.

"What animal came to you both?" I ask.

Kaawishté responds the raven while George talks of the eagle.

"I wish one of those came to me."

"No, wolf is very good," Kaawishté says. "Represents wealth."

When I blink, I see gold nuggets in place of their eyes.

It's time to leave soon and I am given a name by the tribesmen upon my departure, Kahse, which means seeker. I'm unsure if that defines me as a prospector or someone who has now sought a new way of thinking, of living too. Will I take what I've acquired here back home? Will it enrich me and my brood?

I decide I will take it to mean both.

Seeker of gold and what truly matters.

35

That Which Blazes Soon Dims

October 3rd, 1898

Up the Yukon, we wade down a fat and practically frozen waterway, its streams slicking down from the mountains. First, we try the sandbars, using our oars as shovels but finding nothing but flour gold, so fine it's barely worth the trouble. I am, however, getting an education. Kaawishté is a fast hand at washing down a pan, and George adept at a pick-and-shovel. Neither ever complains so that begins to rub off on me. And I'm schooled about how different prospecting is from California where I'd pan on the banks and rivers coming off the Sierra Nevadas. Yukon Territory with its giant mountains and powerful rivers that churn the gold to a fine sand. Nuggets only found in tiny brooks and creeks. I'm feeling disillusioned once again, and George can read that on my face.

"You're thinking of giving up," he says.

"How did you know?"

"Your face wears the mask mine has worn before."

"What keeps you so upbeat, George?"

He takes in a lungful of air. "Smell that nature, crisp like the bite of a fresh apple. Even where you're from, does the air taste like that?"

"Can't say it does."

"Then breathe in that wealth till your lungs are full."

I do as he says and feel a tad better.

"My daughter, Natsanitna, turns five today."

It takes a second for me to recall Little Joe's birthday. I am becoming more and more removed from them.

"Her favorite thing to do is weave," George says, a smile illuminating his face. It's less round since we began our journey. Some might call it hardened. I say it's lived in. "She makes ribbons for the whole tribe. Beautiful color patterns." He pulls one from his pocket, a red-and-blue braid. His hair has grown long and he ties the ribbon into his black curls. "Does it match my ensemble?"

I laugh. George can be such a goof.

"Look at the water, it's glistening."

Sure enough, the tributary at our backs gleams with shiny pebbles.

"Quartz," George says, rubbing his hands. "And where there's quartz, there's often gold."

The creek twists to the right and George taps out the sediment from his pan, squats down, and dips it into the sunny waters. He breaks apart the sand with his fingers and then spits in it for good luck. Like magic, a bright yellow shape appears, very fine, but this flour gold has heft.

"This is near where we'll find our treasure," George declares.

We follow the burbling creek up a grassy hill that feels like a valley of golden dreams. Birds chirp, the sunlight a caress. A strange rock formation juts out at an impasse. George knocks over the damp bedrock and shovels the dirt at his feet into his pan. This time instead of flour gold sit two small nuggets.

"Well, I'll be..." I say, drooling.

That's all the gold we find in that spot, but about a mile up the creek bed, we reach a fork leading to a rapid waterway called Rabbit Creek, and we stay with the tributary for a while until we hit a slab of black bedrock.

"Down there," George says, throwing off his pack and scampering down. Kaawishté and I do the same. In the shallow water, a gold nub shines, big as a minnow. George places the nugget between his teeth as it bends, definitely not yellow rock, the sweet glory of actual gold!

"Come down and shovel," he tells us. "Hi yo. Hurry!"

The gold had been lodged into the nooks and crannies of the rocks. George flings his pan into the air as the gold rains down in sweet delight. Then he starts doing a jig, dipping and twirling and singing like a beautiful fool. Kaawishté and I join, each of us singing our own song of jubilation. All the blood and sweat we've put into this Alaskan jaunt, now in Klondike territory, finally paying off. I wish Adalaide and Little Joe could see my weepy smile. Though I'll settle for my two journeymen. We hug and kiss each other's cheeks and then break off all the gold we can see, which equals a few fistfuls.

But as I've learned from life, happiness sometimes only greets us in fits and starts. For tragedy often follows merriment. Without strife, we would not know the true meaning of gaiety. That's what I like to tell myself to ease the pain. So as George dances his heart out, an axe spirals through the air landing directly in his chest. The blade cuts so deep it hastens to bleed. He falls over on his face, stone dead in an instant.

Kaawishté and I look around for the assailant. A flash whisks by us revealing an Injun savage, hair a dirty mop, blood painted under his eyes, teeth blackened and sharp. He knocks us over, retrieves his axe, and sets to steal our gold.

"No!" I scream, my eyes darting from George to the gold, unsure what to focus on. The savage lunges, the axe held high. Kaawishté and I scurry back. The savage has the gold in his dirty palms. He gives a cackle and takes off, fleeing into the camouflaged trees. Kaawishté pursues him without flinching.

I am left alone with George. Rolling him over, the blood teems from his gaping wound. If he wasn't dead before, he's long gone now. A smile permanently stamped across his face. He died not seeing his death, but ultimately his success.

I give a few blows from my nose as the tears come. I'm crying for the loss of a friend, a true friend, something I haven't experienced in a long time, and crying for his wife and half-breed child left behind, also because it could have been me. Little Joe might have been going to bed fatherless tonight had I been in George's place.

When Kaawishté returns, his hands are painted red with the savage's blood while carrying the gold blocks under his armpits.

"I kill him with his own axe." He grunts, dropping the bloody nuggets at my feet. He bends down and closes George's eyes. "We bury him."

"Of course."

We dig in silence as night arrives with its brisk chill, the light of the moon beaming on the grave. Delicately, we hoist George inside as Kaawishté says a prayer over the body. I hold my rabbit-eared hat to my heart.

"A finer man I've never crossed paths," I say.

"We bury the gold with him," Kaawishté replies.

I'm about to object, but Kaawishté seems determined so I hear him out.

"It never would have been found if not for George," he says. "And he sacrificed his life. By having the gold eternally rest with him, we are showing the gods that we deserve to locate our own. And they will come through because of our sacrifice."

"Fair enough," I say, and help him place the gold in the grave. We shovel until the dirt is piled high and the grave just a part of the earth. It's the faint light of morning when we're done.

"So we head into the Klondike?" I ask, whipping out my map where a red X lies over Dawson City. "Dawson City shouldn't be too much of a hike."

"We go for George." Kaawishté shoulders his pack and is already ten steps ahead.

"Off to the city of gold," I tell the surrounding nature with a sigh. The budding frosts listen with pleasure. Foothills wink, alive with their burning red hues. Crystallized waters lap to the rhythm of my steps. Snow-peaked mountains standing tall and proud with their watching omniscience.

The land that has given us so much but taken mightily.

36

Dawson City, Heart of the Klondike!

October 5th to October 10th, 1898

The trail to Dawson City is a treacherous climb, but Kaawishté and I aren't the only ones making the forty-five-mile journey along a skinny and twisting path replete with cliffs, jagged rocks that could poke out your eye, and swamps thick as quicksand. We pass by hundreds of dead mules crushed by avalanche falls. The acrid stench of rotting flesh mixing with the chill mountain air. We follow a line of other hopeful prospectors inching forward along a morose winding procession, holding onto ropes staked into the ground. At night, we huddle in makeshift tents, our bones burning cold, the freezing temperatures plummeting. I write to Adalaide but tell her none of my troubles.

Dearest Adalaide,

I write to you as my Indian guide and I near Dawson City, the heart of the gold expedition! I miss you and Little Joe terribly and apologize for not writing thus far, but there haven't been many post offices along the way. The adventures I've had are unbridled. I have seen pockets of our majestic country that would rival any painting in a museum. I have become an adept hunter, killing game with a loaned rifle from a steamboat captain in Juneau. I've spent time in an Indian settlement where I've learned to be more spiritual. I've made lifelong friends of similar ilk who also see the world through a golden lens. There is opportunity in these lands, which makes me believe that it was my destiny to embark on this wilderness jaunt. I am not lonely, for I have found the embroidered mirror that you have left me. I keep it close to my beating heart because you and Little Joe have captured that pounding organ. We have come across gold already, but the true treasure awaits us at Dawson City! I will not let you down, my love. I will make you and Little Joe proud.

With all my caress,
Wyatt Emmett Barlow

I place the letter in a sealed envelope, satisfied that there are very few lies in what I wrote, only omissions of the difficult truth we've encountered.

October 11th, 1898

Land ho! Our weary feet arrive in Dawson City, a bustling, glittery, gold-steeped town packed wall-to-wall with prospectors, investors, bosom-heavy ladies, mules and horses advertising performances, tents filled with grimy faces poking out, brothels, arcade restaurants, fruit and tobacco stores, markets, saloons, casinos, photo studios, dance halls, an opera house, the Palace Grand Hotel, the Pavillion, and the Monte Carlo featuring boxing matches. The city loud with the rush of promise. Finger-tips etched in gold dust, gold as the city's currency, the smell of it a sweet tang. Kaawishté and I in awe, not expecting this grand show. It's a city that seems as if it's sprung up out of nowhere, its surroundings nothing more than native Han fishing camps pushed to the outskirts or destroyed. After not socializing with large groups of people for a while, I'm tongue-tied, and I can tell Kaawishté feels similar. George would have probably lapped it all up and celebrated our arrival with a finger of whiskey in a saloon.

"Let's have a drink for George," I tell Kaawishté, because George has been on my mind a lot lately. I'm still unable to process his death, believing he'll magically appear saying it was all a trick.

At a casino, men play poker but instead of chips gold bullions are used. We sit at the bar on swiveling stools and order whiskey. Kaawishté points to two gold bullions on the floor that no one seems to care about. I quickly stuff them in my pocket.

It's good to take off our weighted packs but my back can't get used to its freedom, almost as if a phantom rucksack still plagues.

"The whiskey should help that," Kaawishté says, because he must be feeling the same.

The casino ripe with the jubilation of men who have staked their lives on a dream that's finally become real. These aren't the hardened faces that we've come across on our journey so far. They toss gold cubes at each other like it's all a joke. I want to shake them for their senselessness. They are all drunk with pleasure, squeezing the derrieres of waitresses in prairie dresses and giving them a gold tip.

The bartender is a red-faced man with cheeks like a hoarding hamster and a dot of a mouth that's all smiles. He even has a gold tooth that shines in the sunlight.

"Just arrived to our fair city?" he asks, spit-shining a glass with a rag and pulling out a whiskey bottle to top us off.

"Me and my guide have traveled a long way," I say, and Kaawishté gives an affirmative nod, knowing it's best as an Injun to not say much and possibly cause a disturbance.

"Ah, many of us have," he says. "Cal-i-for-ni-a here. But that land was tapped so I headed north. Opened this fine establishment with every last cent I had. Now I bathe in gold."

"That so?"

"Yep-sir-ee, but I'm afraid you gents have arrived a tad late. Surrounding land is pretty wrung dry. Big city miners come in taking whatever is left."

I scan the room. "Doesn't seem like folks are fleeing in droves."

"Oh, they will. Your best bet is to scurry around the floors like a rat hoping for crumbs."

He lets out a booming laugh that shakes his belly.

"Or maybe you just don't want competition," Kaawishté finally says, and I'm glad for him to speak up.

"Injun's got a mouth on him," the bartender says. "Well, good for you, feather head. But you can ask anyone. Boom here is over, we're all just staying a little too late at the party, not ready for it to end."

I slam my fist on the bar, causing the glasses to rattle. "I won't go home without gold."

"Now, now, son. Calm it down. Didn't say there's no gold left in Alaska, only this area. There's a whole frontier to the West that's been barely mined. *The Unknown*," he says, the word oozing from his lips. "In fact, those who haven't found their fortune here are beginning to head that way."

The thought of more arduous traveling weighs my head down. I want to say I still have the resolve in me, but my last bolt of energy has gone into making it here.

"How far out west into The Unknown?" I ask.

"Around Anvil Creek, the true wilderness. Land of bears and ice and not much else save for gold supposedly."

"Why are you telling us this?" Kaawishté asks.

"Feel bad for ya, I guess. Stream of folks coming here lately expecting miracles. But look around. All the miracles have already occurred and people are just riding out their riches before they head back to reality."

"Top it off again," I say, tapping my glass, needing the drink evermore. Kaawishté does the same and we toast.

"What do you think George would want to do?" I ask.

Kaawishté grunts. "He'd want us to keep going."

"I say we stick around, maybe collect some crumbs so we at least have something. Say, I saw a boxing match being advertised. What do you say we do that?"

At the luxurious Monte Carlo, we hobnob with rich folk paying to see men beat each other to a pulp. I watch with great awe, feeling like I'd want to pound on someone myself. Afterwards, I remember the letter I wrote Adalaide.

"I must mail this," I tell Kaawishté.

We head to a post office grander than any in my tiny Washington town. Kaawishté waits outside while I buy a stamp and can practically smell Adalaide's lilac aroma as I go mail the letter. But before I can, I'm cut short by three middle-aged cowboys with bandanas covering their faces save their eyes who burst through the front doors with rifles pointed at the screaming customers. I crouch low, my hand on a knife blade, but I tell myself, *this is not your fight.*

"You can go ahead and pay us in gold," the ringleader tells the clerk. He stands beside me, smelling of soap. A long mustache trickles from out of his bandana.

The clerk goes to a safe and actually pulls out gold! The post office using that as a currency. I'm drooling as bindles get stuffed with gold blocks. The two other members of the gang wait by the door, one built like a mountain, the other like a long and skinny tree. They monitor the door with guns armed. I've left my rucksack with the rifle outside with Kaawishté.

"Let's go, hurry it up," the ringleader says to the clerk, whose brow is sweating and hands shake as he passes over the gold.

The ringleader pokes the gun at a sniveling man and his wife locked arm-in-arm. "Empty yer pockets, folks." Then he spins the rifle around the room. "All of yous."

Everyone starts obeying, pushing forward wallets and pocket watches, along with golden knobs and jewelry. The gang member built like a mountain waddles over to pick it all up.

The ringleader turns to me, the only one who hasn't complied.

"You hard of hearing?" the ringleader asks, his rifle's nose pressed into mine.

"I barely have gold on me," I say, and turn a pocket where the two small nubs were buried.

The ringleader cackles. "Who let you in Dawson?" He presses his nostril and fires a glob of mucus my way. It lands on my cheek, all moist and runny. He eyes the embroidered mirror and the letter from my other pocket.

"Silver?" he says, like it's some mysterious object. "Boys, do we take silver?"

"Bite it and make sure it's good," the tree bellows.

"I am a bit hungry," Ringleader guffaws. He places my beloved mirror between his lips and digs his teeth in. I squirm as if he's taken a bite out of me. "Yep, that'll do." He tilts his foolish-looking hat. "I thank you for this."

I put one hand on the knife's blade again. It's hidden in my belt and this criminal hasn't noticed. I could whip it out and slice his throat but would still have the rest of the gang to contend with. Mountain and Tree surely firing a bullet to end me.

Then I remember Kaawishté standing outside.

My best chance would be to let the thieves think they've won. They can march out with my beloved mirror and the booty not knowing what awaits. I saw what Kaawishté did to the savage that killed George. He didn't tell me this, but he scalped the man, carrying the tip of the savage's head in his rucksack. I'd mixed our packs up one morning and found it hovering at the top of his clothes.

"I am a wolf," I tell the ringleader, who looks curiously. "Part of a clan. We will not forget."

"What in the Sam Hill you jibberin' about?"

"Go on," I say. I've departed my body momentarily, a spirit taking over. This has been happening more and more since we left the Tagish settlement. Since I've turned lupine.

Obviously spooked, Ringleader starts backing up, eager to get away. He gathers his gang and they go bolting out the door. The clerk yells to get the police, but when I run out, I aim to be the law, knife in my grip. Front Street's packed, Dawson City like a zoo. I spin around trying to locate Kaawishté. There are three horses alongside the post office. The thieves each hop on one, screeching "giddy up," but the horses remain stiff. Kaawishté has his palm out by the horses' noses like he's casting a spell. His eyes white, and the horses get this relaxed look on their mugs and stay put. The thieves go ballistic, kicking at their mules with their boot heels, then turning their rifles on Kaawishté.

"Injun, you better knock off this evil trick and git our horses right."

Kaawishté doesn't respond, uninterested in their threats.

"Charlie, you shoot him good," Ringleader says.

"Soapy, I thought you said not to use our real names."

"Goshdarnit, you just used my moniker!"

"Least no one called me Aaron," Tree says, then realizes his mistake.

"Quiet," Soapy tells them. "Now I will count to three, Injun. And on three, both my men gonna pull those triggers. You release my horses from your foul spell."

"If you kill me," Kaawishté says, "the horses will stay frozen like this. The law will come and hang you."

Soapy turns to Charlie and Aaron for advice, but they shrug. However, he isn't dumb as them. Ringleaders need some merit to get others to follow. Same in a wolf pack.

"We'll cut you in on the take if you release those horses," Soapy says.

"You give back what you stole from my friend." Kaawishté indicates me, none of them realizing I was there. I slide the knife back in my belt loop.

Soapy zeroes in. With the bandana still covering his face, I try to imagine who this man may be. The three of them aren't too quick in mind and stamina. Relics of another time. Aging cowboys unable to let go. The Wild Wild West had ended and never got around to telling them. I picture him with winter in his beard.

"I never really liked silver anyway," Soapy says, tossing me my embroidered mirror.

I cannot explain how it hurt to be without my beloved's gift. The last time I killed a man for making the mistake of stealing. I clench it in my palm until my love line starts to bleed.

"C'mon!" Soapy bellows, turning around and seeing a policeman huffing and puffing his way over.

Kaawishté says something in his native tongue to the horses and the spell they're under vanishes. They buck and bray, ready to roar.

"Deal's a deal," Soapy says. "I may be a criminal but I ain't crooked. Hop on."

Kaawishté mounts the horse behind Soapy, and Mountain pulls me on his before I can argue. I lean down to grab my rucksack.

"Hiya!" they shout, slapping their horses as we thunder off, mud flinging on the portly policeman damn near out of breath.

Front Street's very crowded but the people part to create an aisle for us to pass through. Then Soapy turns off the main stretch, and in a minute we're surrounded by plains and open skies. We hoof past a Han settlement, the clansmen watching us with mute derision until they see Kaawishté riding side-saddle and trickles of smiles appear on their faces. We robbed the very folks who had robbed them, and I've always declared that the enemy of my enemy might be my friend.

After some ways, we pull up to a lean-to shack haphazardly built and hidden by a thicket of surrounding trees. We dismount and I've got my hand on the knife blade, my rucksack firmly on both shoulders too in case they plan to kill us now that there are no witnesses.

The gang remove their bandanas from their sopping faces. Each of them older than I expected. Mountain's completely bald, his head almost too big for his floppy hat. Tree's gone fully gray with thick lines all over his face. Soapy looks the youngest, but only due to his spirit. I was right to guess winter in his beard. One eye of his has a nervous tic while the other shines crystal green. He lets out a cough that could rival any sick man in a hospital.

"We ain't aiming to try anything funny," Soapy says, in his laconic cowboy tone. "Let's get a fire started."

The lean-to smells of soot and fried lard, blackened pans charring on the stove. Mountain lights a match and blazes the kindling in the fireplace. The room fills with smoke and he opens the flume.

"This hellhole," he says, waving his hand through the black soot in the air.

Tree takes the booty, kisses a block, and stuffs it in a hollowed-out space behind a wonky table.

"Time to get arfarfan'arf," Soapy sings, breaking out a bottle of Old Horn Brook Whiskey, taking a mighty swill and passing it over to Mountain who does the same. Kaawishté declines and so do I, still not trusting these men.

"You and the Injun don't like to live?" Tree asks, wiping his mouth from whiskey overflow.

"Been a trying day," I say, hoping that ends it.

It does since the men seem pleased not to share their booze. Now that Soapy's good and snickered, he's ready to divulge his plan.

"See there's a mighty amount of land that miners haven't checked out yet. Trick is to go beyond Dawson City. I met this prospector a few days back. He's traveling alone so having a hard time. He swears he's come across gold in the far plains but has no way of transporting it back along with hauling his rucksack too. Don't got no mule either. So he needs us and the more the merrier because there's likely too much gold for us to carry off on our own anyway."

"We aim to be far from this town come sun-up," Mountain says, and lets out a belch. Tree whips out his gun, fake fires a bullet, then coolly slips it back in his holster. Then the two sidekicks punch at each other playfully before things get more heated and they're rolling around on the ground.

"Boys," Soapy yells, but they don't listen. "Boys!" Soapy fires a bullet that shoots clear through the ceiling. Mountain and Tree finally let go of each other. "Focus on the task at hand." His twitching eye looks over in my direction. "This prospector should be on his way. We just wanted to pick up some small change from the PO beforehand in case his claims turn out to be a bust. You and the Injun wanna be on our side in case he tries anything funny?"

Kaawishté gives me a nod.

"You can count on us, Soapy," I say. "Say, that's a funny name you got. Where does it come from?"

"Ah, Soapy's origin," he says, pressing down his mustache as the tic in his eye turns to a twinkle. "Didn't start as a bank robber. Charlie, Aaron and I been together since the eighties. Used to sell soap but it was really a scam. I'd tell folks there was a dollar bill hidden in some of the soaps and then charge people that amount. Oh, they bought it up like flies on a turd. Go from town to town, city to city, hoodwinking all the rubes. But then the law got involved. I'm in some city where I see my name and face on a WANTED poster. Damn near soiled myself. Figured if being a con man got me on that poster, I might as well go all out and take to banks. But we ain't known in Yukon territory. It's like we're starting over. Spent part of my youth panning for gold during the California Gold Rush, figure we might as well try it up north too."

"Soapy tells us where to go and we just follow," Tree says. "Has worked for us thus far."

"I'm a good man mostly. Who have I really robbed from? The rich banks who barely notice their money's missing. And POs? For what they charge for stamps, they deserve to be bled." He jabs Kaawishté in the arm. "Am I right, Injun?"

Kaawishté gives a tired nod. I can tell he's sick of Soapy already.

Soapy sits back in a chair, kicks his boots off, and rests his holey socks on the table. A big bare toe sticks out, the nail darkened, toe throbbing.

"Good to git a load off," Soapy says, scratching at his filthy sock.

Mountain and Tree have gotten sleepy and Soapy allows the two a small nap before the prospector arrives. They snore like old men on their last few wheezes looking even more aged in their slumber. These men have never truly worked, have lived off the fat of others, created their own laws. In some ways, I hate them for it and in other ways I admire them. They've chased dreams as foolish as they were and lived without any compromise. Something to be said about that. I can certainly relate. I've worked on my farm till my bones ached but gave it up for the thrill of promise. These men and I are more alike than I'd care to admit. But the Wild West ended some time ago. Weather-beaten now, full of wrinkles and gray, products of a bygone era. I have a chilling fear I could wind up like them soon enough.

"What's got your mind turning?" Soapy asks, because I've gone under for some time now. "Tell me your story."

"I just chase gold," I say, with a lump in my throat. "It's all I know to do."

We've all nodded off, except of course for Kaawishté, who never sleeps, whose eyes stay trained on Soapy's men, never believing them to be allies. It's the first I'm able to rest indoors, and while it's not entirely warm, it's better than outdoors and I'm cooking a bit from the fire. I dream in fits, no clear images except for a pair of the wolf's ice-blue eyes, ever observing. I'm being watched over, but the wolf hasn't revealed itself yet. I am certain before this adventure ends, it will.

A booming knock resounds at the door and I wipe the drool from my lips. Mountain and Tree still snore, but Soapy waves for me to go answer. As I do, he puts back on his boot over his dirty sock. I signal Kaawishté, who nods that he'll offer support in case whoever's at the door turns out to be a foe. And sure enough, when I open it, no greater foe stands before me than Frank Allard, the lying, cheating, skilamalink sumbitch who got me to do his dirty work by killing Carl Finnegan Langford aboard the *G.W. Elder!*

Frank's face goes white as a swan, since I clearly am not the man he expects to see. He backs up, ready to squirrel away, but I don't give him a chance.

"You!" I cry, leaping upon him. We tussle as if death is on the line. My teeth are gnashing, someone's bleeding but I don't know who.

A bullet shatters a window to our right. Soapy stands there with a smoky pistol.

"I am guessing you two know each other," he says, a laugh twirling his mustache.

Mountain holds me back and Tree's got Frank. Kaawishté has his knife out. I think my guide's in the mood to stab someone. His eyes ask me what I want him to do.

"This man is a thief, and a scoundrel, and a murderer," I say to an audience that yawns in response.

"Welcome to the club." Soapy's finger digs at the wax in his ear. "Who you think you're runnin' with?"

They all break out in a laughter that turns their faces red. Even Frank, until I lunge at him again and he trips over his big feet. Tree helps him up.

"I didn't do anything to you I wouldn't have to someone else," Frank says, rubbing his skinned knee. "Meaning you shouldn't take it personal."

The spit rises in my mouth. "You tricked me into killing a man."

"You still on that?" Frank blows a raspberry. "More sensitive than I thought."

"I had never…" I lower my head, almost in shame. "I'd never taken a life before."

Soapy claps me on the back. "Well, sonny, it's about time then. You should thank this man." He coughs into a soiled handkerchief already stained with dried blood.

"That's what I figure," Frank says. "I helped you, Wyatt. I bet you wouldn't have made it this far had you not been tried."

I hate to say it but Frank's probably right. What occurred on the *G.W.* caused me to lose my naivety.

"So let's us kiss and make up, shall we?" Soapy says, puckering his dried lips.

"I don't know if this is the type of man you want to align with," I say.

"Sonny, ain't *no* type of man I want to align with," Soapy says. "We all animals, nary a selfless bone in most of humankind. You hook up with who can aid you at the moment. And for now, Frank here's a prospector who may know where the gold might be, and you and the Injun are sure to be good at panning. Therefore, we a gang. The question is, can you let bygones be bygones?"

Frank clears his throat. I recall his phlegmy habit and I'm disgusted. "I sure can," he says. "I actually liked you, Wyatt. And I know you liked me too."

"It was an act you were putting on."

"Life's an act," he says. "We're all just pretending. Tryin' to get by. Fast friends again?"

He sticks out his plump hand, the fingers like sausage links, the nails bitten down. I'd still rather take my knife to his throat, but in the effort of moving along, I spit in my palm and shake his.

"Truce…for now," I say.

"Is all I ask."

After we've faked a renewal of our friendship, Soapy sets out the plan. Tree will wait behind in the shack with the booty and our heavy packs so we don't have to haul. We'll take the horses to the spot Frank found, then bring the booty back here to divide up and we can go our separate ways. I don't like leaving my pack behind, but the idea of carrying it is worse so I comply. Kaawishté agrees as well. We allow ourselves the night to sleep, except for Kaawishté who still stays monitoring. I am glad that no matter what, I can at least rely on him.

It's been an exceptionally long day so when I close my eyes and go under, I'm fully submerged. A cannon couldn't wake me now. I dream of sharing a bed with Adalaide and Little Joe, the warmth of their bodies a reminder I have a home away from this, which should be nothing more than a stopgap until my real life can resume.

***

October 12th, 1898

We eat jerky for breakfast until we're fortified enough to carry on. None of the three men wants to ride with Kaawishté, claiming Injun smells even worse than railroad men, but I'd wager that Soapy's acrid tang is worse than the rest of us combined.

We pack one bag with the essentials: ropes and knives, pans and pick-axes. On horseback, it should take half a day to arrive at Frank's location. I refuse to ride with him so I wind up side-saddle with Soapy while Frank rides with Mountain.

It's a fair day out compared to the weather we've experienced, a reprieve from all our troubles thus far. The plains glittered with various shades of green peeking through the thin silt from the winding rivers. Small mountains capped with snow but no ice in sight, a good sign for when we start panning. Birds reign in this land, yellow warblers setting the scene to music.

Once Mountain and Frank have trotted up ahead, Soapy speaks out of the corner of his mouth. "If your old friend tries anything funny, I'm fit to put him down." He pats the pistol in the holder. Kaawishté and I left our rifles in the shack, but we do have knives as defense.

"I would not object to that."

"I see a lot of myself in you when I was younger," he says, and I wince at that thought.

"I'm no con man."

"Oh really? There's a long life ahead of you hopefully and conning will be imminent. I guarantee."

"I want to provide for myself. My son, he's sick."

"So did I. At least at first, I told myself that. But once you start taking, it becomes hard to justify. It simply becomes a part of you."

"I haven't taken anything that's not mine."

"What about the gold? That's the Earth's, I believe. It's spent many years to refine that gilt to what it is now. No different, sonny."

Soapy and I stay quiet for the rest of the journey. Maybe what he's said has gotten to me, I don't know; I feel guilty as all heck. For being selfish, I guess. But maybe he wants to mess with my mind and I decide to keep him close in my sights, as much as Frank.

With the sun high in the sky, we arrive at Frank's spot, a burbling creek bed with slab runoffs that have a golden reflection when the light hits it right.

"I had walked and walked and walked," Frank says, getting off his horse and scurrying over to the creek bed. "The way the light catches the water, you can almost see fine bits of gold." Panning the stream, he wipes away sand and sure enough a golden knob shines back.

"See!" he says, holding up the evidence.

None of us wait for him to prove there's any more. We get our pans ready and spend the next few hours repeating the same motions over and over until magically each of us has a pile of gold as large as a small child. The sun dips, casting the land in purple lights. Soapy mops his brow and whips out a cigar.

"Stole this down in California off a Cuban so it's the real shebang. I say we share."

He lights it and passes it around. I've never smoked a cigar before. It burns my throat, but I play it off like I'm used to the burn. Even Kaawishté partakes, coughing out smoke rings.

"Hold on, hold on," Soapy says. "I got a flat folding Kodak I took from a gentleman in Juneau. He asked me to take a photograph of him and his wife and I got on my horse and rode away before they even realized!" He slaps his knee. "Get together, you guys." He motions for me to get close to Frank and Kaawishté. "Let's make sure the gold is in the frame too."

I inch close enough to Frank to smell his sweat, Kaawishté on my other side. Mountain tells us to put our arms around each other so we do it while Soapy sets up.

"Oh, what a fine photograph," Soapy says, deliriously excited. "We'll trade addresses and I'll make sure to send it to you."

This reminds me that I still need to mail Adalaide's letter, having been thwarted earlier.

"Even closer," Soapy bellows. "We're all friends."

I have my arms firmly around Frank and Kaawishté neck when I hear a pistol being cocked. Mountain points his gun right at us. At first, I think he's selling us all down the river, but then Soapy tosses the Kodak aside and raises his own pistol.

"It doesn't even work," he says, kicking the Kodak into the creek bed. "But I'd say it's certainly come in handy."

Soapy and Mountain share in a momentous laugh that carries on for too long.

"Since you've already got your arms out, let's keep it going and raise 'em to the sky."

We do so without hesitation. I can tell Kaawishté silently simmers. He probably never wanted to trust Soapy and his men and only went along with it because of me.

"Were you always aiming to turn on us?" I ask.

Soapy scratches his chin with the butt of the pistol. This man is not careful. And if we are to survive this, that will be his downfall.

"Yes, this was a takedown from the start," Soapy says. "We needed Frank to get us to the spot and you two rubes to do most of the work. And look, three extra piles Charlie and I wouldn't have been able to pan on our own. Now we can tie you up and push you down the river, or leave a bullet in each of your heads. But I don't really like to waste bullets."

Soapy gets in our faces, his breath reeking of old jerky.

"So, what's the verdict?"

"Duck," Kaawishté says, under his breath. He eyes bore into mine, even Frank notices.

"What was that, you goddamn Injun?" Soapy asks.

"DUCK," Kaawishté yells, and in one quick move, he whisks the knife from his belt, swings down low and slices at Soapy's ankles. Frank and I dive for the ground as a bullet zings by our ears. Blood spurts from Soapy's boots. With the pistol in one hand, he tries to suture the bleeding with the other, sniveling like a lost puppy.

"Soapy!" Mountain booms, trying to aim his gun but Kaawishté acts too fast. He leaps upon the giant man, knife swinging. The blade catches Mountain's cheek, opening up a wound like a fish's mouth. The two hit the ground hard, wading in a pool of new blood. Kaawishté large and relentless, slicing at every exposed limb while Mountain attempts to line up another shot.

I scramble to get my knife but adrenaline has taken over and I'm shivering from the intensity of the last minute. The knife is slippery and becomes lost in the creek bed, floating away. Soapy crawls on his elbows over to me, presses the pistol into my nose. I hear a click.

"Go to hell," Soapy says. There's blood dripping from his mouth as he gnashes his teeth, close enough to give me a peck.

I wrap my fingers around his neck, squeezing with all my might to choke the life outta him. The cusses keep flyin' from his lips as his face bloats and turns blue. He lets out a bloody hack in my face. Now with the strength of two men, I grasp his neck with one hand while the other latches onto his gun. I attempt to direct it away from me, but he's tough for an old crook.

"Today's the day you die," Soapy tells me, but I disbelieve this proclamation. My story will go on for a lot longer. This will not be my end.

The sun gets sucked up by the night as everything goes black, the moon a paltry replacement. This phantasm of evil hovers over me, and all I have left is my will to keep going, to return to my beloved, to cheat death.

And then the moon becomes blocked by a figure with a heavy branch. The figure swings the branch and knocks Soapy off me. The gun scatters across the earth. The figure picks up the gun and fires a shot. I close my eyes, expecting the bullet in my guts, but when I open them, I'm facing Soapy's dead expression, a nickel-sized hole in his forehead. The figure steps into the moonlight and I see my savior is Frank. He lends a hand to pull me up.

"You saved me?" I ask as a question because I'm confounded beyond belief.

Frank gurgles the phlegm in his throat and spits out a yellow glob. "That I did."

Two shots ring out and we swivel over to Kaawishté who stands over Mountain after firing the bullets in his chest.

"Let's get to the third one by morning to decide his fate," Kaawishté says.

With the little light we have, we collect the piles of gold, replacing most of what we carried in the pack. We swear to one another to take care of the last of Soapy's men without turning on ourselves. I have to believe Frank, since he already spared my life.

In the night, the only sounds we make are the quiet clops from our horses. None of us has anything to say, as if words have been exorcized from our bodies, too stunned and tired to make sense of it all, except that nothing makes sense in this lawless tundra world.

October 13th, 1898

By morning, we reach the lean-to. The plan being for me to go in first and explain that Soapy's gotten hurt. Then with Tree disarmed, Kaawishté and Frank can come in with guns ready. Sure enough, when I enter, Tree sleeps beside the booty so I wave for them to come in and we stand over him with two guns and one knife poking his neck. It takes a few kicks to rouse him, since he's gone to sleep with a bottle cradled in his arms.

"Aw hell," he snorts, rubbing the crust from his eyes. He gets to a sitting position and we take away the gun in his holster.

"I'm sure you can guess what's happened," I say.

His chin quivers. "Soapy and Charlie are dead."

"'Fraid so. The question remains what we should do with you."

At this, he begins blubbering. "I had no idea what they were planning…"

I'm tired of his bawling so I hit him over the head with the butt of a knife.

"Now listen. Soapy gave us two choices, so I'll give you the same. But while he wouldn't spare our lives, we will."

His eyes light up. He clasps his hands together in prayer.

"You all are too kind."

"It involves tying yourself up," Frank says, and tosses him rope from one of the rucksacks. "Get it good and tight."

"Then what?" Tree asks.

"You will see," Kaawishté says.

Tree starts tying the rope around his feet.

"So the booty is ours to decide what to do with it. We debated on turning you in to the law, but the truth is we don't want to deal with them," I say. "Empty your pockets too."

Tree appears hesitant, but Kaawishté slices at his neck so he complies. A few coins and dust balls fall out along with a folded-up map.

"What's this?" I open the map to the same Yukon territory I've locked into my memory, except this map details farther out west to The Unknown I've heard about where a giant red X has been drawn over a particular spot close to Anvil Creek near St. Michael. "This where Soapy was headed?"

"Yes, sir. We were gonna make a try for it. Although the terrain is rugged and hasn't been traversed by many before. No telling what exists out there."

"I guess that's why they call it The Unknown," I say.

After Tree finishes tying himself up, we get the rucksacks sorted with a fair amount of gold for each of us. We decide since the booty has been stolen, it should be returned to the post office. Frank isn't too gung-ho about this decision, but gives in. Tree still blubbers, asking to take him with us, and I'm sick of him so I stuff a rag in his mouth and tie the end of the rope around that too.

"We should go for The Unknown," I tell Kaawishté, who seems off in another world.

"What about me?" Frank asks. "I'm going too."

"Who's says we're allowing you to join?"

"You don't own The Unknown. I could very well go if I wanted to."

"The deal was to take care of Soapy's last man and then go our separate ways."

"We make a team, the three of us," Frank whines. "Look at what we've accomplished."

"I am not going," Kaawishté says, and I turn to him in disbelief. "This is enough gold for my tribe. I do not want to be greedy."

"But Kaawishté, there could be so much more."

"There is a chance you do not return from this Unknown. I have a family back home."

"A family? You never told me that."

"You never asked."

"But I've spoken about my wife and child. George did too. You never once thought to chime in?"

"There is a lot I keep close to my heart, more so than white men do. We Tlingit are humble and pensive. We do not share much about ourselves to outsiders."

He takes the booty from out of its hiding spot. "I will return this to the post office. It doesn't make sense for you both to travel back to Dawson City."

I get in his ear. "Do you really think I should align with this man to The Unknown."

"Wyatt," he says, in his sobering tone, "you have changed since we first met, but you still are restless. I believe you should go back to your family with the gold you've found, but I know that you will not. You will always wonder what lies in The Unknown and it will eat at your insides."

"I know." I'm tearing up now, a little embarrassed, but I just let it flow. "I can't go back yet."

"Then your decision is made."

I go into my rucksack and pull out the letter to Adalaide.

I wipe the drips from my nose. "Will you mail this at the post office? My wife, I would like her to know I'm all right."

He stuffs the letter in his sack. "I will do this for you."

I give him a strangling hug. I don't know why I'm so overcome with emotion, but this Indian and I have been through a lot. I've never had such a unique friendship before and will be hesitant to bad mouth an Indian in any way. They are a great people, wise and brave, and I will never be the same now that we've met. Kaawishté doesn't hug me back, likely because it's not a part of his customs, but he lets me continue the hug until I'm ready to release.

"Good luck," he tells us as we head outside. Kaawishté gets on a horse and gallops away without saying goodbye. I watch until he's swallowed by the white wash of the horizon. I know I will never see him again.

"So, we partnerin' up?" Frank asks. I turn to the new man I'm supposed to rely on, all fat and greasy with a missing tooth. Hardly a comparison to Kaawishté.

"We better get a move on while we have the light on our side," I say. We tie our rucksacks to our horses, slap their hides, and shoot off. Over my shoulder, I see Tree hopping out of the shack and likely cursing at us through his tied-up mouth. I'm pleased that we didn't decide to kill him, my murdering days hopefully finished for good.

37

THE UNKNOWN

October 13th to October 21st, 1898

The weather decides to be as tortuous as the terrain once we leave the area surrounding Dawson City. Providence is telling us not to continue, and for a moment Frank and I remain hesitant. Neither of us is a good rider and if our horses get ill, we'll be done for since it's hundreds of miles to our location. After a moment of warmth in the lean-to, I'm resigned again to the bitterness of the cold that nips at my fingertips and ears like tiny evil bugs.

Within hours, we cross the Canadian border back into Alaska, the first stops being Fort Cudah and Circle City where we take breaks and gnaw on jerky. We stock up a bit with food since this is the last small city we'll hit, but we know to survive the journey, the land will have to provide. At Porcupine River, we strip down and bathe in the freezing waters to remove some of our stink. Then we start a fire and cook beans and fart into the night trying to outdo each other.

"I'm sorry about before," Frank says, mummified in a blanket. "And I don't apologize a lot."

"You talkin' about on the G.W.?"

"It was a rotten thing for me to do." He twiddles his thumbs. "Can't tell ya the amount of times some other prospector has taken what deserves to be mine. I got scared it would happen again." The flames lick at his face, which is rather cherub-like. He whistles though the gap in his teeth. "Anyhoo, I thought you should know this."

"I much appreciate, Frank."

"Other men would've slit my throat first chance they had. But not you, Wyatt Barlow. You're etched from a different kind of stone. Honorable, I'd say."

I pour a little whiskey into a metal cup, take a hearty sip.

"Frank, whatever ill between us is now forgotten, erased, and done away. The two of us are gonna be the first to find this hidden gold, making everything we went through worthwhile."

"Hear, hear," he says, and I swear I can see a trickle of a tear at the corner of his eye.

We clink whiskey mugs, down our poisons, and sleep the day off, awakening with a freshly sealed bond that should carry us well into The Unknown.

October 22nd, 1898

In the middle of the night, I wake from a dream or possibly I am still deep inside one. The fire cooks and morphs into the shape of a wolf's head, ice-blue eyes shining through. Frank is still under as the fire speaks and tells me to be careful who I trust. I wonder if it's speaking of Frank or someone else we will encounter, but it vanishes before I can inquire. When I wake, it has turned back to a dying flame.

I'm less conversational with Frank this morning as we set off. He's telling me a story about his wife Rosalie. I guess he hadn't been lying about her before on the *G.W. Elder*, although I'd assumed everything that came out of his mouth then had been a falsity. But he tells me of plump Rosalie who's always cooking biscuits and usually has a speck of flour dusting her cheeks. That neither of them has any money, and he's not sure if they'll still have their house when he returns, since the bank's been sniffing around to collect its loans.

"You're quiet today," he says. I'm eager to cross the Romantzoff Mountains along the Yukon River. They stand tall and craggily, threatening except it looks like we can swing around them without having to climb. The altitude still rises and I'm a little light-headed when I see what appears to a bear but I wonder if it's simply a vision. The bear winds from out of a blueberry bush. It's so massive that it only takes a few steps to be right in our faces.

"Don't make a sound," Frank says, bringing out a rifle.

"If you shoot, you better hit it, Frank."

Frank closes one eye as the bear sniffs. Then it opens its mouth, sending a big roar our way. Frank fires, but due to the kickback of the rifle, he's knocked off his horse and the bullet sails away. We all watch it become lost in the clouds, bear included. Then the bear charges. Frank's horse gets spooked and attempts to back up, but the bear roars and swipes at the horse with its claw. Scratch marks bleed from the horse's body, gaping wounds that won't heal in the cold. The horse buckles as Frank's rucksack with his gold flips over the side of a snow bank. We hear it reach the bottom of a cavernous hole many feet down. No way to get to it.

I'm unsure whether to dismount my horse and try to help, or to save my life by kicking its sides so I can flee. I think of the wolf's warning from the fire. This would be an easy way to part with Frank for once and for all, but then, it would only be me and the horse traversing this land, surely not good odds to make it out alive. So I dismount as quietly as possible, slip a pistol from out of my rucksack. The bear charges at Frank, saliva dripping from its mouth on his face. He covers himself with his arms pleading to be saved. I fire right into the bear's behind as it lets out a howl loud enough to cause an avalanche. It spins its head, trying to locate its attacker, enough for Frank to wiggle out from under. When it sees me, we lock souls, each knowing that only one of us will make it out of this fight alive. I fire again, hitting its shoulder, as a burst of blood paints the snow. Frank has a knife out and stabs the bear in the back. He removes the knife and does it again and again until its blood reddens his face. He's still stabbing even after the bear has stopped roaring and is obviously dead. He's yelling and cursing and sadistic in his knife cuts, organs spilling every-where. I want to tell him to stop but I don't dare, lest he turn the knife on me. Finally, the knife gets stuck in the bear's flesh and he can't pull it out to mutilate anymore. Only then does he relent.

He's breathing heavily as he looks my way and there's the devil in his eyes that I pretend not to notice.

"Let's roast and use what we can from the rest of it," Frank says.

So we make a fire and I work to skin the bear like I'd been taught by the Tagish. We use the snow to wash away the sinew from the fur until we have two separate blankets. Then we roast a few cuts, our bellies distending, fuller than I've ever been.

"We'll split the gold that's left," Frank says, almost as an order.

"Since mine went over the snow bank."

"That's fair."

"I'm glad there's no argument."

That's all we say to each other that night. I don't want to speak, only sleep. We set up separate tents and I curl up beneath the bear blanket. A glittering snow falls, the only sound in the night, except for Frank who's muttering to himself in his own tent. Part of me wishes I had gotten on my horse and fled, but this is the choice I've made and now there ain't no going back.

October 23rd to November 8th, 1898

For weeks, Frank and I share a horse as we pass the Yukon Mountains and the Kaltag Mountains. Once we saw a steamboat toot by and we waved and cheered for the sign of other humankind. No prospectors got off, the boat filled with ghosts, no idea who was even steering. I think we are going mad. The food has had to be rationed since we lost half of it, much of the protein, and I'm sick of eating beans. I'm gassy like you wouldn't believe, and each night I feel like worms chew on my insides. Frank is no better. He smells vinegary like a hobo and has taken to having full conversations with himself. Oftentimes it has to do with devils and serpents. I try to shut my ears off and think of Adalaide and Little Joe, but I appear to be losing them. The edges of their faces blur; the sound of their voices fades. I know Adalaide has a melodic Irish lilt, but I can't capture the sing-song pattern just right. And as for Little Joe, I'm remembering more of him as a baby than the little child he is now. I wonder if he's forgotten me already, his brain unequipped for this long an absence.

As we reach November, the cold changes from a nuisance to a penance. Winds batter our weary horse. I don't remember the last time I could feel my fingers. My face burns red, each snowflake like a blade. Where we'd been able to travel for many miles a day before, now we can only hit a few before fatigue sets in and one of us needs to lie down. I'm constantly nauseous and cramping as all hell. The blood isn't flowing properly through my veins anymore. Frank has lost a good chunk of his fat while I've turned gaunt, my cheeks sunken-in so much that there are bite marks on the insides. I wait for the wolf to tell me what to do, but it never appears. And I know we might be dead soon.

At St. Michael, we pick up a few provisions with the little money we have left. The town is practically empty, a few Indian settlers who don't speak a lick of English so we can't inquire about where to head from here. I search my brain to recall some Tlingit or Tagish phrases, but come up empty, even after we're fed a seal stew. On the map, it seems as if the red X appears north of St. Michael because to the south are just bays. We pass through a town made up of a shipping port right on the water of the Norton Sound. The snow reflects and blinds us. We can't even see our hands in front of our faces. We tie up our horse and trudge inside where a very old man sits behind a counter. A candle glows in front of his face.

"Don't track in any snow," he says in an accent I cannot place. "Take those boots off."

We do so, our socks sopping wet with ice chunks. There's a tiny fire emanating from the fireplace and we hold our hands out to warm them.

"We're sorry to bother you," I say, because I can tell our presence has upset him.

"This is a shipping port," he says, in that weird accent. "Nothing more. Ships come in, I take in shipments and put shipments to go out."

"We were looking for Anvil Creek."

The very old man takes his candle and comes over to us. Upon closer inspection, he has no teeth and appears so thin that his skin hangs on his bones.

"Anvil Creek? You after what the Three Lucky Swedes found?"

"Gold?" Frank gulps.

"Came by around summer." He gums his lips. "Don't get many visitors other than ships come in with shipments. Been my job for decades."

"And the Swedes?" I ask.

"Yes, the Swedes. They found gold. Don't know how they knew to come up around here. Not by horse like you two neither."

"We've traveled a long way," I say, but he silences me.

"Anvil Creek is about thirty kilometers north. There's a large creek, probably iced over by now. It feeds into a lake that's probably iced over too. The lake is many kilometers long, so you won't miss it when you see it."

"Thank you, sir. That's really helpful."

"Many will come to this area. The wind told me this. When you are alone for so long you begin to listen to the weather. It told of the Swedes and the two of you."

Frank glances over at me and crosses his eyes. *This man is crazy.*

"But the Swedes have left with their bounty. You two will not."

"What?" I ask, my throat suddenly dry. "How do you do know this?"

The wind beats against the door, begging to get inside. "Like I said, the wind."

We both look at the door that seems as if it's about to burst open.

"And many more will come by next year. The turn of the century will bring droves to this land and what I knew of my home will be no more. But I will be dead by then. The wind told me that too."

All of a sudden, I'm leaping up and have this old man by the collar. I'm shaking him and his head is bobbing from side to side, mouth wide open in a scream. I don't want to be doing this, but I cannot help myself.

"Why do you say we won't make it back with our bounty?" I yell. Frank is trying to pull me off the man, who's wheezing and choking. Frank's telling me this man is bonkers, to let go of him so we can head off. I remove my shaking hands, apologizing over and over to the old man, to Frank, to myself.

"Too much blood has been shed," the old man says, as a declaration. "And you must pay. Each sin has a cost."

"But he tricked me," I cry. "The life I shed was not my fault!"

"The wind does not know of particulars," the old man says, picking up his candle that has fallen to the floor. "Now you must leave."

"C'mon, Wyatt," Frank says. "I have a bad feeling about this place."

The old man has returned behind the counter, the candle creating an orb of light around his face.

"No, I want more answers," I say, and Frank tosses his hands to the ceiling and leaves the room.

I go over to the old man, stare into his rheumy eyes.

"I am a good person," I say, demanding for him to agree.

He shrugs.

"Tell me I am good!" I thunder.

"Time has no meaning. Birth, death, and everything in between. We are simply in debt, paying for every mistake. You may not realize it but you are paying for things that haven't even occurred yet."

I'm a quivering mess, ice running through my blood. "What will I do?" I ask. He doesn't answer. "Tell me. Please."

He sighs. "While your sins may have been accidental before. In the future, they are premeditated, despite what you will tell yourself."

"You mean Frank?" I ask, indicating the door where the wind still whips.

"No, not just Frank."

"Who else?"

"Your very own blood."

I hear a scream bellowing from outside, Frank's girlish squeal. When I turn back around, the old man has gone, only the candle remaining in his place.

"What the...where did you go?"

I peer around the counter, knocking over the candle, as it ignites against the wood. A fire spreading.

"Wyatt!" I hear Frank cry.

The flames consume the wooden walls by my next breath. I speed out and find Frank mourning over our horse that has fallen over, already covered in snow. He looks up and I see the flames from the shipping port in his eyes.

"C'mon, c'mon," he says, grabbing my arm. I shoulder the heavy rucksack and we run from the port. We're a few feet away when it ignites and explodes, a dark cloud touching the sky. We're hugging each other, icy tears in our beards.

"Forget about this," he says, "Anvil Creek. No other distractions. Thirty kilometers. We can do this."

I nod, words zapped from my body. We give the horse water and warm him with our hands until he eventually gets up. We grip onto one another, limping north. I'm trying to exorcize the very old man from my thoughts, but he's bored in, infiltrating like a spy.

November 9th, 1898

We go straight through the night on our horse to Anvil Creek. A blizzard accelerates, punishing in its downfall. The horse's legs are shaking from exertion and I know it won't live for much longer. There's no light save for a tiny beam from the moon, marking our way as if we're the only two beings on Earth.

Frank talks to keep our spirits up, telling of wild times from when he was younger. Booze and girls and prospecting before he found a family. I'm slipping in an out of consciousness, so I lean on his back like it's a pillow and allow a semi-sleep to wash over me. I do not dream, but I am no longer in the realm of the awakened, straddling in between. The giant lake off Anvil Creek spills forth, and beyond it, the mouth of a cave opens wide. The cave hidden to most who would pass, looking like a patch of ice with a hole, but I can smell the gold inside, its perfect aroma. I've been to this cave before in my mind while on the *G.W. Elder*, and when I entered, the gold was so blinding I could barely see. This cave exists and we will spelunk.

When I come to, a thin band of sunlight pierces the horizon with its golden sword. The snowbanks glitter from its reflection, warming exposed skin. We hug a thick band of water that I hope is Anvil Creek. After about a mile or so, the creek parts open to a giant iced-over lake that sparkles. Our horse collapses with a dying wheeze, as if it had been engineered to bring us as far as we needed to go before it passes on. Once we dismount, it sucks in a final breath but never exhales. We divide up the pack and I use a tied blanket to shoulder my half—the gold nuggets clinking with a pickax, a knife, and some dried beans.

We skate out onto the lake that spans for miles in its circumference. I spin around to try to locate a sign of the cave but only a forest surround us. Frank stamps down on the ice with his boot.

"Gotta be fish under here," he says. "I'm starving."

He takes out his pickax and hacks until he's created a serrated hole. He dips a few fingers in.

"Cold as a witch's tit."

He uses a fishing rod with some dried beans as bait.

"We're pretty much in the center," he says. "We should take a minute to fuel up and try to figure out which direction to head."

I'm lost for words and out of ideas, so I simply nod.

After some time, Frank gets a tug on his rod. He pulls up a tiny minnow, catching it flapping in his fist. He chews on it whole.

"Don't worry I'll catch one for you too."

He's a man of his word and soon enough I'm chewing on a raw minnow too. I hadn't realized how hungry I've been, the tiny fish making my brainwaves pulse. Frank's yammering on about some story I don't care to listen to. I'm chewing the last bits of flesh from the fish and trying to locate the cave in my shuteye. As I spin around, all I see is darkness, but to the left I spy a glowing.

"That way," I say, still with my eye closed, hitching the tied blanket over my shoulder. I walk and hear Frank scurrying behind, asking a thousand and one questions.

The glowing gets brighter the more I pursue and my feet step off the frozen lake onto squishy land. I keep my eyes shut as I move aside branches. I'm running now, taking flight, creating a snowstorm in my wake. In the darkness, a pair of ice-blue eyes emerge, the wolf returning.

Beware, it tells me as it lets out a powerful howl.

I run straight into something blocking my path. I'm thrown back as my eyes flutter open. Before me, a gaping dark mouth of a cave. I jump to my feet, about to rush in as the wolf returns, this time in the flesh. It licks its salivating teeth.

Do not let the other traveler know of what you found, it tells me. I spin around but can't see Frank. I brush past the wolf, about to leave my tied-up blanket by the mouth of the cave, but then open it to remove my knife and stick it in my belt loop.

The inside darker than when my eyes were closed, but when I walk farther, a faint glimmer surfaces. I feel my way as a beaming glow intensifies and before me stands a wall of pure gold. I touch it to see if it's real, that I haven't become trapped in a hallucination, but the gold is tangible because I break some off. It shimmers in my palm, this elusive treasure that will give my life meaning. I kiss it as if I'm blessing it over an altar, as if I've finally found God.

"Hands to the sky," I hear echo through the cave. When I turn around, Frank steps out of the darkness, his face lit by a dangerous light that reveals a pistol in hand. He must've taken it from Soapy. His eyes shift from me to the wall of gold, pupils dancing. The wolf's howl enters our chamber.

"There's more than either of us could ever ask for," I say, face flush with tears.

He spits at his feet. "Don't matter."

"But you couldn't even possibly take it all with you."

"You fool, I'll come back again and again until I chip away."

"Leave me a few bars," I plead. "I'll never return. I don't want to leave my family anymore."

"Hogwash, you'll race back here the first chance you can."

"You have my word."

He steps closer. "Words mean tiddlywinks." He cocks the pistol and presses it right against my heart. "I'd say it's been nice knowin' ya, Wyatt.

But it really hasn't. You're like a gnat I swat at that never goes away."

The wolf's voice whispers, *Now!*

I swipe the knife from my belt loop and plunge it into Frank's belly. He drops the gun so he can use both hands to wrench it from his insides. With an agonizing moan, he thrusts it out but loses his footing, his fat body falling right on top of mine and we fly back into the wall of gold. I go to get out from under him, but the sleeve of my mackinaw coat becomes caught in a groove between two gold chunks. I twist around trying to loosen him off, but he's too heavy and I'm too weak.

"Frank!" I yell, but his eyes have ascended to the top of his skull. I'm drenched in blood and he's already dead. "Frank," I whimper, trying once again to wriggle free but knowing it's useless.

A day passes like this. I know because of the way the faraway sun descends and then trickles in as it rises again. My stomach grumbles in agony, I've soiled myself multiple times, and Frank's body has begun to stink from the excess of spilled blood. I don't want to, but I begin to gnaw on his ear, lamenting my situation, knowing it's all I can do to survive. Eventually the ear rips off and I chew it disgusted with myself and how my saga will end. Each day, I nibble what I can of Frank, but dehydration soon sets in, my tongue turning into a metal plate, dreaming only of drinking water. By day four, I know I am done for, too emaciated to even open my eyes so I live in darkness. I ruminate on what I've done to deserve this fate, cursing the old man in the shipping port who proved to be correct with his proclamation. Had that been the devil? Had he recognized a kindred soul from the sins I committed? My final vision— the wolf's eyes, brilliant and bluer than the most ideal sky, telling me that this will not be the end, that time is vastly different than I believed it to be and I am not like everyone else. I will not succumb to time's cruel measure. My heart will maintain its beautiful beat.

Days keep going by. I am dead by all accounts, but the tiniest pulse of my heart perseveres. I know not why or how, only that the wolf is correct. Years pass as a rainstorm eventually flushes me out of my entrapment, sending me down on a luge, spinning out on the lake and tossing me over a snowbank, where the blizzard of all blizzards sweeps across the land, forming me into a block of ice and suspending me for the next century. People are born, grow up, and give birth to children, then die as their children have other children, who then die too, much like my own blood will. The world continues spinning into the future while I stay preserved.

Do I have any memories of this miracle? If I do, they are not accessible. My last thought being that it had to have been the devil I encountered in the shipping port, causing this long punishment cast on my soul. Had it been a benevolent God, he would've let Frank shoot me in the heart rather than allow it to linger with a miniscule thump.

38

Jolted from his heroin slumber, Wyatt comes to in Aylen's bath, which has a browning ring around the tub. She's lit a few perfume candles and sits on the ledge dabbing his forehead and cheeks with a cold compress. His eyes unglue and he wipes the tearing salt away, leaning over and retching between his legs.

"Good, get it all out," Aylen says, rubbing his back.

After he retches once more, she turns on the shower, the water scalding. She apologizes and cools the temperature as they watch his sickness spiral down the drain. He steps out and she wraps him with a fresh towel, then leaves the bathroom.

He erases the steam from the mirror in the medicine cabinet. Gets a good look at himself. For the first time, he sees a reflection that truly resembles all of him. His past finally rounded, many of the nagging questions eliminated. He is tenacious. He'd known that already, but never how much.

When he enters the kitchen, Aylen's smoking a cigarette in the dawn light that seeps rusty into the trailer. She's propped one leg up on her chair.

"You find your gold?" she asks, as two Pop Tarts ping in the toaster and she finds two plates in the sink. She passes the hot sugary treat over.

"Gold and then some," he says, between munches.

She leaves the cigarette between her lips and hands him his notepad. Flipping through, he notices he's scribbled in his entire journey in a herky-jerky script.

"I took it away from you when I moved you to the tub, since you were boiling. Never seen anything quite like it. Like you couldn't get the words down fast enough."

With the string attached to the notepad, he puts it around his neck.

"Thank you for this."

"Don't have to thank me, Wyatt."

"I'm gonna get this gold and give you some."

Her expression doesn't change, but the cigarette burns down and she stabs it against the bottom of a rocky table.

"I'll be on the edge of my seat."

"Don't know what that means."

"What a surprise." She removes her tank top, and he covers his face to avoid seeing her nude out of respect. "I have to go to work."

She slams her thin bedroom door. He goes to put his plate away and spies a pair of military dog tags on the counter. *Oxendine, Tohopka. 165-98-7777. B Pos. No preference.* He puts back on his clothes from yesterday left in a pile on a chair, stuffing the dog tags in a pocket. Never hurts to have something over someone else, should he need it.

A car horn bleats outside. It sounds again, lasting longer this time. When he peers through the broken blinds, Trav's pickup idles right by the trailer.

He finds Aylen sitting on her bed and putting on stockings.

"That's my ride," he says, but she chews her lips in response. "Did I do something to make you mad?"

He joins her on the bed, attempting to kiss her cheek.

"How about the next time you see me, it isn't because you need something," she says, adjusting herself so his lips catch her hair.

"*GunalchEesh, Ax eet ilatUowu,*" he says. "Thank you for helping to teach me."

She whips her face toward him, mouth agape. "How did you know that?"

"It's a Tlingit phrase. I spent time with your people and the Tagish on my journey. They taught me many things. They turned me into a wolf. Saved my life more than once. I'm sorry if I ever made you feel lesser because of who you are."

"I..." She pulls out the rubber band holding her hair in a ponytail. "I don't know what to say."

"I'm going into the wilderness as soon as I can, but when I return, you're the first person I want to see."

He kisses her. This time she doesn't turn away.

"Wyatt!"

But he's already out the door, jumping into his boots, his heart thumping soundly with the notion of telling Trav the good news.

* * *

"So you know where the gold is?" Trav asks, one hand loosely on the wheel. No other cars passing this early in the morning.

Wyatt presses down his wild bush of hair. "There's a giant lake in the wilderness attached to Anvil Creek—"

"Yeah, I know it. Stu used to take us ice fishing there. Like nothing around for miles."

"There's a cave off of the lake where the gold is." Wyatt's about to tell him that's where he became trapped in ice, but he remembers he hasn't been completely honest with Trav yet. "I saw it clear as day."

"On heroin?"

"I needed access to the memory. I'm done with that stuff."

"Really?"

"Swear. So you'll come with? Cause I'm aiming to leave as soon as possible."

"I got work today."

"Call in sick."

"Papa's in the hospital—"

"We leave now, we can be back by tomorrow."

The proposal sits between them until Trav sports a goofy grin, and Wyatt knows he's in.

"Ah hell, gotta tell Callie first before she leaves to take Eli to Miss Evelyn's."

Wyatt rubs his hands together in delight. "Fizzing!"

Callie proves tougher to convince. Eli's throwing a tantrum and it's not the right moment to ask. Wyatt stands by the front door. He's out of sorts, since he's interrupted a private family time. He doesn't like feeling this way.

"You want to go into the wilderness to search for gold?" Callie asks. She's trying to put on Eli's coat. "C'mon, Eli, work with me."

"Coats are for boogers," he screams, tearing his arm out of the sleeve and running into the kitchen. She's left holding the coat as if it belonged to a ghost.

"That child is on my last damn nerve this morning."

"Gimme it," Trav says, in his most calming tone possible. "Wyatt, you sell her. I'll take care of Eli. Honey, just think of it like an overnight camping adventure."

"What about work?" she yells at him, but he's already around the corner. She gives Wyatt a pleading look. "Is this really necessary now? With his grandfather in the hospital?"

"Trav is under duress."

"Duress?" She blows the bangs from her eyes. "Yeah, that's true I guess."

"I'll take good care of him, Mrs. Barlow."

"You're so weird," she says, and then bites her tongue. "I'm sorry. Mornings are crazy 'round here."

"I can recall." He clenches his fists. "I mean, it's been some time, but I remember how it is."

She leaves her hand on his arm. "Okay, Wyatt. You two go and have your boys' adventure."

"Trav sure is a lucky man to have such an understanding woman as you."

"Yes, me good woman, good wife," she grunts.

Wyatt tilts his head, confused.

"Coat's all set," Trav calls out, holding up a giggling but bundled Eli upside-down from his ankles. He spins him right side up and pats his butt as he shoots out the door to their car.

"Okay, you can go, babe." Callie kisses Trav and chases after Eli. "Eli, stay right by the house. Don't dart out into the road." And turning back to Trav, "You better bring me back some of that fine gold so we can live like kings and queens. I'm getting tired of this aluminum siding décor."

Trav pats a drumbeat on Wyatt's shoulders. "Let's grab our gear and get to it!"

Wyatt watches Callie's car pull away, in awe of her tough nature, her unpredictability, and how every time he interacts with her, he falls in love a little bit harder. He squelches a dark thought that lies dormant at the base of his mind. One he's afraid will fester and spread.

39

Wyatt hears Trav calling Smitty to tell him he's under the weather before they reach Anvil Creek, knowing his cell would have no reception that high up. It's the first day he's missed since starting the job so Smitty doesn't question. They take some barebones camping gear in case they'll need to spend the night. Trav turns on some country tunes, affecting his twang as he croons to the radio. Wyatt bobs his head, in awe of the music coming from the vehicle and sounding as if it's being played live just for him. The modern world never ceasing to amaze.

Trav tells him he can't remember the last time he's been so excited. Had to set aside the fish shack but the chance of gold could allow it to revive. It's not as if he isn't happy on the *Cutthroat*, simply that he wants to be working toward a goal, something to really make Callie proud.

Part of Wyatt feels overjoyed too, deserving the gold after it eluded him for over a century. But he can't deny becoming affected by what he learned from his past. Its vivid highs and lows. If Kaawishté was able to mail his letter to Adalaide, the last thing she heard from him would've been that he found gold and everything was peachy. Then when he never returned home, she might've assumed staying in Alaska with the gold became more fascinating than returning home to be with her and Little Joe.

"Why so down?" Trav asks, lowering the song.

"Thinking about my wife now that the gold is close."

"Maybe finding it'll wind up bringing you two back together?"

"'Fraid that's an impossibility. Callie, she reminds me of her in some ways. Your son is like mine as well. But more so the idea of a tight family."

"Hey, buddy, hang in there. You got a long life ahead of you. Plenty of time for a new family if that's in the cards."

When they reach Anvil Creek, Wyatt experiences a dual sense of déjà vu from being there a century ago and returning only yesterday in his mind. Since summer's closing in, the creek isn't full of ice chunks but runs crisp and smoothly into the giant lake that's still iced over.

"We're at such a high altitude that lake always stays frozen," Trav says. "This is as far as we can go by car."

They exit the vehicle, each with a pack on their backs. Trav taps his foot against the lake.

"Just making sure it's solid and we won't fall through."

They trek out to the middle where they take a break and set their packs down. Wyatt smells the air, as if it could tell him which direction to head. A forest still hugs the lake's edge, all of it looking the same.

"Do you remember where?"

Wyatt shakes his head. "When I was here last, I got more of an intuition that led me there."

"Why don't we fish and catch some dinner? Maybe your memory will spark?"

Trav removes an ice saw from his pack to cut a circular hole. Then he hands Wyatt a light fishing rod with a small brightly colored jig and wax worms as bait.

"A lot of it's the waiting game," Trav says, using his pack as a seat and motioning for Wyatt to do the same. "Often, when I'd go with Stu it wasn't about catching fish, more like experiencing the wilderness. To quiet our minds. Maybe it could still yours?"

"My mind races like you wouldn't believe, Trav." He picks at his cold nose. "Your father really doesn't like me."

"He's fucked up. Bobby did that to him. And in an odd way, you probably remind him of my brother. He had a beard like yours and a similar wild look in his eyes."

"You think your father will ever find out who killed him?"

Trav gets a small tug on his line, but it turns out to be an ice chunk. "I certainly hope so. I fear it eats away at him. You have to remember, he's the sheriff. He's supposed to shut open cases."

"What do you think happened, if you don't mind me asking?"

"Naw, it's cool. It's like good to talk about it, 'bout Bobby. I've bottled him up for too long. I think Bobby got mixed up with the wrong people and got in over his head, but he was ingesting a lot of substances and stupidly went swimming high in the dark and drowned. Every night I went to bed thinking I'd be awakened with news he died. My folks weren't living in reality, they thought he could be cured. But not when you're that addicted. It's why I was so concerned about you doing heroin, Wyatt."

"I told you I'm done with that junk."

"Many have said that before and relapsed. It's a tough drug to kick. Bobby was on it. Had marks all up and down his arms, even between his toes."

"It was the only option I had to go back so far in my mind." He gnaws on his lip, bristles of beard caught in his tongue. "I haven't been completely honest with you."

"Oh?"

"I've been to this area before, but you don't understand *when* I was last here. I'm afraid you'll think I'm crazy."

"Wyatt, if I haven't already thought that nothin's gonna change. We're out here hunting gold, for Chrissakes."

"Okay…" Wyatt's nervous but wants to be forthright with Trav, the best and only friend he's made since George and Kaawishté. "I was frozen right in the cave that I found gold."

Trav's smile drops. "I'm confused."

"You know like how you preserve meat? That caribou you caught, put it on ice, right? Well, same thing happened to me. 'Cept it lasted a century."

Trav cackles, nearly losing his grip of the fishing rod. "And here I thought you were about to be serious."

"Oh, I am. In 1898, I came to Alaska searching for gold. I traveled on the *G.W. Elder* from Washington State, to Sitka and Juneau, stayed in Tlingit and Tagish settlements, saw Dawson City at its peak, fought a bear around the Yukon Mountains, and then a wolf led me to my treasure where my traveling partner tried to gun me down, and I became trapped in a pile of gold only to resurface in present time."

"You're fucking with me. Now I thought you were serious…"

"Trav, I am gosh-darn serious as I'll ever be," Wyatt yells, his voice trapped in the echoing silence of the lake, lingering. "I'm not cut from the same cloth as you, or your wife, or your family. It's because a century separates us."

Wyatt's about to go further and tell Trav he's his great-great grandfather, but that would be too much information too soon. Dole it out in pieces.

"You think I should be in an asylum?"

"You're really not fucking with me?"

"Don't really understand the use of that term. Half the time, don't understand what most of you are saying. And lots of things are strange. I see people around town glued to things they call cells? It's like an extension of their arm. And the women are so different. The men too, but the woman more. Back in my time, they'd be completely covered up. I didn't see Adalaide in the flesh until our wedding night."

Trav gets a tug. "Shit, got a fish." He reels in a baby Arctic char, takes it off the line and puts it out of its mercy by crushing it against the ice. "Wyatt, I don't know what to fuckin' say."

"I wanted to be honest with you."

"But it's impossible, get it? We preserve meat from spoiling, but once you freeze something that's alive, it's kaput."

"Not me," Wyatt says, thumping his chest. A lull sweeps between them. "You're looking at me differently."

"I think you believe this. Really, I do. I get you're not messing with me. But as for the truth? Sometimes we want to believe things that can't be. Because it may be easier than dealing with what actually is."

Wyatt sniffs a frozen ball of snot up his nose. "Meaning?"

"You've spoken about being separated from your wife and son. Maybe you've created—now don't jump down my throat—you'd made up this fantasy to avoid the hard truth?"

Wyatt's pupils go wide. "Wyatt? Wyatt, man, you with me?"

"Wolf."

"What?"

"Wolf," Wyatt growls, indicating across the lake to a wolf that watches them from a point at the far edge.

"It's too far away to pose a threat," Trav says.

The wolf's ice-blue eyes glimmer from the reflection of the high sun.

"It's calling us. The gold is this way!"

Wyatt jumps up, gliding across the iced lake toward the wolf.

"Wyatt! What the fuck, Wyatt?"

Past the lake, the wolf gets spooked, darting past a fence of a trees. Wyatt blocks his face as he breaks through as well, Trav close behind. Once Wyatt's through, the wolf paces in front of a cave. Wyatt has his palms out, attempting to calm the wolf, who licks his chops.

"Careful, man," Trav whispers.

"He is not our enemy. He is no different than me."

The wolf nudges the cave with his nose, signaling for them to enter.

"Come," Wyatt says, walking past the still wolf as it makes no attempt to attack.

"Jesus H.," Trav murmurs, tiptoeing past the wolf too.

The darkened cave appears much like in Wyatt's vision. Unable to see your hand in front of you the further you descend. But then a tiny orange glow, nothing more than a few dots puncturing the blackness, until the glows spreads, blinding like a brushfire. And before them, a wall of gold, not as massive as Wyatt previously encountered, possibly due to erosion and earthquakes and avalanches that may have moved large chunks of gold to another area.

Wyatt dislodges a shimmering brick, heavy in his hand, passing it over to Trav who stands there slack-jawed.

"Believe me now?" Wyatt asks.

A grin emerges from Wyatt's thick beard that had trapped it for so long.

40

Wyatt stays watch over the gold while Trav goes back across the lake to get the car. No way to carry that many bricks for such a long distance. The plan is for Trav to drive around the edge of the lake until he comes across a marking Wyatt has left on the pathway leading to the cave. They sawed down a small tree shaped like a fork and stabbed it into the earth, which will be tough to miss.

While Wyatt waits, his mind travels to sinful thoughts. The last time he was in this cave, Frank betrayed him. Not that Frank ever proved trustworthy, but can anyone really ever been trusted? Sure, George and Kaawishté hadn't turned on him, but maybe that's because they never had the chance. Should he have traveled with them longer, they could've backstabbed. But then the good side of his conscience directs him back. How much gold could he possibly need? And none of these other men was kin like Trav, who's been nothing but kind and welcoming into his brood. He wasn't even judgmental when Wyatt recounted his frozen tale. Still, they're far enough out in the wilderness that neither man would ever be found should the other get greedy. A terrible thought, but one nonetheless.

This is who you are, Wyatt tells his reflection in a golden brick. *You have been through too much adversity to not solely rely on yourself. You are the only one you know who is sure to have your back.*

He drops the gold brick, shocked at the lengths his mind runs. This is what gold does, changes a person. The promise of riches overriding all else. Likely Trav ruminates over the same moral dilemma too. He desires a fish shack, and building a business never comes cheap.

But they've discovered so much! Piles of gold, less than he originally found, but enough to at least begin to live again. He could get out of the abandoned goods store and find a real home. Help Aylen out so she wouldn't have to stay with her troublemaking cousin. What more does he need?

An image of Adalaide fades into Callie. Similarly, Little Joe morphs into Eli. What would it be like to come home to them? Could they be enough to satisfy his restlessness? Eventually replace his beloveds? Time would do that for him, just like it kept him alive. He'd done the hard work of returning to himself. Doesn't he deserve to be fully complete and loved?

Right? he asks the wind, not blowing hard but stiller than ever. Barely a sound. So he ceases asking. He bottles it up and pushes it deep down, only existing as a bubbling in his belly.

Travis skates across the frozen lake having grown up on ice as an Alaskan native and adept at good balance. He scoops up their packs and swooshes over to the pickup, tossing them in the back, and hugging the edge of the lake looking for the tree shaped like a fork. He can't believe the fish shack a possibility now, since there should be at least enough gold after splitting it in half for a down payment. He could even kick some Stu's way to help with any gambling debts and Papa's health care should he make it out of the hospital. Wyatt had been right, as insane as it might've sounded. But another nagging thought arises. If Wyatt was right about the gold, does that mean he'd really been frozen for the past century too?

"No fuckin' way," he tells the rearview, as he shoots past the tree shaped like a fork and has to back up. He drives through a wall of branches and parks right outside the cave. Wyatt sits beside the wolf, petting its coat as if the animal was his pet.

"Jeez, Wyatt," he says, getting out of the pickup.

The wolf observes with his ice-blue eyes.

"Be careful, man."

At the sound of his voice, the wolf takes off, skittering across the snowbanks until it's a furry blur.

"He was friendly," Wyatt says, disappearing into the cave.

They spend the next hour and change chipping away at the bricks of gold and hauling them into the pickup. When they're done, they've created a few nice piles. They do one last look for anything left in the cave, but it seems like they've tapped it dry. It's night when they finish.

"I say we head home rather than stay over," Travis says, turning on the brights that pass over the wolf. "Ah, there's your buddy."

The pickup heads down the pathway, turns at the tree shaped like a fork, and travels along the lake until it reaches Anvil Creek.

"Dude, I can't believe we found mothertruckin' gold! There must be thousands and thousands dollars' worth there."

Wyatt stays quiet, watching the sweep of the dark trees as they travel out of the wilderness.

"Wyatt, man, you cool?"

"There's a sadness in finding what you spent your entire life searching for. What do I chase now?"

Travis is all wide smiles. "You bask in it, bro. Treat yourself."

"I feel old."

Travis finds himself about to joke that Wyatt has lived over a hundred years, but keeps it to himself. He shakes Wyatt by the shoulder instead.

"Glass half full," Travis says. "Always. Every day we're older than we were the day before, but not every day we strike it rich!"

As they drive onto a main road, Travis's cell starts buzzing.

"Your machine is making a lot of noise."

"Probably Callie checkin' in, even though she knows I might've not had reception."

With one hand on the wheel, he digs into his pocket and takes out his cell.

"Ah shit, I got like a dozen messages. Callie, Pop, even Grayson. That's never good."

He dials his voicemail and puts it on speaker. Callie's voice comes up first.

"Babe, call me back as soon as you can. Papa just passed. We're all at the hospital. I'm so sorry. They say he went peacefully. Okay, call me. I love you."

Stu's voice comes up next but Travis mutes it. When he looks over at Wyatt, the man's eyes are red with tears.

"Hey, Wyatt, don't cry. Papa was ninety-three. It's sad but it's a life well lived. Really. He would say that too."

Wyatt allows the depression to wash over. Most never knowing what it's like to live long enough to suffer your grandson's death.

"You don't know what he was to me, Trav. You couldn't understand."

41

"I'll take you back to the abandoned store before I head to the hospital," Trav says to Wyatt, once they hit the outskirts of Laner.

"I'd like to go to the hospital too," Wyatt quietly says.

"Shit, Wyatt, after what happened with Stu the last time, probably only family around is best."

Wyatt wants to shout that he *is* family, but chews on a hangnail instead.

"I would like to say goodbye to the body," Wyatt says.

"There'll be a funeral and an after service. Plenty of time for that."

"But I could help with your grieving—"

"Wyatt," Trav snaps, the first instance he's lost his cool with him. "Dude, my grandpa died. Gimme a minute, will ya?"

Wyatt goes to speak, retools his thoughts. "I know what it's like to lose someone close."

"I know, man. You've told me before. Can we be quiet for the rest of the drive?"

"I've upset you."

"No. I just don't wanna talk."

"I apologize."

Trav doesn't respond. When he sees Wyatt about to speak up again, he turns on the radio. The same country station with a different crooner. He turns up the volume until it dwarfs all other sounds.

When they arrive at the abandoned goods store, Trav gets out to help Wyatt haul the booty inside.

"You don't have to," Wyatt says.

"I'm sorry I snapped at you."

"You hurt my feelings."

"I know. I can do that sometimes. This was wonderful today. Really. We found fuckin' gold. Let me deal with my family stuff and we can celebrate when the time is right."

Trav grips a few bricks under each arm. He peels off the tape from the garbage bag covering the window and slips the gold through the hole. Wyatt comes in dragging the rest.

"My condolences to you and your father," Wyatt says, and begins putting away the bricks behind an island in the middle of the store.

"I'll let you know the funeral details."

"Please do."

Trav extends his hand. Wyatt takes a moment to shake but does. Yet something has changed in the air between them. The easiness they experienced with each other is gone. Wyatt's aware of this. He sees exactly who he is to Trav, an acquaintance but not a true friend. It will make whatever he decides to do down the road that much easier. His options multiplying.

"Make sure you hide that gold well," Travis says, halfway out of the hole in the window. He keeps walking without waiting for a response from Wyatt, finding that spending an elongated time with the man and his idiosyncrasies can be hard. Wyatt's someone who's not only daunting to read but also difficult to gauge what will set him off. It might not be the worst idea to create some space between them. But then he feels bad for even thinking this. Here Wyatt helped him land a literal goldmine and he doesn't have it in him to be at all thankful. He can admit to being an uncaring son of a bitch at times, not always taking others' feelings into consideration. Something he wants to work on, especially toward Callie. He ruminates on this as he pulls up to the hospital in the dead of night, the only other cars in the parking lot being Callie's, Cora and Stu's, and Grayson's deputy wagon.

Grayson's in the waiting area when Travis arrives.

"Ah hell, man," Grayson says, giving him a strangling hug.

Travis's eyes begin to water, having tried to keep them dry since he heard.

"That man was the toughest SOB I knew," Grayson says, and Travis can smell the beer on his breath and spies the two remaining bottles in a six-pack squirreled away under the seat. "You okay, buddy?"

"I'm all right. How's Stu?"

"Hasn't really said much. Which I think means he ain't doing so well."

"You can go, Gray. Thanks so much for tending to my folks when I wasn't here."

Grayson picks up his bottles to leave. "Where were you by the way?"

"Out in the wilderness with Wyatt. Went camping."

"Dude, I don't understand. That guy is freaking weird."

"He's a friend."

"I don't know about that. I'm your friend. Me. Since grade school. *He's* a stranger."

"Can I go see my grandpa now? Huh, Gray? Is that okay?"

"Just watch yourself is all." He clinks his two bottles together and backs out the electric doors. "That's all."

In Papa's room, a white sheet has been draped over the body. Stu sits close while Cora and Callie have their arms around one another.

"Hey," Travis says, as all eyes glance up. Callie first with a hug. She smells like apples and he loses himself in her flowing hair. Next comes Cora who can't stop touching her only son, fussing with his appearance.

"Go to your father," she whispers, scooting him toward Stu.

"Pop?"

Travis has his arms out. Stu stays crumpled in his chair, his eyes displaying his grief. This was a man Travis never once saw cry before Bobby's death, now he's enveloped in a permanent sadness, ready to weep at any moment. He hugs his father, not letting go even when Stu squirms to break free.

"I love you, Pop."

Finally, Stu embraces back, placing his chin on Travis's shoulder.

They mourn in silence until a doctor comes inside. He explains to Travis that the family has taken care of all the funeral arrangements. They can go whenever they're ready or stay with the body as long as they like.

"It was peaceful, right?" Travis asks.

"Very," the doctor says. "In fact, all accounts indicated he had died yet his heart continued beating ever so softly for a while until finally it just stopped. He was a very strong man, your grandfather. Only the superhuman of our race make it into their nineties. It is an accomplishment."

"Thank you, doctor."

Cora convinces Stu it's time to go and Travis leaves with Callie after many more hugs. Everyone seems ready for bed. On their drive home,

Callie holds his hand while he steers with the other.

"Eli's at Miss Evelyn's. I'll pick him up in the morning."

"Yeah, please tell her thanks."

"So how was your camping adventure?" she asks, managing to give him a smile she surely thinks he needs. "Or if you don't wanna talk..."

"There's something I need to show you when we get home."

And when they pull into garage, Travis makes sure the door gets fully closed. Then he removes a heavy tarp revealing the piles of gold.

Callie gasps. "Is that...is that real?"

"It's the purest thing you'll ever see, baby."

She leaps, knocking him to the ground. He bangs his head, but they're laughing until they feel bad to be happy during such a sad time, but they can't help it. They go to bed, giggling under the covers, exploring parts of each other's bodies that they haven't in a long while, not even noticing when morning sneaks up on them before they even have a chance to sleep.

42

The funeral's a small affair, immediate family only. Callie has Miss Evelyn watching Eli at the house where they'll receive visitors afterwards. Father Clayton gives a nice speech about Papa being connected to so many moments in history. How even though Papa wasn't a regular at church, Father Clayton was always glad to hear his jokes when they met in town. How everyone loved Francis and how she emanated pure goodness. How wonderful it was to see them sitting on the bench off Main Street sharing a thermos of soup. And how they enjoyed the water and used to take their boat out to go cruising, the one they called Honeybell, Papa's nickname for Francis.

Stu speaks briefly, never a man for long speeches. He tells a memory about when he was a small boy Papa took him fishing for the first time, and how he was bored at first but Papa explained to enjoy the silence because silence is difficult to find. How Papa got him to truly love the quiet, appreciate their isolated existence in Alaska.

Travis has a sense of vertigo when the coffin is lowered, an urge to dive inside the grave. Like once when he was on a roof and for a moment he thought what it would be like to jump, not because he wanted to die, but because it allowed him the sense of being in control. Father Clayton says his final words and they drive back home.

When they arrive, Miss Evelyn bustles around, busy plating the food with Elson and Lorinda, who cater the event. Plenty of pizzas with various toppings along with Mondo Burgers that Papa always liked to takeout when he was still eating full solid meals. Eli squirms in his little suit until Travis remarks that it's unnecessary for anyone to dress up. With a "weeeeeee," Eli flings off the suit until he's running around in his underwear.

"Gotta put on a shirt and pants, buddy," he tells Eli, who defends being nude but eventually gives in. "Good boy," Travis says, hugging the child and holding onto him for longer than normal, not ready to let go.

"Are you okay?" Callie says, rubbing his back while Eli's given enough room to break free and flees into his bedroom.

"Yup, hate funerals, though. Give me the willies. Death and all."

"You have a long life left, Travis. You ain't cutting out on me soon."

Arm-in-arm, they walk to the table eyeing the food. Travis swipes a salmon pizza.

"There's plenty of pies in the fridge," Lorinda says.

"Thanks so much, Lorinda."

"Ain't nothing. Just when Gray arrives, I'm gonna pop out. Think that's best for everyone."

"Probably."

The town soon shows up. Smitty with his wife. Cora's book club ready with kind words and casseroles. Old Charlie with a flask. Tuck along with Jesse, who stands awkward and gangly in the corner. A couple of other fishermen talking business after they finish paying respects. A few men from the retirement community who are all ten to twenty years younger than Papa but knew him from playing canasta. Grayson's wagon pulls up and Lorinda spies it parking so she makes a beeline for the back door.

"I'll talk to you later, girl," she tells Callie, with a kiss on her cheek.

Grayson lumbers in, embracing Cora who appears the most devastated out of anyone. Stu receives a handshake since that's all he offers.

"How ya holding up, sir?" Grayson asks, which is the last question Stu wants. An introvert at heart, the notion of everyone focusing on him, monitoring his emotions, proves too much. He longs to escape down into the basement.

"Part of the cycle, right?" Stu says, the same phrase he tells anyone. "We live, we die, nothing more can be done. Papa had a full life, most of it healthy as a fiddle. We should all be so lucky." He's growing tired of this rehearsed speech, but at least he can do it on autopilot.

"Beers in the fridge?" Grayson asks.

Travis runs into Grayson in the kitchen. "Ah, how's it going, Travis?"

They hug and Travis mumbles he's fine. Grayson swipes a beer and one for Travis as well. They cheers to Papa.

"He gave zero fucks, didn't he?" Grayson says, and Travis confirms. "Did whatever the hell he wanted to do at all times. I admire that."

"Me too."

"So what you've been up to? Haven't seen you in some time."

"I'm around, Gray. You know, been on Smitty's boat—"

"And hanging out with that hobo."

Travis shakes his head. "I don't understand your beef with Wyatt."

"Something about him I don't trust. I'm trained to spot liars, criminals. He don't add up to me."

"He's a good guy. We went camping."

"I know, bro." Grayson drains the bottle and grabs a second, or likely he's had one or two before he drove over. "But that's *our* thing. Hunting and shit. I feel like I'm being replaced."

"Gray, buddy, ain't no one can take your place."

"It's just…Okay, you know with me and Lorinda on the fritz, I need some cheering up."

"You do? It's my Papa who died."

"Dude, I know. I'm not trying to be a jerk-off. But I feel like you don't have time for me anymore. And I miss you, man."

Travis sighs. "It's been a weird time for me, Gray. Being out of work, going back but not doing what I want." He leans in close. "I'm opening my fish shack."

"Oh yeah? Since when?"

"I've come into some money."

"From Papa?"

"I've put this dream aside for too long."

"Shit, man, that's awesome. I'm happy for ya."

"But it's gonna monopolize my time even more. I know I'll get flak from Callie, can't have it from you, too."

"No worries here. But if I see you with that hobo…" Grayson parts the floral curtains that reveals a view of the backyard. "Speak of the devil. You invited him?"

"Course I did, he's met Papa."

Wyatt raps on the screen door while already stepping inside. He's combed his hair, beard too, a slightly more presentable version of himself.

"My deepest condolences," he says, embracing Travis. Grayson hangs back, looking like he wants to punch Wyatt.

"Thanks for coming."

Wyatt presents Travis with a bottle of whiskey. "Only thing I could think of to bring."

"It's kind of you, Wyatt."

"Deputy," Wyatt says, extending his hand. Grayson gives a half shake. "I apologize for any words we had before."

"I'm gonna check on Stu," Grayson says, spinning out of the room.

"He's tough with new people," Travis says.

"He's a horse's ass." A pause fills the space between them.

"How was the funeral?" Wyatt asks, and then punches his skull. "What an insensitive question. I'm sorry."

"No, Father Clayton did a great job. It was…I think we're all at peace from it. Talked about Papa's legacy and being a part of so much history."

"All that he must have seen in his lifetime," Wyatt says. "Makes me proud."

"How so?"

Wyatt doubles back. "That someone can live such a long life."

"He would've been tickled to know about the gold we found," Travis says. "I knew I had prospecting in my blood, since I believe his father tried at some point."

"I want to transfer it to money."

"Sure, I can do that for you at the bank. Since I'm guessing you don't have any ID?"

"Thank you, Trav. And I'll be moving into a new place soon. No need to stay in the abandoned storefront."

Callie pops inside. "We're already out of pizza. The Mills's brood came with their six kids. Oh, hi Wyatt."

"Ma'am, I am so sorry for your loss."

"Thank you, Wyatt. Travis, help me."

"Sure thing, babe." Travis puts down the beer and grabs a few boxes of pizza from the fridge.

"Those kids'll eat it cold," Callie says. "Excuse us, Wyatt."

Trav leaves with Callie, and Wyatt stands there alone in their kitchen. The smell of the family permeating. He breathes them in like a drug, then unscrews the whiskey cap and takes a nip, as Grayson swings back inside.

"I have your number," Grayson says, pointing with his beer bottle.

"Don't understand what that means."

"What do you want from the Barlows? Always hanging around like a leech."

"Their friendship."

"Bull honkey. You're after something more. A lawman can tell. What's your last name?"

"My last…" Wyatt goes to say *Barlow*, his true surname, but holds his tongue. Had he made up one before when he first met Grayson at Elson's? He doesn't remember. "Killian," he says.

"Wyatt Killian? What the fuck kind of name is that?"

"The only one my daddy gave me," Wyatt says, bumping Grayson with his chest. "You got a problem with that?"

Grayson makes a gun with his thumb and index finger. "I'm gonna check you out. See who you really are."

Grayson exits the kitchen, not allowing Wyatt any type of comeback. He's aware Grayson could prove a problem, should he go digging. At some point, he must tell Trav the truth of how they're connected. Soon, in fact. He has to find the right way to broach the topic, but it's better if he explains rather than Grayson warning Trav that Wyatt Killian doesn't exist. He's worked too hard to live for it all to blow up.

The main room filled with people now. He overhears stories of Papa, people working to keep his memory alive. Stu's in a chair, cold beer in hand, others are talking to him but his eyes show he's not present. Wyatt wants to tell him he's lost a father but found a great-grandfather. However, this is not the right time. In fact, he seems to be creating more strife here than if he leaves, so he does, quietly out the screen door, past the dog house where Chinook nibbles on a bone, into the forest which comforts him with its silence, rounding him whole again.

43

Spring in Laner means hundreds of migratory birds returning to their breeding and nesting grounds. The sight of them pouring in after months of its residents encased in ice proves revelatory. But this spring has lower temperatures than usual so the birds don't flock until closer to summer when the uptick in heat combined with the nonstop midnight sun warms the Bering Sea to a tropical feel—for Alaska. Even the town's biggest hermits can appreciate the greenery, the budding of flowers, the way the sun uplifts. Summer is Laner's true rebirth, and no one experiences this more than Travis Barlow—at first.

Plunging into the legwork to get his business up and running, Travis spends sixteen-hour days on the abandoned goods store he's turning into his fish shack, The Goldmine. Wyatt had moved to a tiny house with the gold they found and once Travis exchanged his share, he had eighty-eight thousand dollars to sink into the restaurant. He finds some part-time contractors recommended by Elson to do the heavy lifting. A good majority he does on his own, wanting to outlay as little money as possible, since his newfound savings are depleting fast. Anyone who likens owning a restaurant to a loveless marriage sure have it right; the shack takes, takes, takes, and has yet to give. The hours at home are spent fretting over the licenses he needs to obtain, hiring a cook, a waiting staff, setting up a menu, a website, fixing a leak in the basement. The sheer number of boxes that have to be checked never seem to end. Even sleep brings fitful dreams full of more problems, and when he wakes up gagging in the middle of the night, Callie is ready to call quits on the whole venture.

***

While initially supportive, Callie soon becomes a single parent since Travis assumes that opening a business means he could shirk all other responsibilities. It's not like she isn't on her feet all day and the last thing she wants to do is to chase Eli around rather than take a bubble bath with a joint. Initially, Travis seems so excited that she can't say anything, but soon, he turns more miserable than when he wasn't working at all. One night after he wakes up choking, she speaks to the ceiling about her fears, and while the ceiling listens, Travis takes offense and starts sleeping on the couch. The sex between them has already dwindled, but the idea of not having him close, even smelling his fogged breath first thing in the morning, bolsters a depression she can't shake. On the outside, she's still the same strong Callie, but inside, her wires no longer connect. She wonders if they ever will again.

Wyatt starts showing up to the Pizza Joint every day on his lunch break. He still washes dishes at Elson's despite their windfall—his money going into renting a house, a wardrobe of new clothes, and saving the rest since he isn't foolish enough to believe they'll ever find gold again. The local paper runs a story about the two friends striking it rich up by Anvil Creek where settlers from a hundred years ago sought their own fortunes. For a few weeks, everyone in town have their names on their lips. Soon others travel into the wilderness, none finding any treasures. It's considered a fluke, and while some remain jealous, talk soon dies down.

Wyatt figures his upward mobility would finally bring happiness, but the idea that he'll never find gold again—the well tapped dry—messes with him. It had proved a distraction from missing his wife and child, now they plague even more. While Trav has fitful nights, Wyatt's are worse. He dreams of his family vividly, loses them in mornings. Feels them aching, the guilt a steady throb. From the letter he had Kaawishté send, Adalaide's final thoughts of him were that he gave her up for gold, since he lied about his success. It would have been better to simply believe he perished. He'd forever be punished because of his lies.

Callie and Eli become replacements again. With Trav so busy, Wyatt rarely sees his old friend unless he goes to the abandoned store, and even then, Trav rarely has time. Wyatt offers to help, but the tools used are too modern and he finds himself lost. Trav never outright says to not come by, but his body language becomes clear so Wyatt supplements the lunch break he used to help Trav by going to Pizza Joint instead. Callie waits on him even when he isn't technically her table, and the two begin talking. Normal chit-chat at first, but it's clear something has been bothering her and eventually she speaks about Travis being absent, how it's taking a toll and she needs a break. They talk about California and it seems like she wants to go back there, if just for a little bit. Wyatt pushes her toward this, wondering if time away from Trav might unsettle their relationship even more. He doesn't want to break them up—well, that's not true—he does, but wants it to seem organic, and for her to come running to him. If Trav won't appreciate her, he could. So he listens at those lunches, rarely speaks of his own sorrows. He tries staying with Aylen more, except Tohopka has returned and always makes him feel uncomfortable. Aylen says she never enjoys sleeping in his new house because she's used to the settlement, and on the nights she does, they fight often. It boils down to her being a poor replacement for Adalaide. There's little of his wife in this woman, while Callie radiates more of his past than he can sometimes stand.

Stu stays steeped in the past as well. First with Bobby, now Papa, both deaths not entirely settling. Stu wanted to solve Bobby's murder while Papa was still alive, show his father that his life's calling had not been for naught. Papa sometimes remarked that the sheriff of a tiny town like Laner spent too much of the day veering moose off the road and drunks back into their homes. Papa's life had been insular for so long that he wasn't aware of dangers that existed on the edges of Laner, which had darkened in the past decade. He refused to believe that Stu actually did real police work. So Stu finds himself seeking out that danger, spending nights amongst the underbelly without any backup.

Grayson is too far up his own ass to notice Stu's descent while becoming a regular at Raye's and pining over Lorinda by sometimes standing out of her apartment singing "In Your Eyes" at the end of a bender. He only stops when she threatens to file a restraining order.

While Cora feigns sleep and worries about her husband, imagining all kinds of gruesome outcomes that could arrive with a knock on the door.

She throws herself into pickling like she did before taking care of Papa became a full-time profession, until she runs out of places to store the jars.

So it's summer, but a lot of the residents of Laner behave as if it's still winter: cold and isolated, melancholy and morose, with no hope that the sun could part the clouds.

44

In the kitchen, Stu shakes his head at the sheer amount of vegetables Cora pickles. Radishes and turnips, gingers, and something that looks like severed pinkies. He's finished his regular shift and Cora went to bed after watching an old episode of *Murder She Wrote*. He loads his gun, sticks it in the holster, and munches on some vinegary bites in each jar until he's full. There's a poker game happening in the basement of a house on the outskirts. Even though he owes the guy who runs the game a shit ton of money for the last five times he lost, he begs to be invited again hoping this time someone connected to the heroin trade might be at the table. A start to getting closer to any connections to Bobby.

He wears a cap low over his eyes and uses Cora's Hyundai so as not to arouse suspicion. This man's house is in the middle of the woods, not a soul around to hear any screams. He could use this to his advantage if need be. The basement smells of water damage, but the stakes are higher than the surroundings might reveal. Thousands of dollars in the pot.

The game is run by a Russian ex-pat named Grigory, a trunk of a man with a dark mustache like a brush, tiny dots for eyes, and puffed-out cheeks. He speaks in a thick accent, his expression never revealing his poker hands. Three others at the table. A Native American barely older than a teenager, but not one Stu recognizes from the settlement, not the one he's been searching for. None of the other players will recognize Stu either, since Grigory's place is past the border and not in his jurisdiction. The two others are brothers from Nome. They've been at games before. Big spenders who wear fur coats, smoke thin cigars, and sport sunglasses indoors like they're celebrities in hiding.

"We're waiting for the sixth," Grigory says, taking a sip of brown liquor. He offers it to Stu, but Stu always declines. "Also, do you have my money in case you lose?"

The fur-wearing brothers snicker.

"I got you covered," Stu says, slapping his pocket with a wallet protruding as if it actually holds the ten-or-so-thousand he owes.

"Pass me one of those cigars," Grigory says, his voice sounding like he's gargling. He clips off the end. "That will be your dick if I don't get what's due."

The fur-wearing brothers guffaw and even the Native American boy chuckles. Stu laughs as well to fit in but stops as he hears mice scurrying in the walls.

"Don't mind them," Grigory says. "They eat up the dead bodies I keep behind the dry wall."

"I don't have all night," Stu says, his hand floating toward the gun, seeing how fast it'll take him to line up a shot and kill the ringleader. But who is this man's boss? He must find out even if it destroys him in the process.

"Patience, my pet," Grigory says, puffing away.

The door at the top of the stairs swings open and an unruly light shines in. The sound of feet walking down the creaky stairs. Darkness shades the owner of the body until he reaches the table. Tohopka, who ran out on him that time at the settlement when he knocked on his trailer to ask questions. They've never been this close to one another before.

Stu's first instinct to charge at the guy, stick the gun in his face, and make him spill any names. But no telling who else at the table might be packing, so it's best to hold off doing anything impulsive.

"Tohopka," Grigory says, as Tohopka nods.

They begin playing. Stu winning some early hands: a full house, a flush. He finds that Grigory enjoys it when others think they have the upper hand. Then Grigory strikes. Stu will use the early rounds as a time to gather information.

"I don't know if this is the right crowd," Stu begins, the baseball cap kept even lower over his eyes so he won't reveal any nervousness. "Lookin' to purchase some tar, if anyone knows a hook-up."

The fur-wearing brothers tilt their chins at each other, clearly in the know. Except they come from Nome, not the ring he's after. Let the bigtime police force deal with their own mess. The Native American boy looks clueless, no different than how he appears during every hand. But Tohopka has a connection. A band of sweat drips from his forehead.

"Don't know what you mean," Grigory says, petting his mustache. "This tar you speak of."

"H," Stu replies. "Heard there was a main seller in the area."

"And where you from exactly?" Grigory asks, eyeing Stu over his cards.

"Bismol," Stu says, a town about twenty minutes west. Nothing much there except for an Eskimo settlement and a petroleum plant.

"Ah, work at the plant?"

"Yes, sir," Stu says.

"And you're looking for a little...vacation?"

"Sure am."

"'Fraid I can't help you," Grigory says, raising his voice as if a microphone listens. "Got *no* business in drugs. Never had. Now can we play cards?"

The rest of the table agrees, but Tohopka watches Stu differently. Does he realize he knows this man but is unsure how?

"Tohopka, I believe it's your turn," Grigory says.

Tohopka pushes a chip forward.

"What about you?" Stu flat-out asks Tohopka, who twitches in response. "Who's your supplier?"

"How do you know he uses?" one of the brothers asks.

"Can tell from the fat black sacks under his eyes," Stu says. "Dead giveaway."

"I might," Tohopka says, his voice a peep.

"Would give you a finder's fee."

Tohopka tugs at his lip. "That so?"

"No," Grigory says, waving his hands like a conductor. "When you come here, you here to play, not make side deals. Do that on your own time." He gestures to one of the brothers to bet.

"I know you from somewhere," Tohopka whispers. He goes to reach for his gun, but second guesses and flips the table instead. Chips and cards are launched to the sky while Tohopka makes a run for it up the stairs.

"What the hell?" Grigory shouts, as Stu whips out his gun and charges after.

"Stay right here," Stu yells. "The police are on the way and it's best if you all comply."

His bum leg burns as he runs, the pain shooting up his thigh with each stair. He radios in backup, giving the coordinates as best he can since the house is camouflaged by the woods. Once he's outside, it's impossible to see far ahead of him. The moonlight obscured by clouds. He freezes, listening for any movement. A twig snaps and he pursues the sound, but when he arrives at the spot, only darkness awaits along with a pair of boots. Tohopka has gone barefoot to mute his footsteps. A rush of wind circles, masking any chance to pick up more movements. Faintly in the distance, he hears someone scurrying away. But they're already too far. He's forty years Tohopka's senior and doesn't stand a chance.

"Fuck," he shouts, creating an echo. He can still hear it in the trees, shifting throughout the woods.

Backup arrives about a half hour later. Grayson along with two other police officers, Cole and Bickley, two guys who recently joined the force barely out of school. Stu monitored the front door with his pistol trained, but no one emerged from the basement. They were smart to listen because he would've shot to maim.

It's three in the morning once they take the rest of the table down to the station. Cole and Bickley brew muddy coffees and then get to grilling. The Native American boy weeps and offers nothing. The brothers act cool, having been through this questioning before. They call their lawyers and refuse to talk. Stu requests to be alone with Grigory.

"I assume this means I am not getting my money," Grigory says, fishing for a cigarette and having a hard time being in handcuffs.

"Here," Stu says, directing the cigarette to the man's mouth and lighting it with a match. "No, you aren't getting that money. The kind of games you're running are illegal with those stakes. And you were profiting from the pot since there's a buy-in to you to play."

"Okay, I am guilty. But is this really worth all this racket? I love cards. I am immigrant trying to make his way."

"You aren't my target," Stu says. "But you have to pony up some information. That man you play with, Tohopka…"

"Yes?"

"He's a derelict with thousands to play poker. Where does he get that kind of money? He's dealing drugs. But he's not the main supplier."

Grigory blows a smoke ring. "Yes, yes. That whole settlement is addicted."

"Where are the drugs coming from?"

"I have heard a name spoken about."

Stu leans in close, his lips wet. "Tell me. I'll let you off."

"The boy at the table is used as a ringer. I pay him to play. He doesn't know anything."

"Fine, he'll walk too. The brothers in fur as well. None of you are my targets."

Grigory inspects his cigarette, takes a long suck until it burns down to a nub. A long ash like a caterpillar still hangs.

"The Hand."

"The what?"

"This man, the supplier, that is what he is called. The Hand."

"Are you fucking with me?"

"I am not. I have heard this name. I do not know what he looks like or where he lives. But The Hand controls all the H in this area, runs guns too. Tohopka got me a piece through him, that is how I know."

"If you're lying…"

"Then book me." He puts out his cigarette, rubs his tired eyes. "These handcuffs are chaffing. Could you?"

Stu walks to the door.

"Hey. Hey! Mister, we had a deal."

Stu knocks and the metal door swings open. "Your friends were right to have their lawyer present. They're smarter than you, Grigory."

Grigory's threats rattle the tiny room, but Stu chooses not to hear a criminal's pleas. The guy has to be guilty of something more than cards.

45

"We're going out," Callie says, shaking Travis by the shoulder because he's come home early like he said he would, but already passed out on the couch with a beer in hand. "Miss Evelyn's gonna watch Eli."

Travis burps in response.

"Get the fuck up." She kicks his hip, causing him to let out a howl. He rolls over to the floor.

"Baby, I'm so tired. How about we cuddle on the couch instead?"

"And watch NASCAR?"

Travis's eyes light up. "Really?"

"Of course not. I'd rather be tarred and feathered."

The doorbell rings and Miss Evelyn lets herself in with a chocolate pie in hand.

"Oh, thank you, Miss Evelyn," Callie says. "Eli's napping now. I already made tuna noodle and left it in the fridge."

"We'll be fine, honey. Have your night out without the wee one."

"Tell that to party pooper over there."

Travis sits up. "Miss Evelyn, I work hard. I just want a night in."

Callie stomps her boot into the hardwood floor and heads into the bathroom, slamming the door.

"Now, son," Miss Evelyn says. "You got a lovely one there who's at her wit's end. You take her out for a nice meal, listen to all her stories, and make her feel special."

"You're right, you're right."

"And don't run home neither. If it's before midnight, I'm leaving the deadbolt on."

Travis lumbers into the other bathroom, takes a quick shower, and dresses as nicely as his wardrobe offers. A tucked-in shirt for once. Hair combed. Five o'clock shadow trimmed. Splash of cologne Callie bought him on his thirtieth birthday that he never used. She comes out in a blue dress.

"Wow," he says, gushing. "When did you get that?"

"I have my secrets. Where do you wanna go?"

"Elson's."

"Elson's? I mean, don't you want something different for once?"

"I like Elson's. I know what I'm gonna get there."

"I'll look foolish dressed up like this."

He winks. "Nah, you'll be the star of the place. All eyes on you."

At Elson's, there's a hockey game on the tube as per usual and country music on the juke. All the regulars present. Tuck and Jesse having a beer at the bar. Smitty and his wife eating pastas.

"I should have chosen the place," Callie says. "We've never tried The Angler in Nome."

"Look, we're here," he says, his tone exasperated. They're nipping at each other more than ever, enjoying pushing buttons. "Let's get some drinks and make the best of it."

Drinks not being the best way to go, since the wine at Elson's is always suspect so they order gins. There's some famous painting Travis can recall of a town split in half between gin drinkers and beer drinkers. The gin side are all fighting, the beer side hugging. Travis knows gin makes him and Callie mean, but sucks it down anyway.

Travis orders a Mondo Burger while she chooses a fried fish and they split jalapeno poppers.

"Haven't had dinner together in some time," she says, because Travis hasn't been home before ten in weeks.

"Usually skip dinner, or eat a bag of chips and Oreos or something."

"Making good headway?" she asks, perking up.

"Found out I'll need a loan."

"Shit, Travis. You think that's wise?"

"Too far in now to go back."

"But the gold was like a hundred thousand."

"Not quite that much. Bills are piling up fast."

"Okay," she says, after a breath. "Whatever you need."

"I know you've felt shortchanged recently."

"I have, but this is your dream. So I'll be supportive."

They finish the rest of the meal without talking. He can tell she doesn't mean what she says and already resents The Goldmine. But he's too tired to think of how to make it better between them, and he's starting to get drunk.

A country song comes on the jukebox and Callie squeals.

"Oooh, this is my favorite!"

"What is it?"

"Don't know, but I love it. C'mon and dance."

"Callie, no one's dancing."

"So, we'll start the train. Please, Travis, I need to move. I need to step out of my body."

He doesn't know what she means, but he can't think of one thing he hates more than dancing. He shakes his head.

"You suck, you fuck," she says, with a fingernail between his eyes.

"I can't dance for shit."

She jumps up. "So what? Just hold me, rock me, I don't care!"

"Cal, c'mon, sit back down."

"I'm dancing! And I'm gonna find someone who'll do it with me."

She scans the bar, zeroes in on Jesse, who's alone now swigging a beer.

"You, my friend," Callie says, her hand on his knee. Jesse gulps. "Don't be like my stupid hubby. Get those legs moving!"

She pulls Jesse from his stool and captures his tall and wiry frame in her arms.

"Mrs. Barlow, I don't think…" Jesse mumbles.

"*Mrs.* Barlow? Am I that much of an old maid? Now dip me."

Jesse obliges and she whirls in his arms, kicking her leg out and eyeing Travis, who's fuming at the table.

"You're not a bad dancer, Jesse."

He's stepping all over her toes, but she laughs anyway.

"Your husband's coming over," he says, his voice hitting a high octave.

"So?"

Travis pulls the two apart and Callie watches as Travis sends a fist into Jesse's jaw. The boy crumbles upon impact, his thin arms not standing a chance to fight back. He covers his face as Travis keeps pummeling.

"Travis, stop," Callie says. "Travis!"

She hits him from behind, but he pushes her away. She nearly pitches over and screams. Elson gets between the men now, and Smitty helps to hold Travis back.

"This isn't what I signed up for," Callie cries. "None of it."

Jesse has curled into a ball on the floor, holding his bleeding nose.

"You're out of here or I'm calling the cops," Elson tells Travis, who flings them both off and heads for the door.

"Travis!" he hears Callie calling after him. "Travis!"

He keeps walking. Since he's feeling shitty, he wants everyone to feel shitty too. Always been like this. Selfish. Rotten. He punches his skull, winding down Main Street and turning on Platen toward The Goldmine, which pisses him off even more. The place a disaster. Nothing finished. Not even close.

"I'm such a fuck-o," he tells the walls. "I should go back to her."

But what would he say? The loan he'll need to take out will be at least fifty thousand dollars due to unexpected expenses. And that's if the bank agrees to give him one. He has the meeting on Monday, and his gut tells him that they'll pass because of his lousy credit. The gold he found winding up being more of a curse than a prize.

"Trav," he hears from outside. He peers out of the window.

"Trav?" Wyatt asks, as he comes inside, kicking aside some loose flooring. He hasn't seen Trav in a while and gets concerned that the restaurant looks the same as when he was last here. Trav has rings around his eyes that weren't present before. He seems as if he could fall asleep right here.

"You don't look well," Wyatt says.

"I could say the same about you."

Wyatt's sleepless nights have affected him. He's been hallucinating but maybe that's also due to the heroin he's been snorting. He swore not to inject, since that's for true addicts. It's a way to return to his past and Adalaide and Little Joe. But they have yet to materialize, like he's wrung out all the memories of them and nothing remains. He's avoided mirrors. For his reflection shows the man he was. Someone who's killed twice in cold blood. He's unable to line this up with his current self. But a hundred years isn't likely to change what a man's hands are capable of doing. And all for gold, which robbed him of everything truly important.

"Was it all worth it?" Wyatt asks. He's trembling like he's been caught in a downpour.

"No, Callie's probably pissed as hell," Trav says. "I shouldn't have swung at Jesse."

"I meant the gold, but no you shouldn't have. I was finishing up a shift and saw her driving home."

"I need to go after her," Trav says, starting to walk out, but Wyatt stops him.

"Let her cool down. You'll make it worse."

"I always make it worse."

"Maybe the two of you aren't meant to be together."

"What the fuck, Wyatt? Why would you say that?"

Wyatt paces around the gutted store remembering when it was his home. Seems like a lifetime ago.

"I thought I was meant to be with my wife forever. Life had another idea for us."

"Callie and I run hot and cold. Always been like that."

"So was the gold worth it for you?" Wyatt asks, struggling with his own answer.

"Not sure." Trav wipes the dirt off a stool and sits. "It's mostly sunk into this place and I still need more."

"We always need more," Wyatt says. "Nothing ever satisfies. I'm learning that now."

"I'm getting a sense you haven't been happy with our bounty."

Wyatt towers over Trav, rests his large hands on his great-great grandson's shoulders. "There's something I've wanted to tell you."

"Wyatt, you're scaring me."

"I don't mean to. No. But you need to know who I am. My last name is Barlow too."

"What the...?" The room inverts and then widens. Trav has to hold onto the stool to stay upright. The gin soars up his throat, bile seeping through teeth.

"I knew about the gold because I had been to the area before, but not like how you think. It was over a hundred years ago."

"That don't make no sense."

"Trav, listen. Don't speak, open your ears. I was frozen in time."

Trav cackles as he seems to get his bearings. "My funny friend Wyatt."

"I am serious."

Trav's laughs build, evil in their growth, hurting Wyatt to the core. Wyatt smacks him across the face. The stool spins from out under and Trav lies splayed on the floor. He looks up, petrified.

"Wyatt?"

"Get up!"

When Trav doesn't rise immediately, Wyatt pulls him to his feet.

Trav pokes the inside of his cheek with his tongue. "You hit me?"

"I slapped you, there is a difference."

"I was just laughing."

"But it's not a joke! You are my great-great grandson. I left my wife and child to find gold and became trapped in ice. My son traveled to Alaska, either to find me or gold for himself. He was killed as a young man but had a child. That was Papa Clifford. Papa told me this."

Trav rubs his head. "*What*? What the fuck are you talking about?"

Wyatt shakes him, his strength making Trav flop around like a ragdoll. "It's the only explanation I have! It's how I knew where that gold was! A century passed to bring us together, for me to reunite with my family."

"No one can be preserved in ice, that's impossible."

"Not for us! Not for Barlows. My son ran cold too. And I am the same. Feel my hands, go on!"

Wyatt grabs onto Trav, palms icy cool. Trav yanks away in shock. Wyatt guessing he doesn't want to admit his power.

"And Papa too," Wyatt continues. "His heart was still beating, wasn't it? Even after the doctors declared him dead."

"How did you know that?"

"I went to the hospital afterwards. I told them I was family. They explained how uncanny..."

Trav steps back, beyond spooked. "Wyatt, this isn't cool, man."

Wyatt takes a step forward for each step that Trav retreats. He doesn't know what he'll do when he catches up. Only that he needs Trav to understand.

"My family is gone," Wyatt thunders. "But you are my family that's still here. We look alike, you and I. That's what united us."

"Sometimes people resemble each other."

"It's because we're blood." Wyatt digs into Trav's arm with his sharp fingernail until dabs of red trickle.

"Wyatt, man, stop!"

"Your blood is my blood. See?" He smears it over his palm, holds it up as evidence. "Don't deny who we are."

"You're fucking crazy."

"Any crazier than us finding that gold? I've defied logic for you. I've changed the way you think."

Wyatt palms Trav right over his heart. "The way your heart beats. It's like mine. Powerful thumps that can withstand frigid temperatures. I was born in 1860, and it kept me alive this long."

"I need to go."

"No, not until you hear me out!"

"Wyatt, you're getting blood all over me." He glances down at his shirt that appears as if he's been knifed. "Are you taking heroin again? Like, what is going on?"

The bloody palm lessens its hold on Trav's heart. Wyatt's face forlorn, irrevocably destroyed. The closest person in his life won't hear his desperate truths. And Trav'll never look at him the same way again.

"I see," he says, quietly, shriveling.

"Wyatt, we can help you. There's rehab facilities."

"It has nothing to do with heroin," Wyatt roars. "Heroin has given me more than anyone else has in this present time...even you."

"It can control you in a bad way."

"I will mash your face in if you don't stop your yammering. I will beat on you until you howl for release. I should go before I do anything I will regret."

"Wyatt, you sound high—"

Wyatt grabs Trav by the collar, fury rolling in his murderous eyes. The two breathe in the tension hovering between. Neither knowing what might occur. But then Wyatt lets him down, fixes his collar, and bolts out of The Goldmine's door.

"Goddamn," Trav says, as Wyatt punctures the night at full speed, running away on all fours.

It'd be easy to write off what happened as a drunken delusion, but Travis quakes when he returns home. He strips down bare and slides into bed, tracing his finger down Callie's back. More than ever he wishes they hadn't fought and he could climb on top of her and forget about any weirdness that occurred with Wyatt. But he doesn't deserve to have her and she makes that clear by wiggling away from his probing finger.

"I'm gonna go to California for a while," she says, halfway between sleep and lucidity. "And I'm taking Eli with me."

His finger feels as if he's stuck it in a light socket. Sucking its tip to ease the pain, he swallows every tear left until he's fully dry and morning arrives without her there.

46

Aylen's obsessed with watching those true crime shows into all hours of the night. She returns from Raye's, gets under the covers, and toggles between *48 Hours*, *Snapped*, *Disappeared*, *Cold Justice* and *Dateline*. Better to get sucked into these strangers' tragedies, her own seeming manageable. No one's outside her door with a cleaver. When Wyatt arrives, she has no desire to get intimate. Pisses her off that he's not a fan of television, finding the idea of it spooky along with his tired excuse, "It wasn't around in my time."

He pants after running the entire way over. She removes his sweaty coat, finds some clear space amongst the clutter to lay it down.

"I told Trav the truth," he says. "Who I am."

"Hmm." She lights a cigarette at the burner, blows the smoke away from his face because he hates the smell. "How'd he react?"

"Didn't believe."

Wyatt's glummer than when they first met. Like a wet towel that's been wrung and discarded on the floor. He's a true crime show, making her own life seem better. She's stayed up at night wondering what she really wants. Orphaned so young, raised by various members of her extended family if they felt like it that day. A childhood spent wandering. The settlement used to be bigger, filled with enough children to create fantasies. To swim in lakes during the summers, make snow angels in winter, stay out all night experimenting: cigarettes, alcohol, sex, pot, cocaine, acid, whatever caused flight, got rid of unwanted babies, aged her dramatically. As a teenager, she'd already lived multiple lives. At twenty-three, she has no energy for any more.

But she liked Wyatt because he was different. And caring when he wanted to be. Sex always the last thing on his mind. Being held was paramount. She'd never been the rock in the relationship. She'd never had a relationship. She had regulars but most were only silent partners.

"Would you dye your hair red for me?" he asks.

She knows where he's going with this. His wife. She's slipped into this role before, never fully comfortable in that woman's shoes, his exalted idol.

"I'd look trashy with red hair," she says, stabbing out the cigarette. She doesn't want to talk tonight. She wants pure silence, a lifetime where neither ever has to speak again. Two monks living in blissful unity, saying all they need to each other with their eyes.

They hear a rustling coming from outside. She can tell from the patter of feet against snow who approaches. She has lived with Tohopka for too long.

He bolts through the door, practically knocking it off its hinges. A whirling dervish oozing narcotics from his pores. Babbling in the devil's tongue.

"Move," Tohopka declares, pushing them both to the side and dashing into his room. They follow with their eyes. His bedroom an explosion of junk, a soiled mattress its nucleus. He tosses it aside and rips up a floorboard.

"Tohopka, I..."

She's aware of his hiding place that contains a Smurf lunchbox with a gun and a stack of bills. Wyatt had offered her some of the money he got from the gold but she refused. Told him she never wanted to feel beholden. She'd rather pilfer some bills from Tohopka's stash, assuming he's in enough trouble to stay away for a long time.

The gun still remains, but the stack of bills dwindled since he last checked. About two hundred left in total, a far cry.

"Where is the rest?" Tohopka says, quietly at first which scares Aylen even more. "WHERE IS THE REST?"

He's grabbing her by the shoulders, spitting in her face.

"Get offa her," Wyatt yells, leaping between them, holding Tohopka back while pushing Aylen toward her freedom. Tohopka cocks the gun. Sweats pours off him like it's raining. His pupils dilated to cartoon levels.

"I had almost a thousand dollars in that lunchbox—"

"Six hundred," Aylen replies, flipping her hair.

"What did you do with it?"

Aylen disappears and returns with a negligée, writing it off as a business investment. She throws the silk attire in Tohopka's face.

"Take it, you motherfucker!"

They charge at each other, animals wanting blood. She scrapes Tohopka's arm, he rips a chunk of her hair, she digs her teeth in refusing to let go even after Tohopka cries out wounded. A bullet goes off, shooting out a light. Downpour of glass. Wyatt enters the arena, punching Tohopka in the face. The gun bobbing between them but Tohopka has a better hold.

"And where are my dog tags?" Tohopka yells. "You took them, you sneaky bum."

"That's right, I did." Wyatt still fights for the gun with one hand while the other constricts Tohopka's throat.

"I was a solider, I was…I don't have time, no time, no time," Tohopka says.

"I want you to leave here and never return."

Tohopka wrenches out of Wyatt's grip, looking down at his frozen feet.

"Give me your boots, you'll never see me again," Tohopka says.

"I'm not giving you my—"

"Wyatt," Aylen says, so he sits up on the kitchen counter and chucks his boots at Tohopka whose feet are too small, but he'll have to make do.

"You'll pay for what you did to her," Wyatt says, snarling. "Retribution."

Tohopka weasels past him. "Fuck your retribution."

He bounds out of the door waving the gun mightily, running off into the night. Aylen inspects the chunk of hair her cousin ripped out.

"He's not allowed here anymore," Wyatt says.

She lights another cigarette, calming her nerves. After a few puffs, she realizes she's not freaked out, only titillated, enamored by Wyatt at the moment, her hulking hero. No one has ever stood up for her like this before. She pulls him in her bedroom. The tiny TV replays a *48 Hours* she's already seen as she strips him down and climbs on top, in the middle of riding him when the sheriff pokes his head inside with the second gun trained on her for the day.

Stu allows Aylen and Wyatt to put on some clothes while he inspects Tohopka's room for any clues of where he may have gone. Once the lovebirds get themselves together, Aylen wears a negligée and Wyatt pants but no shirt. Stu can't help but notice that Wyatt has the same build as he used to when he was younger. Before muscles started to sag and a gut sprouted in their place.

"He was here about an hour ago," Aylen says, filling some plastic cups with cheap whiskey. Stu declines.

"Any idea where he might be?"

Aylen shrugs. "Ain't his keeper."

"He's not welcome anymore," Wyatt says, the first he's spoken since Stu arrived. The voice catching Stu off guard. "Ripped out a chunk of her hair." He nods to the ground where a black patch of hair appears like a ball of yarn.

"Is he running drugs?" Stu asks her.

Aylen shrugs again but then shakes her head. "I mean, to kids and stuff, but he's not the supplier or nothing. Same thing most around here do."

"Not her," Wyatt says.

"I'm not after your girlfriend. Miss Oxendine, your cousin comes up in our database with a few priors but nothing too troubling. Yet I believe he's connected to a bigger organization. Does the name The Hand mean anything to you?"

"The Hand?" She gulps a thick swallow of alcohol.

"You say it as if there's something familiar?"

"Not with the name, but..." She looks out of a tiny open window, the wind creating a harmonica hum. "There's a man living past the settlement. I know some drugs used to come from him, not sure if he's at the top."

"It's a start, Miss."

"He has a mangled hand, like a claw. Or more like a chicken's foot. Gives me goosebumps."

"You've seen him?"

"Once, talking to Tohopka, but never again. He doesn't leave his cabin. That was a few years ago when Tohopka got back from the Middle East, when he was just starting to slide. He's not naturally bad. None of us coming from here stood a chance, ya know."

"Could you locate where this man lives?"

"It's far in the woods, but I heard Tohopka giving someone directions once. Some middleman. I think I'd remember enough."

Stu sucks in a sharp intake of breath, the sensation of being so close to what he's sought for an eternity.

"I'd have to be in the car," Aylen says, dragging her toe across the floor. "Like, I wouldn't be able to just tell you."

"I need to go right now."

"I don't sleep," Aylen says, and Stu wants to reply the same.

"I don't want to put you in any danger," Stu says, flicking between her and Wyatt, gauging how both will reply.

Wyatt strokes his massive beard, holds both of their attention as if he requires the final say.

"She ain't going without me," Wyatt says, already walking toward the front door that's off its hinges.

"Wyatt, you have no shoes."

"I've suffered worse."

"I'm gonna get his coat and one for myself," Aylen says, as if this kind of reconnaissance happens with them all the time.

Stu reaches for her plastic cup with a ring of swill remaining. He knocks it back. Pours another gulp for the extra kick of bravado.

47

In the haze of an Alaska morning, all foggy, white, and contained, Callie scoops up a sleeping Eli and drags a suitcase to a called cab. There's no sun, but she will get some soon. Two tickets booked to Los Angeles, a fortune last-minute but her parents promised to pay her back. When they found out she was coming without Travis, they would've spent anything.

The Nome airport with only a few travelers. She has to steel herself for the bustle, having not been to California in years. When she had Eli, her parents visited for the second time after the wedding. They bumped into each other for a few days in their small house until Callie sent them away. Occasionally, she'd Skype with them, and so that's how Eli knows of their existence. Two digitized images waving from his iPad.

On the plane, Eli finally wakes up, complaining about his ears. She points out of the window and he watches as they sail through a cloud.

"Wooooo," he says. The stewardess comes by and asks what he wants. Emphatically, he tells her "apple juice" like it's his coffee and he needs it to function.

"Cute," the stewardess says, through her smile. Callie notices a lipstick stain on the woman's front tooth. She brushes a finger across her own, but the woman doesn't catch on. Time for a break from simple Alaska.

But L.A. proves too much too fast. Eli plugs his ears in the LAX terminals, his eyes wide enough to pop out. She hates herself for rendering him so helpless. She checks her messages and gets one from Travis. He got her note. He hopes they have a great time in California. The bank passed on the loan. Did she really need to know that? Travis, always the bearer of chagrin. She buys a cranberry muffin for her and Eli to share.

Her parents, Ken and Patricia, not the type to pick her up at the airport. They'd pay for a cab so what's the difference? She'd grown up in a giant house in Los Feliz that used to be owned by a silent movie star. The house gothic and filled with winding hallways and nooks, places a small child could create worlds. Without siblings, she spent her time fantasizing with imaginary friends. She longed to return to that house, but her parents had bought a bungalow in Venice Beach when she left for Alaska. Her mom taught yoga, her father dabbled in investments after retiring from being an entertainment lawyer. They became the true hippies they were destined to be who rubbed scented oils into their feet and talked of chakras. Always into crystals, but now Ken wore Zen beads and Patricia started a raw food diet. They liked to talk about detoxing as if everyone else should be ashamed of their poor choices. Except for marijuana, which they consumed with an outright vigilance.

Callie finds them stoned and smiling on their front porch, away from the main strip of Venice Beach, and the sound of a drum circle forming.

"Cal," Patricia says, stretching her arms so her caftan flows like a parachute. She's wearing sunglasses as big as her face and a statement necklace that makes her look like a warrior.

Callie smells patchouli as they embrace briefly. Patricia never one for giving too much love.

"And this one," she says, with a bony hand on her hip. "My grandbaby. C'mere, handsome."

Eli's tuckered out but folds into her. Ken greets him with a tough handshake.

"Let me put him down for a nap," Callie says, after a hug with her father that's nothing more than pats on the back.

In the guest room, a thin slice of space with two double beds and an overstuffed closet, she lies down to gather herself before she has to emerge.

"Why are we here, Mama?" Eli asks by her side, nudging her cheek with his nose.

"I don't know," she tells him. "But I'm gonna figure it out."

When Callie finally gets the confidence to greet her parents again, they've moved inside since the sun's setting. Her father looks good, as usual. Trim and sockless in expensive shoes, a collared shirt opened at the neck. Her mother thinner and veinier than she remembered, poof of hair like a seventies starlet. Both still wearing sunglasses indoors.

"So Travis didn't want to come?" Patricia asks. The tone is sweet but the underlying implication palpable.

"Mom, I..." Patricia's foaming at the mouth, almost whispering the word *divorce* with delight. "We needed a break from Alaska."

"Well," Patricia says, turning her nose, "I don't know how you live in a dead-end like that. Look at your skin."

Callie wants to say, *Look at your skin, you two are leathery like lizards*, but she glances at her own hands that are ivory-colored and dry AF.

"Lotion, darling," Patricia says, whipping out a bottle from her caftan like a magician. She squirts some into Callie's palms. "Rub it in good."

"Bug," Ken says, "you can tell us what's really going on."

"Everything's fine," Callie says, raising her voice. Her parents eye each other. "Everything's wonderful. God, you haven't seen Eli since he was born. Is it so crazy I wanted to come?"

They both wait a beat and give a nod.

"Sweetness, don't stay in Alaska to spite us," Patricia says.

And Callie almost wants to leave right then and there. She grinds her teeth.

"Can you watch Eli? I want to go for a walk. I want to be by myself."

"Of course," Ken says, rotating the prayer beads on his wrist.

She takes in the home décor, which she's never seen beyond being background in a Skype call. They have so much clutter, paintings competing for space, coffee table books they'll never read, tchotchkes from their travels, not because they loved the pieces when they were there, but so they can say to friends, "Yes, we got that in Marrakesh, I believe," and then tell a long-winded story full of asides and misdirects until they arrive at procuring some stupid little statue on their mantle of an elephant with a fez hat.

"Here," her mother says, after Callie already stood. She slips a gummy bear into her hand. "The sunset will be beautifully enhanced."

"Eli will be up in two hours."

"Take longer," Patricia says, pushing her out of the door. And now Callie loves both of them for noticing her stress and giving her a tart gummy that she gobbles, immediately feeling high once she swallows even though she knows that's impossible. She takes long strides to the beach, wandering away from the dozens of vendors hawking their art, or tarot cards, or perfumes, and finds herself by the drum circle she spied from her parents' balcony. About fifty kids, ten years younger than her, still firmly kids without spouses, or children, or worries, stoned under the pink and purple setting sun, drumbeats accelerating, all of them dancing, united.

She tells herself the gummy has kicked in and flings her arms to the sky. It's warm enough and she can't recall the last time she's been outside in short sleeves. Two teenage boys dance around her, their moves polished, their rhythm divine, and she dances like she's auditioning for a spot in a troupe, smiling at her ability to still hang. The song continues because a drum circle never ends, its eternal beat glistening, wild thumps over and over until finally the sun sets and the California night comes in cool and sweet, the air smelling of salt and pretty sweat. She waves goodbye at the two teenagers, takes off her shoes and runs down to the tide that licks her toes, and after a good cry, scoops some salt water onto her face, and returns to the girl she left here years ago.

Callie's baked and being stoned alone proves no fun so she dials an old friend of hers, Madison, blond and tan and always up for getting wasted.

"Cal?" Madison chirps, before Callie has a chance to say hi. "No way! OMG."

"Way. I'm in L.A."

"Alaska melted?" Madison asks, and then laughs.

"Yeah, I guess."

"I'm having a party right now in the Hills. I'll text you the address."

"Okay!"

"Hop in an Uber."

Callie doesn't have that app on her phone but is too embarrassed to say it. "I'll come over right now!"

She beams, all exclamation points. Since she's on the beach, there are plenty of cabs so she gets in one and tells them Madison's address. On the way, she calls her parents who vaguely remember Madison because they never paid attention to her friends, but tell her it's fine and to stay out as late as she wants.

The cab climbs up Havenhurst Drive to a new construction in WeHo with a boutique collection of townhouses: modern, white against glass with views of the city and the sky. The party in full force on the deck filled with outdoor couches and a DJ with oversized headphones. Callie pictures Laner where neighbors gather around a television with canned beers that aren't meant to be ironic. Talk of fishing, guns, and weather. Here house music plays, girls wear bikinis covered in glitter, guys with their pecs and abs out, everyone having just come from trainers. She locks her arms around her own stomach, abs a thing of her past.

"Callie!" Squeal from a pig's tail being pulled and there's Madison, golden tan, blond hair with extensions down to her ass, righteous bod and angel wings protruding from her back. She has a tattoo of a fairy on her shoulder, her lipstick an unnatural pink. "What a blast!"

"Hey, Mad," Callie says, and the two hug. Madison steps back to get a good look. "What are you wearing?"

Callie peers down, a T-shirt she got in an outlet mall, jeans that didn't taper enough, a lavender crystal hanging from her neck. She looks like an uncool mom.

"I just got off the plane," Callie says.

"Let's get you a cocktail."

Callie instantly feels better with the cold drink glued to her hand. Something red, cloyingly sweet but also with a heavy pour of good vodka, not the cheap shit Travis picks up at the packy.

"Elena," Madison yells, calling a girl over who has bug eyes from being so thin. She's all protruding bones.

"I didn't even recognize you," Callie says, finally placing the face. She had roomed with Madison and Elena along with one other girl for a year after moving out of her parents'. Most of them waitressed while trying to score auditions, making enough for booze and tacos, hooking up with whatever guys meandered in their direction. Elena had been much larger then, and sometimes Callie and Madison would speak of how bad they felt for the girl to be in their hot posse. "You look great."

"I had my stomach stapled," Elena says.

"Ouch."

"What are you doing here?" Elena asks, like she's accusing Callie of some terrible act.

"Visiting my folks. They're with my son."

"You have a son?" Elena asks, and she and Madison squeal but not from excitement.

"A human being is never coming out of this," Madison says, indicating her vagina.

"Are you married?" Elena asks.

At first, Callie's offended. How could none of them know this? Hadn't she been the hot topic amongst their circle? The girl who fled to Alaska. To them, it was far from exciting news.

Callie shows her wedding ring, a small band with a diamond like a pinhead. The girls plaster on smiles, afraid of seeming cruel.

"What's he like?" Madison asks.

"He's a fisherman. Well, he's opening up a fish shack. He hunts…" She tries to think of what else to say but finds herself stumped.

"You never liked to color inside the lines," Madison says, as if that explains Callie's entire existence. "Come." She hooks a finger with Callie's and directs her over to a table where a pyramid of coke sits on a glass tray. "My boyfriend is a producer, he—"

Callie shuts off while Madison boasts of her boyfriend who produces some reality TV show that Callie never heard of and is writing some spec script with some actor she didn't know who has a PJ, which she later realizes means a private jet, and they fly to Vegas and Aspen all the time, and get the best coke in the land. She chooses to listen to the last part and replies with a good long sniff.

"Amazing, right?" Madison asks, and winks. Her eye gets stuck due to her gummy, oversized eyelashes and she has to use her manicured nails to pry it apart. "Oooh, this is Julien."

Callie gets introduced to a skinny guy with a weird mustache and saggy pants that look like he took a dump in them who's a songwriter. He starts singing in an embarrassing falsetto.

"Julien is so talented," Madison beams.

"Where's your boyfriend?" Callie asks.

"Dubai. I think. Yeah, Dubai. Securing financing. Girl, I'm opening up an athletic wear company."

"In Dubai?" Callie's having a hard time following. People speak so fast here, and yeah she'd ingested a line of coke and probably everyone here snorted more, but it's like no one can take a breath before they start talking more.

"You should follow me on IG," Julien says.

"What?"

"I said you should follow me—"

"I need a bite of food," Callie says, and pushes past them into the kitchen where two models discuss the calories they consumed that day and which one cheated more. Callie finds a cooked chicken in the fridge, rips off a drumstick, and gnaws. "Oh fuck, that's good." She tosses the bone in the sink and rips off the other drumstick.

"You should take a napkin," one of the models says.

"You're dying of jealousy," Callie replies, munching in the girl's face.

When she gets back to the party, she spies Elena, who walks in the other direction, clearly fleeing. She thinks of how Travis would view these people: moochers and showoffs. He'd go off on them and this makes her laugh because he's right.

Madison slides her palm up the back of Callie's shirt. "Em and Jeslene just told me you ate an entire chicken in front of them like a savage. What gives?"

Callie belches in response. "Thanks, this was great." She kisses Madison on both cheeks, leaving chicken grease. "Bye, doll." She hugs Madison and the half-eaten chicken bone gets lost in Madison's mane of hair. Since Madison doesn't notice, Callie decides to leave it.

"You're going already?"

Callie wipes a solitary tear. "I'm an alien here."

Madison shakes her head. "You're just out of practice."

"For what?"

"Mingling, angling, networking. There's opportunity on this deck."

Callie wipes the sweat from her forehead. "It's so fucking hot."

"Yeah, it's summer in L.A."

"I miss the cold."

"You've been here two seconds."

"I just want to be with my husband on the couch."

"Then why did you come?"

"Because I'm a fool."

"All right, bye girl. Enjoy your mooseland."

"I will, Madison. I fucking will. Enjoy your fantasy."

Madison drops her mouth wide open. "Bitch, I was on a PJ yesterday drinking Cristal."

"And on your deathbed, if that image makes you happy, then by all means give over your soul."

"You were always so…"

"So what?"

"So unsettled, Callie."

"Well, you have a chicken bone in your hair."

And in the middle of the night when she gets back, her parents asleep, Eli out cold, she has a glass of wine on the deck observing the still Pacific. How it gives her the silence she's longed for since she got here. Its lapping waves, its quiet conversation. Telling her to get in her spaceship and fly back to the only home she's ever known.

48

Stu has second thoughts about taking Wyatt and Aylen along to go after The Hand, but they're almost halfway to the cabin and there's no chance of turning back. Aylen directs him from the passenger seat while he keeps Wyatt in his sights through the rearview. This man who his son has befriended, an odd choice. He can't quite pinpoint why he doesn't trust him. Thirty-plus years on the force, his gut saying to get as far from him as possible. But for now, a much larger fish needs to fry.

"I'll stop when we near the cabin," Stu says, crawling at a turtle's pace because there are no worn paths. "Then you two take the car back. Leave the keys in the sun visor."

"Won't you need a way out of here when you apprehend him?" Aylen asks.

Stu whistles through his bottom teeth. "I ain't planning on only apprehending him."

"He do something to you personally?"

"That's what I'm gonna find out."

Wyatt clears his throat. "Trav's wife…What you think of her?"

Both Stu and Aylen furrow their brows.

"Where the hell did that come from?" Stu asks.

"Seems like they've been having problems as of late," Wyatt says.

Aylen gestures to the right. "Turn here."

"Marriage is hard," Stu says. "Cora and I hit our share of rocky patches. But the good outweighs the bad. I'm sure my son feels the same."

"Callie said she wanted to go to California."

"When were you talking to her?" Aylen asks, crossing her arms.

"We talk all the time. I have lunch every day at Pizza Joint."

"Travis is starting a business," Stu says, keeping his eyes trained.

"They have a young child. Wears on anyone."

"But do you think they're right for each other?"

"Wyatt!" Aylen hisses. "Stop poking."

"Do I think they're right? Well, no. California and Alaska don't mix well. In fact, nothing mixes with Alaska well."

Stu lets out a yawn, delirious. He counts the hours since he last slept, almost reaching a full day. His bones heavier than normal.

"We're close," Aylen whispers, and gets a visible chill.

"Why are you so concerned about my son?"

"He's like family. At least that's how I think of him."

"And does he think of you this way?" Stu asks.

"There." Aylen directs a shaking finger up a bump of a hill where the cabin sits. Shades drawn, mostly camouflaged by a ring of trees.

Stu eases his foot off the gas as the car rolls to a stop. "This is where we part ways." He opens the door in slow motion so it doesn't make a sound. Aylen inches over to the driver's side.

"Don't you want backup or something?" she asks.

Stu observes the cabin. Creepy even if it didn't house a baddie like The Hand. The wood stripped of color, nothing more than gray slab. Weeds birthed from the landscape and crawling up the sides like tentacles.

"Only way I'll get the answer I want is if I go in alone."

"If I hear anything about Tohopka—" Aylen begins.

"He ain't the puzzle piece I'm after. Just call the station if you find his whereabouts."

"Sheriff," Wyatt says, with a salute.

Stu doesn't salute back. He closes the car door, slips his gun from the holster. Waits until they back up and disappear.

Driving away, Aylen has no interest in speaking to Wyatt. If she has to hear about Travis's wife one more time, she'll scream. It's bad enough he drones on about his own. His obsession with the Barlow family began as amusing. Fixating on them as if they're his own kin. Now it's borderline twisted.

She'd done this before with guys. Excused their deficiencies, made excuses. Stayed too long. Same thing with Tohopka. The rent's cheap, even if it costs an occasional chunk of hair. Sometimes she disgusts herself that she has so little self-value.

If I had a mother, a father? she often thinks. Someone to guide. A child has no business in raising themselves.

"You've gotten quiet," Wyatt says. They've almost reached the settlement. "The sheriff'll be okay."

"I'm not thinking about him. How do you really feel about me?"

He hunches forward, his massive forearms resting between the front seats.

"How do you mean?"

"You speak of your wife and this Callie so often."

"She reminds me of her."

"I don't?"

"Not at all."

"Then what are you doing with me?"

"She is with him."

"Fuck you." She doesn't want to cry but her tears betray, hating that she doesn't appear strong.

"What are you doing with me?" he asks.

"You're different, I dunno. I spend so much time in these false relationships, I don't know how to act in one of my own. That's the most honest I've ever been."

"You've been very kind to me, Aylen. I was broken when I met you. I'm almost pieced back together."

"Glad I could be of service."

"But I'm no one to hitch yourself to, at least not now. To me it seems as if it's only been months since I was with my wife. And my son. I can't describe to you—"

"I'm not asking."

"When I'm around Trav and his family, it's like I'm with my own. I don't love Callie any more than you, she just allows me to transport."

"I get it—I understand. Well, I don't. But I'm trying."

"It's not me being mean."

"But you are."

"Stop the car."

She does and shuts off the engine, places her face against the steering wheel. Tiny toot from the horn.

"I need to leave here," she says.

"You should. Nothing is keeping you."

"I thought you might want me to stay."

"Go. You deserve better."

She lets out a bark of a laugh. "I do."

"You are lovely and would be a dream for most guys to call their girlfriend. I am damaged. I've killed, Aylen. These hands have been responsible for gruesome acts you couldn't imagine. And I'll do it again."

"But that was in the past." She smiles awkwardly. "A hundred years ago, right?"

"But it's like yesterday. And I'm not finished. Because I'm not complete."

"What would make you complete?"

"You don't want me to say."

"I do."

"No, I don't want to speak it out loud. Because that will make it true. And I'm trying everything in my power to change the course of what I think will happen."

Aylen starts the car again. They roll for a while until the settlement comes into view.

Part of her wants to fight, not just for them, but for him to see his own self-value. But she knows if she can't find hers, his will be even harder to locate. Left behind in a different era, unable to thaw.

49

As small children, Bobby Barlow formed differently than Travis. Even when Travis was four and Bobby two, Stu and Cora could tell the boys had divergent personalities. Travis amiable, always eating his food, quick with his please and thank yous. Bobby never would laugh, or cry, or express much emotion. As he grew older, he took to slaughtering small animals in their backyard. He refused to leave his room. He fought at school. Unlike Travis with a dust-up during recess, Bobby maimed. Broke a student's arm. Touched a girl inappropriately. Yanked on a teacher's dress until she fell over. He was himself when he followed his darkest impulses. He was a soul who needed saving.

Cora, master of denial, summed him up with one word: boy. She didn't have girls, and while Travis had been well behaved, most boys were not. Bobby would grow out of his rebellion. And he could be sweet when he really tried.

Stu attempted to treat the boys the same. Taking them hunting, fishing, letting them alternate shotgun in his squad car. Bobby was master of talking himself out of trouble, and while Stu wasn't in denial about his son like Cora, he found it hard staying mad for too long. When middle school rolled around, Bobby traded mauling animals for alcohol and pot, by junior high he was doing bumps of cocaine, hanging at the settlement on the outskirts. Dropping out of high school, doing heroin, getting arrested for petty robberies. Stu kicked him out on many occasions, but Cora always coaxed him back. She'd wet a towel over his forehead during withdrawals. Make him mac and cheese with spicy cream sauce to get in his good graces. After he hit eighteen, he pretty much left for good, meandering back when he needed money. He and Travis fought those times. Travis considering him poison. The boys had never been close, but when they were younger they coexisted. Adulthood made them enemies.

Yet Stu loved his youngest son fiercely. Stu began life as a bit of a miscreant, bucking authority, not getting into drugs but certainly dust-ups. Alaska-bred wild men, he and Bobby were alike in that respect, while Travis was always the more sensitive one. Times spent hunting alone with Bobby were some of the happiest of Stu's life. The power of stillness to unearth Bobby, hunting giving him focus. Without distraction from friends or family or drugs, Bobby was at his purest—his beautiful young son.

He ruminates on those days as he waits outside of The Hand's cabin. The shutters are down so it's hard to see inside. He listens for any sounds from within. Not a peep. The sun passes overhead a few hours later, and he decides The Hand is not home. He finds a package of walnuts in his front pocket and nibbles, since his stomach starts to concave. Hiding behind a thicket of leaves, he spies his opponent. A massive man lumbering through the woods carrying three dead hares by their ears. No shirt, rug of fur coating his back, likely pushing forty but could be older. Identifiable face: nose, eyes, and mouth smushed together. His other hand just as described, whittled down like a sad chicken's foot. The Hand swings open the cabin door and barrels inside.

Stu pursues, gun ready. He charges for the door, catching it before it fully closes. Entering, he's hit with the powerful slap of rot rendering him dizzy. The Hand swivels around, dropping the three hares with scooped-out eyes.

"Police," Stu barks, spit flying from his lips.

The Hand holds up his claw, shaking a thin E.T. finger back and forth. Then he dives for the floor, scurrying under the bed. Stu keeps the gun trained on the box spring as it bends under the mass of The Hand's body. He's about to fire, but afraid to kill this man and never receive the closure he seeks.

"Come out from under there!"

Stu cases the joint. A wall of guns ranging from Uzis to AR-15s. Another wall displaying samurai swords. A half fridge with a burned hot plate and a pot already boiling for the bunnies. The hiss and spit of water as the pot bubbles over.

"I said to come out."

A round of bullets shoot through the mattress and puncture the ceiling. Stu dives down, hugging the soiled floor. He only makes out a dark shape moving under the bed until the mattress and box spring get thrown in the air and The Hand leaps like a wrestler, coming down hard on Stu. They roll around fighting for the semi-automatic until it slips through The Hand's grasp and pirouettes across the cabin. The Hand tries to dig his giant thumbs in Stu's eyes. He's got over a hundred pounds on Stu, crushing his bones. Stu drags his gun so it lands in line with The Hand's shoulder and fires, the bullet trapped in flesh, the wound coughing up blood.

"AAARRRRGGGGGGHHHH!"

An ogre's cry, The Hand's breath oozing like rotten yogurt. Stu slips out from under the man, scooches back. Keeps the gun set right between this devil's eyes.

"My son was Bobby Barlow," Stu says, composed.

The Hand clamps his good hand over the wound, blood running through his fingers.

"So?" The Hand says, with the voice of a pipsqueak. Not what Stu imagined.

"Did he work for you?" Stu shouts. "Running drugs or guns?"

"I've retired now."

"Two years ago Bobby drowned, or was drowned. Is that name familiar?"

"My shoulder," The Hand says, as if he's just realized.

"I will kill you if you don't give me answers. There will be no jail for you unless you comply."

The Hand chews on his lip, mangling it good. "No jail."

"Bobby Barlow. He…" Stu thinks of how to describe his son to make him familiar, but nothing rushes out. He feels this missed opportunity like a pang in his stomach, a cancer building. The hisses and pops of the boiling water prick at his ears.

"Yes," The Hand says, resting his bowling ball head against his little chicken foot, the fingernails tapping against his chin. "He worked for me."

Stu's face turns cranberry red. "Doing what?"

"Odd jobs. Whatever I needed him for. One of many workers. This was some time ago."

"I need you to be more specific. What jobs?"

Stu wants this man to tell him more about his son. Any anecdote a gift, even the most brutal.

"Drugs mostly," The Hand says. "I'd send him to other towns."

"He was murdered two years ago."

The Hand shrugs.

"Was he working for you then?"

"I've farmed out my business to others. See, I was shot." His chicken foot reaches for his hair and rips off a toupee. Underneath, a hodgepodge of a skull clearly stitched back together like Frankenstein's monster. The Hand knocks against his skull, sound of metal pinging. "Got a plate in my head. Brain working slower. Hard to do everything I used to."

"Did Bobby make you angry. Did you turn on him?"

"Who?"

"Bobby Barlow, my goddamn son!"

The Hand shrugs again. Stu jumps to his feet, pressing the gun into The Hand's right temple.

"I will blow your fucking brains out all over this dirty cabin. No one will find you. No one will care."

"That is probably true."

"Please," Stu says, his voice hitting an octave that mimics The Hand's. "Please, is there anything you know about Bobby's death?"

"He'd talk back. A lot."

"Would he challenge you? Did you not appreciate that?"

"You are putting words in my mouth."

"Stop talking in riddles, you goddamn monstrosity. This was my baby boy, don't you see? And we have no idea why he was taken away from us."

"Did a lot of drugs too."

"Bobby?"

"Yessir. Took the drugs he was supposed to sell."

"Did you have him killed because of that?"

The Hand shrugs again.

"If you do that one more time." He thwacks The Hand across the face with the butt of the gun. The Hand licks blood from his cut lip, replies with red teeth.

"I have a plate in my head. It makes me forget what I am talking about sometimes. What were we discussing?"

"You son of a bitch. You're goddamn fucking with me."

"The water."

"What?"

"The water!" The Hand roars, his tiny chicken's foot indicating the pot that reaches maximum capacity and falls from the hot plate, crashing to the ground.

Stu takes his gaze off The Hand for a millisecond too long. The Hand charges, belly-flopping on top of Stu, banging the sheriff's head into the floor. Stu pokes the gun around The Hand's midsection and fires. The Hand's eyes bug and blood seeps from his mouth. Stu rolls the heavy body off him and gets to his feet. He aims the gun between The Hand's eyes.

"Did you kill my fucking kid?"

A bloody smile as a response. Stu fires the bullet, creating a third eye. No firm answers, possibly never a chance. But what did he really think he'd get from this beast of a man? Cold cases can exist for decades, eat at loved one's hearts like worms on the dead. That will be the tragedy of his life.

50

With Callie and Eli gone, Travis takes Grayson up on an offer to camp in the wilderness with Chinook tagging along. It's been a long time since they've been there and even hung out. Travis keeping his distance; Grayson doing the same. Friendships mutate as life becomes more complicated and childhood ones are usually the most fragile. They pack their gear along with a cooler of hot dogs and beers. Some hunting rifles too in case they get the itch. Marshmallows for s'mores.

In the summer, the wilderness has a different pull. Not threatening, no longer encapsulated in ice. Trees with leaves, the landscape shades of green. The animals out to play. Birds in from the winter, the sky a chorus. Travis and Grayson park near where they shot the caribou in the spring, set up their tents, and get to cracking beers.

"We got Molson Ice, Bud, and Natty," Grayson says, making a face at the last one. "You trying to kill us with battery acid?"

"Natty gets a bad a rep. And I'm trying to save some dough."

Grayson opens a Molson and flicks the foam to the dirt. "Don't I remember you finding a shit ton of gold recently?"

"The Goldmine's eating it up. Nearly all gone."

"A hundred grand!"

"More like eighty. And the bank's not giving a loan cause my credit history sucks."

"What're ya gonna do?"

"Torch the place. Collect some arson insurance. Hell if I know."

"Buddy, we can forget about it for the weekend."

"Cheers to that." Travis cracks a Natty Light and they clink cans. He lets Chinook lick his beer-laced finger.

"Last time we camped was with the wives, I think. I mean, you and

Callie and me and Lorinda."

"You over her yet?"

"I'm trying out this new philosophy. If something wasn't meant to be, then it wasn't meant for me."

"Poetry, Gray."

"There once was a girl from Nantucket…"

"Oh jeez, there's the Gray I know."

"I missed you, buddy. Don't mean to sound like a pussy or nothing. But I did. So there."

Grayson squeezes Travis's shoulder. The fire cooking between them. Night soon arrives and they break out the hot dogs, spearing them with a stick over the flames.

"So what's your boyfriend doing?" Grayson asks.

"My what? Dude, I don't wanna go into it about Wyatt."

Grayson puts his hands on his cheeks. "Oooh, do tell. What happened between you two?"

"He's not in a good state of mind."

"Dude, what did I tell you?"

"Save it, Gray. He's good, deep down. He's been through a lot. He lost his wife and kid. I don't know what happened exactly, he never fully went into it. But like, they're gone from his life. I can't imagine."

"Callie and Eli are gone right now. You're more alike than you think."

"Just gone for a few days. She'll come back. She gets pissed and it wears off."

"So what did the hobo do to get your knickers twisted?"

Travis tells Grayson everything, not to make Wyatt look bad but as an outlet. He hasn't really been able to express what he's feeling about Wyatt to anyone. Callie knew a little, but she liked to see the good in people, at least she used to, and would tell Travis to be patient with Wyatt and to remember they wouldn't have found the gold if not for him.

"He's a fucking nut," Grayson says, well adept at the art of being a dick. "Your great-great grandfather? Frozen in—*what?* His screws are loose."

"Sometimes we want to believe a thing so bad it becomes real."

"I didn't want to tell you this, man. Well, I did, but I was gonna save it. Anyway, I looked him up in the database. No record of a Wyatt Killian."

"That's not his last name."

"He told me—"

"He said it's Langford, but maybe it is Barlow."

"Do you actually believe that?"

"No. I dunno. He knew where the gold was, right?"

"Doesn't mean he's from the Gold Rush days."

"Well, why don't you look up Wyatt Barlow and see what that brings?"

"Even if that person exists, it don't mean it's him."

"That's true."

"Listen, Travis, I've been deputy for a good chunk of my life and you get these senses about people. Who are just not right. Who could snap. He gives off that vibe."

"He's never shown he could be dangerous."

"Really?" Grayson kills the Molson and pops open another. "Even Stu thinks so. That time at the hospital?"

"Emotions were running high and Stu was in the wrong."

"Stu's also said for you to watch out for him. Problem is, you don't listen to advice."

"Nope." Travis belches and opens another Natty. He stares at the sway of stars, a light show as their ceiling. "Callie's coming back, right?"

"What makes you even question?"

"She's never taken off like this before. But when it's good between us, it's real good. Right now, it's just not."

"I used to say the same about Lorinda."

"You two fought all the time."

"Yeah, we got off on that." Grayson shifts on the log he's sitting on and slips off. He rubs his ass with a laugh. "That smarts."

"At least one part of you is smart."

Grayson swings to hit Travis in the shoulder but misses. "She'll be back, man."

"What makes you so sure?"

"Because if you guys fail, then all relationships are doomed."

Travis clutches the cold can, takes a nervous sip. "I miss her. Eli too. What's the saying, 'Don't know what you got 'til it's gone'?"

"Yep, amen to that, brother. No one except Lorinda could stroke my balls just right."

Travis whaps Grayson on the head with his half-cooked hot dog on a stick. "You're a fucking nightmare."

"I'm your brother."

Travis bites his cheek. "Yeah, you're my brother, Gray."

"Love ya, knucklehead."

"Let's get some food in us before we throw up and leave a Goldilocks trail for bears."

They eat like animals, allowing their stomachs to stretch. The fullness comforting when Travis isn't feeling fully comforted. What it's like to be in a type of limbo. Travis hates this insecurity, the absence of a wife to spoon, a child to wake you up at the crack of morning.

"Don't fuck things up like I did," Grayson says, six beers in, rocking back and forth on the log.

"What was—*hic*—what was that?"

"With Callie. Don't treat her like I treated Lorinda. Treat her better than you'd treat yerself."

Travis gives an A-OK sign.

"I'm serious. You have a good thing goin', an enviable thing. Most would kill for what you have."

The word *kill* cutting through the midsummer night, echoed by the mighty birdsong.

51

To duplicate someone takes skill, and above all, dedication. Most importantly a need must exist, a reason to turn. In his new house, with his new clothes bought from gold riches, Wyatt stands before a tall mirror asking all the questions required for such a dramatic metamorphosis. But he's been shedding skin since he woke in the wilderness. This should be no different. From egg, breaking through the burden of amnesia, to hatching with a fully realized past. He clenches his fists, calloused and scarred, knuckles like knobs, these hands who chose to kill twice. All for the shine that's been his obsession.

"Have I descended so far that nothing else I do matters?"

He asks this to the floor, but really Hell remains the target. Not that he's ever believed its existence. But still, he fears. People are often frightened by the imaginary, the unknown.

And somewhere tucked in another pocket of his brain, another question lingers. The mystery of his eternal stay on this planet. The reason he was able to freeze for so long. Upon opening his one eye months ago, the answer was paramount above all else. Now that seems naïve. Enigmas are often unsolved. They give us focus, keep us questioning, even youthful. Answers are closure and that's not always what is best. For once we have no questions left, we might as well be dead.

Wyatt finds himself on 201 Elk Road lingering at the door. It's the weekend and only Callie's car is in the driveway, the pickup truck gone. If Trav had been home, Wyatt has no clue how the afternoon would shape. Better for Trav to have vanished for all their sakes. He spent the morning practicing Trav's gait. The way Trav's shoulders hunch forward when he walks, his voice that tends to mash words together like he's too lazy to separate them. That sometimes Trav lightly hums in the absence of speaking. All the quirks that come together to form a human.

He knocks on the door before he loses his nerve. Callie appears in a sweater too large for her frame. Her red hair in a clip. No makeup on, an appearance he prefers.

"Wyatt," she says, and gives a long yawn. "Travis isn't here."

"Oh yes," he replies. "I…I wanted to see how you were doing."

She scrunches her nose, holding onto the door, not yet welcoming him inside.

"I know you went to California, and I was curious how your trip went."

She rests her cheek against the doorframe. "Fine. Super jet lagged even though there's only an hour difference."

She laughs, but he has no idea what jet lagged means.

"I know Trav is running into difficulty with the restaurant. I was hoping we could speak about it?"

Callie glances at her watch, scrunches her nose again. "Eli's down for a nap. I was planning on taking my own."

"Won't be too much of your time."

"All right," she says, swinging the door open. "You plead a good case."

Upon entering, Chinook growls in the corner, fangs bared. Wyatt has never seen the dog behave this way, usually being so taciturn.

"I'm sorry," Callie says, corralling the dog by the collar. "'Nook, I'm gonna take you outside if you don't stop."

Chinook snaps at Wyatt, saliva dripping.

"Stop it!" Callie says, and leads the dog out the screen door before closing it. She returns, reenergized. "I have a pot of coffee brewing."

"That would be lovely."

She pours two mugs and they sit at the coffee table in the living room. Wyatt lets the steam tickle his nostrils, alerting his brain to what exactly he needs to say.

"I haven't seen much of Trav lately," he begins, hanging his head.

"I wouldn't take it personally. The Goldmine has eaten up all his time."

"No, not personally. Well, somewhat. See I believe I can help his woes."

Callie takes a deep sip from her mug. "How so?"

"I could invest in the place."

Her eyes widen. "Oh. Didn't expect that." Her tone shifts to a more singsongy lilt akin to Adalaide's.

"What did you expect?"

She smiles. "I can't say I know what to expect with you. You're an enigma." She lets her hair out of the clip, shakes it until it falls into place along her shoulders. Rubbing a sore in her neck appears to change her demeanor. "You know Travis and I aren't too much alike, but in some aspects we are. I won't be fine waiting tables my whole life. I had dreams too. I thought I was gonna be an actress. That it would be so easy. But it was horrible. Lecherous men in casting couches. Directors poking and prodding like I was cattle. There were so many girls like me. But I never really had drive. I did when I was acting in *Our Town* in high school. I left myself up on that stage, acted the shit out of Emily Webb. But when things weren't working out, I had zilch motivation. And I've accepted that. I never would have made it, just become a basket case. And Travis is the same. Because Travis has drive when things are working in his favor, not otherwise. And that's dangerous for a business. But did I say anything? No. Because it was found money, right? What would we do with it otherwise? A college fund for Eli? By the time he's old enough, eighty grand won't even cover dorm dues. Money appears out of nowhere, so you take a chance with it, right? But I'm losing my husband. The Goldmine has become an obsession. And you want to donate to this?"

"I want what is best for your family."

"See that's what puzzles me, Wyatt. Why?"

"Because you all have been so kind."

"Have we? You're the one that led him to the gold, what have we really done?"

"I assume he hasn't spoken to you about who I am."

"And who are you, Wyatt Langford?"

"For one, that's not my last name."

"It's not? So what is it?"

"Well—"

"Daddy?" asks a small voice. Eli pajama-footed and rubbing the sleep from his eyes. He flops over to them, hugging Wyatt's meaty leg.

"No, that's not Daddy," Callie says, coaxing Eli toward her.

Eli blinks a few times, the netherworld of sleep further and further away. His eyes brim with tears, sobbing into his mother's sleeve.

"We've been gone a few days and he hasn't seen Travis yet. Flew home this morning and the pickup was gone along with camping gear. Guessing he and Grayson are having a boys' weekend."

"Eli," Wyatt says, mimicking Trav's voice. The boy perks up his head and observes this strange man with a mix of curiosity and disdain. "Come sit on my lap."

"Wyatt, that's okay—" Callie begins to say, but Eli wobbles over and climbs onto Wyatt's knee. He begins bouncing the boy as the tears dry and a giggle erupts.

"No need for crying, Little Joe. Hush, hush now."

He sings the song, *"Too-ra-loo-ra-loo-ral,"* the same one Adalaide sung to calm Little Joe. Eli pops his thumb in his mouth and relaxes against Wyatt's chest.

"You're very good with children," Callie says. She seems eager to pull Eli away, uncomfortable with the situation, but also, mystified with how peaceful Eli's demeanor has shifted. Eli's tiny eyes shut. He's asleep again.

"Let me put him down," she whispers, taking back her child and carrying him into his bedroom.

Wyatt observes the room while she's gone. The kingdom he craves. They could be so happy, or at least a version of what he remembers as happiness, a slice of it, enough to soothe. When Callie returns, she tucks her hair behind her ears and sits across from him.

"How much are you willing to go in?" she asks, business-like.

"That's a conversation Trav and I would need to have."

"It'd be a godsend for us."

"That's why I would do it."

She sips again, staring into the black coffee as if it can foretell the future. "Your name, your real one that is…Are you running away from your past?"

"I'm running back toward it. Fast as I can. Head-first."

He longs to tell her that he can be everything Trav doesn't have it in him to be. Provider, protector, true lover, confidant. Everything that united him and Adalaide. Callie's not fulfilled with Trav, this crystal clear. She escaped to California, and yes, she returned, but not much will change between them. She just said they are nothing alike.

"So what's your last name?" she asks again.

Better to keep the enigma alive, even if for a little longer. Keep her guessing, more important to have her thinking about him than knowing every secret. He can be that itch that never ceases, the stirring in the night, so he speaks of himself as that *enigma*, and she smiles because it's now their inside joke, and there's something about him that keeps her attention. She's divulged her woes during lunch sessions. He knows some of her innermost feelings. There's danger in that knowledge, a palpable attraction, this version of Trav who's rougher around the edges and sweeter at the same time.

"Coffee was delicious," he says, rising. And she's flustered, face as red as her hair. She stands to say goodbye and he takes her hand and leaves a wet kiss atop, his bristling beard causing a nervous tickle.

It's been a month since Callie's made love to Travis, not since Papa Clifford died, and her loins are screaming. Let this mountain man Wyatt lie her down and do unspeakable things. He smells of the earth, deeply rich, aromatic in an all-consuming way. And he's ready for her too. The heat between them vibrating. But he leaves before a collision occurs, making his way to the door with the same gait as Travis, shoulders hunched, this mystery wrapped in a package so similar to the one she knows better than anyone else. She'd never repeat what she does next, even to her girl Lorinda, but after Wyatt leaves she slips into her bedroom and curls a finger into her underwear with her other hand clamped over her mouth so she won't wake Eli with her bucking moans.

52

Stu's long walk back to the Native American settlement is interminable. No closer to answers in Bobby's death than before. And even worse, no more clues—The Hand being a last hope. It's afternoon when he arrives, shell-shocked, as if returning from battle. A wounded warrior limping toward a bonfire. The usual teenagers gone. It's summer and they don't need its warmth. He lets the flames direct his thoughts, absorb his frustration. His face soiled with a layer of dirt and clean lines of tears dripping into his stubble.

An old man observes from his trailer. He saw Stu when he sat down for lunch, oftentimes watching the goings-on in the settlement, never one for television. After a nap later, he finds Stu still standing there cooking in the sun. The white man's face red from the fire. If he stays too much longer he'll start to boil and peel.

The old man feels his age every time he rises. His quivering knees first, a back that stings. Grasping his cane, he goes outside to retrieve the white man because he knows of his face. The sheriff who comes by to root out the evil in the settlement. The one who has never succeeded.

"Come," he tells the sheriff who blinks in response, seemingly unable to talk. He takes the sheriff by his elbow, leading him toward the trailer. Inside, the sheriff has to duck his head for the old man is short and the trailer's ceiling low. He sweeps the dust off a seat and sits the sheriff down. In his fridge, he finds a sliced egg in a cream sauce, slathers it across a grainy bread, and serves it to the sheriff who wolfs it down.

"Thank you," the sheriff says, rubbing his stomach.

"Qaletaqa," the old man says, pointing at himself with a finger twisted by rheumatism.

Stu wipes the crumbs onto his plate. "Stu."

Qaletaqa has lived alone for some time. A wife passed many years ago and he never had it in him to search for another, part of him dying with her. So he became an observer. The pain that travels through the settlement appears in various colors. He sees his neighbors in different hues, assesses how he can help. Those teenagers who sleep around the fire are bathed yellow. There is hope for them because they are so young. They can one day be freed from the spirit they ingest in the form of drugs. He'll perform smoke ceremonies in the back of his trailer, a room kept precisely for that. Filled with herbs and clay pots. He hasn't healed everyone who has entered, but at least he has tried.

"You are at an impasse," Qaletaqa tells Stu, who nods to this stranger. "Come," he says, directing Stu into his ceremonial room that smells of freshly cut grass.

Without explaining, Qaletaqa places herbs in clay pot to begin the smudging ritual. Smoke being a medium between the higher and lower realms, creating a good space for positive spirits and removing the negative ones. He mashes together sweet grass, tobacco, white sage, cedar, and his secret concoction. Each of the herbs a gift from the Creator. The leaves bound and placed in the clay pot. With a lit candle, he ignites the herbs, sweeping his hand across to extinguish any fire. Tendrils of smoke rise from the smolder. Cleansing himself first, he cups his hand and draws the smoke around him. Starting from the top, the smoke brought around his head, down his torso, all the way to his feet. His breathing slow and relaxed. With a feather, he wafts the smoke into the corners of the room, then focuses on Stu. He blows the smoke into the sheriff's eyes, his treasured eagle's feather directing it around the sheriff's body until he becomes encased.

Qaletaqa's room morphs from a hole-in-the-wall trailer to a plane on another realm. It appears to look the same, but Stu can tell he's traveled far. Qaletaqa's chanting like a bad phone connection filled with static. The old man dances around but is invisible, only present by the music spilling from his lips. Stu's son enters this plane too. Bobby with a beard that appears to have kept growing in the two years since he's been gone. It flows down his chest, sparkling. Stu goes to speak but his mouth stays closed; Bobby's as well. Yet they can communicate, minds in sync. Stu asks him how he died, his own life's burning question. And Bobby explains that it's a mystery because even he doesn't know. *But were you murdered?* Stu wonders into the universe, and the universe answers that one night Bobby's eyes were open and a second later they closed forever. Stu explains his two-year quest, his basement wallpapered with newspaper clippings, the man he just gunned down who won't be found for days and days, but nothing has brought him closer to the truth.

You cannot stop what is inevitable, Pop. Bobby hangs his head low. *Whether I was murdered or did myself in, it was always bound to happen.*

Stu wants to reach out and shake his son's image. *But if they killed you?*

Then they beat me to the punch. You can't save someone who is already dead.

Stu's bloodshot eyes narrow in response.

What will you gain from answers, Pop? If you're looking to alleviate your guilt, you shouldn't have any. You and Mom did all you could. You treated me with kindness more than I deserved. You allowed me to make mistakes to teach me a lesson. None of it worked. Some souls are doomed. It's the toss of the dice. I was a born with a mark. For some, the mark is poor health, an expiration hanging over their lives; my mark was a different type of sickness, an evil sprout. And I nurtured this bad seed, watered it often, watched it grow until it took over. I've done terrible things. Things it's best you don't know.

Stu chokes on a sob. *I failed to guide you correctly.*

If not for you and Mom, I would've gotten lost earlier. I would've destroyed more lives than I already did. You two, Travis, you all are better without me. I would've only dragged you further into the pits of hell.

Stu stares at his palm, the crisscrossing lines that change in lengths, showing him a variant future, then reform back to their original map.

I saw what you did to The Hand.

Stu looks up from his own hand into Bobby's face, absorbing every millisecond of this final reunion.

Whether or not he was responsible for my death, he caused many others. Whether or not he would cause any others, he deserves to be no more. The universe has decided this. I helped you destroy him because you never would've been led to that cabin otherwise. This I can swear to you.

Qaletaqa's chanting gets louder, less staticky.

So it's time for you to leave with peace in your heart. If you don't, then this is the end for you, for Mom. What you are carrying around will be the albatross that sinks you both. But that's not what the universe envisions. There is a window at my side and through it I see you returning to Mom, and she's worried because you've been gone all night and day, and even though you do this sometimes, she worries and doesn't sleep. So you can't do this no more, ya hear? But I see you go to her and show her your basement; she hasn't opened that door since I died because it used to be my room when I got older and came and went. It was easier to have me home but out of the way. For all of us. And I see you show her the last two years of your life and together you take down those newspapers along with every last shred of paper you scribbled on. You'll burn that pain away and emerge healed. You'll take her on a vacation, you'll enjoy your twilight years. You'll remember the good times we shared, though they were few, but that's what you'll allow to remain. And now I say goodbye.

It's nighttime when Stu gets back in his car, finding the keys under the sun visor. Windows down, cool breeze thickening his hair, he drives home to the woman he loves. He finds her knitting by the television watching an old episode of *Perfect Strangers*, but she's not laughing because she's worried and she's been worried about her husband ever since she lost her son. He can tell she's been upset because he hasn't called and that's a rule between them, to always call. She made dinner and had eaten hers and left his plate in a cold oven to warm when he got back home, like she always does. There are flecks of blood on his shirt, his hair smells of smoke, and he hasn't bathed since he left.

"I can run you a shower," she says, because it's better to face him once he's cleaned up. But he takes her down into the basement instead. He knows she's nervous, not having been there for months. She's let Stu have his carved-out space. A tiny lamp on his desk beams a cone of light across the wallpaper headlines. It's like a hit to her stomach, she has to kneel. Her cheeks puff and he can tell that because she's nauseous, but he says it's time and begins removing the wallpaper, throwing it in a trash bin along with the journals and the scribblings of a madman who lost his son. They fill three trash bins. Each one he brings up to the backyard and won't let her help. She waits in the yard holding back tears. When he comes up with the last trash bin, he carries a can of gasoline too. He dumps the gasoline over the trash and lights two matches, one for each of them. He tells her he's not ready to retire but he's ready to retire from this. She says, "Good." And then they toss their matches and watch the flames eat up the last remnants of the horror they'd faced. He holds her close and they cry together, for one last time. He understands they'll be sad again because they've been unlucky, but it doesn't need to define them anymore. They don't have to be the parents of Bobby who died too soon. They can be Stu and Cora again, who enjoy bird-watching, hikes, old country music, waking before sunrise, and when Alaska shimmers at its coldest and most silent, so quiet at breakfast that you can hear the turning of a newspaper page, to a headline with good news because the world isn't always unfair.

People can drift far away from themselves but eventually tether again.

53

Wyatt doesn't trust Grayson as he spies the deputy's car pulling up to his front yard. The two alike, since Wyatt bets that Grayson doesn't trust him either. Walking to the house, Grayson knocks the dirt from his boots, rotates his hat in his hands, and spit-licks a pestering curl sticking up. Wyatt grabs Tohopka's dog tags that sit in a bowl in the foyer. Just as Grayson's about to knock, Wyatt swings open the door keeping the deputy on his toes.

"Was headed out," Wyatt says, pointing in the distance.

Grayson attempts to step inside. "Like to ask you a few questions if you don't mind?"

"Ain't there something called a warrant?"

"Really? That's how you want to play?"

Wyatt crosses his meaty arms. "What's this regarding?"

"If you'd let me in—"

Wyatt snorts. "I cleaned. Place is sparkling. Don't want you mucking it up. How about a drive instead? You can drop me off in town."

Before Grayson can argue, Wyatt's bounding toward the deputy's car.

"On second thought, show me some of the outskirts," Wyatt says from the front seat, as Grayson goes to get on a larger road into town.

"I'm not your personal driver."

"Coulda fooled me," Wyatt says, slipping on a pair of gloves.

"You cold?" Grayson asks.

"Always," Wyatt replies, without missing a beat.

So Grayson banks a left and the car skids past the turnoff. Only miles of woods instead. They weave through paths barely big enough for the car to fit. Grayson agrees because he plans on utilizing some shady police tactics. This man was never who he said he was. And he won't let Wyatt out of this car until the mystery gets solved. He parks so the men can face each other, takes out his gun.

"What is this?" Wyatt asks.

"A truth session. Meaning I let you go if I'm satisfied with your answers."

"How do you believe I've been deceptive?" Wyatt asks, winking. Grayson hates that wink.

"For one, there is no record of a Wyatt Killian in our database."

"Doesn't mean nothin'."

"It means you haven't been honest!"

The aggression Grayson's felt since Lorinda left leading him to dark places. He has a boxing bag in his basement that he pounds with fury each night. He's imagined Wyatt in place of this bag.

"Let me see your driver's license," Grayson says, snapping his fingers.

"Don't have one," he says.

"Fine. An ID. Gimme your wallet."

"Don't carry one."

"Tried another name," Grayson says, mopping his brow with the hand not holding the gun. "Wyatt Langford, which you told the Barlows. No record of him either."

"I don't appreciate that gun pointed at me."

"And then a final name, Wyatt Barlow. And you know what came up? Born in Washington 1860, no record of death. This is the guy whose identity you've stolen. The Barlows' ancestor."

"It's my identity," Wyatt thunders.

"You're nuttier than I even thought. That would make you one hundred and sixty years old."

"Time doesn't work like you think it does for me. I was suspended—"

"What the fuck you mean, suspended?"

"In ice. I've told this to Trav. I've come clean. He *is* my great-great grandson—"

Grayson responds by hitting Wyatt in the forehead with the butt of gun. A trickle of blood slicks down Wyatt's nose.

"Travis doesn't need a bullshit scam artist like you in his life right now. He's got a business to open, family that needs him. You're a dead weight."

"I'm a better friend than you have ever been."

Grayson goes to hit Wyatt again, expecting Wyatt to throw up his hands in defense. But Wyatt stays stoic.

"Travis is like a fucking brother," Grayson says. "We go back to the schoolyard."

"But I've given him gold. I've changed his life."

"He's blind to a con man like you. And I see the way you've looked at Callie. You've wanted a piece of that."

"With the way you've treated women, you don't have the right to cast stones at me."

"I was good to Lorinda," Grayson wails.

"Tell that to the girls at Raye's."

Grayson punches Wyatt in the jaw, feeling the crunch of teeth. Wyatt responds with laughter. Grayson knows the only power he has is if he kills Wyatt. He could make up some excuse and bring Wyatt in for questioning, but nothing would stick.

"You may have loosened a molar."

"Good." Grayson reaches in his pocket and passes over a handkerchief. He's a good man overall. Always had a wandering eye, but never abused his police privileges. And yeah, he drinks too much. You try living in a frozen world where people hibernate like bears for most of the year. Find someone who's not a drinker in this town and he'll give them a prize.

He watches Wyatt mop up the blood from his gums and wedge the handkerchief in his pocket. In its place, Wyatt removes the dog tags.

"What are those?"

They sit in Wyatt's palm, the letters too small to read from where Grayson sits.

"Were you in the military?"

Wyatt gives a solemn nod. He shakes his palm, indicating for Grayson to take the tags. Grayson picks them up with his free hand, still directing the gun at Wyatt but with less precision, for his eyes stay glued to the tags that will finally reveal this man's true identity.

"To-hop-ka Oxendine?" Grayson asks.

"That's not me either."

Wyatt lunges, grabbing Grayson by the throat. He squeezes tight enough for Grayson to gag. Grayson flaps his arms wildly attempting to direct the gun closer to Wyatt. A shot rings out shattering the window, but Wyatt doesn't relent.

The gun goes off a second time, the bullet puncturing the ceiling.

Wyatt digs his knee into Grayson's stomach until Grayson can feel the contents of what he digested roiling. He spits up vomit that spews through his teeth. Wyatt squeezes his neck even tighter, digging fingernails into flesh through thin gloves.

"This is who I am," Wyatt declares.

Grayson's eyes bugging. He had seen the devil from the start in this man but didn't take the threat as seriously as he should've. None of them will.

His body goes slack, twitching as it clings to the last bit of life. A layer of film covers Grayson's eyes, his murderer nothing more than a phantom blur. He doesn't have a flash of all the great moments from his existence. Death doesn't allow this pleasure. It only brings forth excruciating pain and it's hard to focus on anything else. The gun slips from his fingers, bouncing around the floor. His last hope hiding under the seat. In the brutal haze, he visualizes Wyatt leaving his human form. Turning into a wolf, primed only for survival. No other instinct allowed. Grayson's body stops twitching, his soul detaching.

Wyatt climbs off, dipping the dog tags in Grayson's blood, and leaving them by the seatbelt for the police to find. The car remains running so someone might locate this terror even sooner. But he will be far gone, satisfied by destroying two of his enemies with one solid blow.

54

Lorinda has gotten used to Grayson phoning her every day around the time she'd close up Pizza Joint, so when three days pass without a word, she thinks it weird. Granted, she hasn't answered his calls since she kicked him out but can't help worrying about him. On the fourth day, she mentions it to Callie, who's been taking some time off after getting back from California. Callie explains that Travis and Grayson went camping for the weekend, but Travis already came home. So she calls the police station where the receptionist says that Grayson took off to go camping but hasn't returned or gotten in touch. The sheriff gave him a day pass, figuring maybe he'd gotten sick, or was sleeping off a weekend hangover.

By the fourth day, Stu is concerned as well and heads over to Grayson's to see what's going on.

Stu hopes he's wrong about Grayson's proclivities, but no one answers the door. He's ready to ream the lug nut for being such a fuck up. It scares him that the lights are off and two days' worth of newspapers have piled up on the doorstep. Meaning Grayson returned to pick up the weekend edition but hasn't been back since. His deputy's wagon isn't parked either, indicating Grayson hasn't set off on foot. Easier to find a car than a missing man anyway.

He puts out an APB for the plates.

Another day passes before it's called in. Two hunters had been out in the woods past Main Bluff and smelled car exhaust. Approaching the car, they found the engine killed and the dead body of Grayson Hucks. Stu first thinks it's suicide by carbon monoxide. Grayson had been depressed as of late, especially after being dumped by Lorinda. He drank too much and one night could've decided on this terrible fate. Stu brings his deputies Cole and Bickley to the site where it's clear from the marks on his neck that Grayson had been strangled. They call in the crime scene investigators who discover that two bullets had been shot from Grayson's gun into the window and the ceiling. There's blood on the seat from the scuffle, but no major arteries had been hit. Dipped in the blood is a pair of dog tags belonging to Tohopka Oxendine.

Stu's knees go weak when he hears this. Over the past two years, Stu mentioned his private investigation into his son's death even when the rest of the local police gave up. It'd been deemed a drowning early on, no sign of foul play. Yet Grayson was always supportive and listened about the underbelly in Laner that had hooked Bobby. Stu even spoke about the Native American settlement he'd visit frequently for clues. He can't remember if he'd brought up Tohopka by name, causing Grayson to decide on his own type of vigilante justice.

He goes back to the settlement to bring in Tohopka's cousin Aylen for questioning. Wyatt isn't there, which makes it easier for her to comply. They spend hours grilling her about Tohopka's whereabouts. He's unsure how innocent she may be, but unless she's a spectacular actress, she seems to know nothing about his dealings. Toward the end, a thought pops in her head and she mentions the town of Elwer, where Tohopka used to go to score meth. She assumes he would want to get away from the immediate area and Elwer is about an hour and a half up north. A tiny town with a motel that was a stop before the oil port of Valdez. Stu figures it's as good a shot as any to try.

He waits to tell Travis the news. Better to have the perpetrator behind bars first. He can't take both Cole and Bickley, since that would leave Laner with zero police force manning the town, so he chooses Bickley because he's a year Cole's senior. Bickley drives while Stu asks for complete silence until they reach Elwer. He thinks of the years spent with Grayson as his deputy. Bickley would take Grayson's place and do a fine job, but Stu doesn't have the history with Bickley like he did with Grayson. He'd watched the boy grow up. Grayson came from a tough home. A dad who drank himself to death early on. A mother that did whatever possible to scrape by. Grayson lost his mother to cancer a few years back, so at least Stu wouldn't be left with the unfortunate job of breaking the news that her son had been killed. He's not ready to watch someone's face as he'd destroy their life like that. And while Grayson was far from perfect at his job, he was loyal and he tried. He would be missed.

Elwer makes Laner look like a bustling metropolis. A literal one-stop-light kind of town where only the yellow and green lights work. Almost telling whoever is driving to *not* stop here. The only motel has a diner connected on the ground floor where they find a few oil workers who stopped for a bite on the way to Valdez. The cook takes their orders and they ask if he'd seen a Native American man, twenty-five years old, lean build, possibly on drugs. The cook says someone like that was staying at the motel all week, so they tell him to keep their meals warm while they inquire.

At the Elwer Motel, a pleasant woman mans the desk and hands over the keys to the room where Tohopka stays. She says she hasn't seen him leave for days and he'd refused maid service. She says the maid described a weird odor coming from there but eventually it went away, so she didn't bother to investigate.

The room is at the end of the second-floor balcony. The blinds shut but they can hear a rustling inside. Stu indicates for Bickley to hug the rim of the balcony in case Tohopka shoots out when Stu enters. Bickley gets his gun ready. As quietly as possible, Stu puts the key in the hole and turns. The lock opens and Stu catches a glimpse of a tweaked-out Tohopka naked and yelling before he raises his own gun and Tohopka crashes through the front window. Bickley fires once and misses.

Tohopka leaps to his feet, body cut up from the glass, and runs toward the edge of the balcony. Bickley fires and the bullet catches Tohopka clear in the back, spinning him over the railing where he falls head-first twenty feet below. His skull cracks open upon impact while Bickley and Stu run down the stairs and hover around the corpse.

"Ah shit," Stu says. The plan had been to take the sumbitch in alive. Bickley apologizes over and over, the kid practically crying, but Stu tells him it's okay. This was as open-and-shut a case as they come. Grayson had likely picked the perpetrator up and Tohopka had snapped. Maybe he couldn't cut it running for the rest of his life. Maybe he wanted to end it in a way that wouldn't lock him up for good. It's not a case to lose sleep over. The son of a bitch had taken away a man Stu considered like a son, so he hocks up a good hunk of phlegm and spits it on Tohopka's brutalized face. Then they go and have the lunch that the cook kept warm, a country-fried chopped beef steak in gravy with two eggs, hash browns, a side of reindeer sausage, and two tall beers, before they called into the station with the details.

55

Aylen's spent the last couple of weeks getting her life in order. She sold the trailer since there's no highway system to make it possible to drive straight to California. Only way out of Laner is flying from Nome, and she's tired of living in a trailer anyway. Her whole life fits in a suitcase, which actually makes her kind of proud. She says goodbye to Raye, who's been like a mother, and to all the girls who have been like sisters. They all tell her she has a place if she ever decides to come back, but she knows she'll never return.

The police stopped questioning her shortly after Tohopka died. She reacted more strongly than she would've thought. When they were children, Tohopka was like a brother. They would wander the settlement catching critters. Tohopka grew up without parents as well, similarly raised by whoever felt like it. They had a bond that even in his brutality was hard to deny. He's the last link to her past and, now that he's dead, it's time to sever the rest.

She packs up her small loom in a separate bag from her clothes and mementos. She's flying to San Diego where she hears it's forever seventy-three degrees. She wants to make blankets and throw rugs, intricate quilts with Tlingit designs. She will be leaving her past but not where she came from. Proud of her heritage, she will use it to help her succeed. With a ticket in hand for an afternoon flight, she drives her piece of shit car to Wyatt's place for one last goodbye before she drops it off at the lot to turn into spare parts.

Wyatt attempts to get rest whenever he can, since he hasn't been sleeping. The most he can do is nod off for a moment of peace. There's an element of guilt. He didn't like Grayson but can't say the man entirely deserved to die. He wonders if anyone does. Did Carl Finnegan Langford? Or Frank? Soapy and his men? Or even Wyatt himself? He certainly didn't deserve to freeze and lose his family, so why should he feel upset over anyone else's fate?

To make use of the long nights, he spends the hours mimicking Trav. Getting the pitch of his voice perfect. He's got the man's walk down pat. He's ready to no longer be himself anymore, slip into another's shoes. Maybe that will stop the madness.

The doorbell rings. A curious sound since no one has ever rung it before. An element of fear makes his hairs stand on end. That somehow the police traced Grayson's death back to him. He had pinned it all on Tohopka, but did he make a mistake at some point? He's relieved when he opens the door to Aylen.

She looks beautiful as usual, but lighter than normal, like a weight has been lifted. Her long hair is parted down the middle. She wears old jeans and a heavy purple fleece. Even in the summer, Laner barely hits over fifty-something degrees. Been some time since he's seen her, too preoccupied. Or maybe he felt they had said all they needed to each other and it was best to let things end.

"Can I come in?" she asks.

He sweeps his arm out. "Of course."

She observes his place like it confuses her.

"It came furnished," he says, cracking his fingers. "Easier."

She picks up a large shell on the mantle and listens to the roll of the ocean.

"I'm leaving," she says.

He motions to her suitcase. "I figured."

"With what Tohopka did to the deputy. It's a glaring sign for me to go."

"I'm sorry about your cousin."

"I'm not. Well, that's not true. I'm sorry his life took a turn. He should've had a better one."

"Shouldn't we all?"

She narrows her eyes. "I'm going to California. San Diego. Trading these fleeces for tank tops."

"What will you do for work?"

"Not what I've been doing. I want to weave, make things. Feel good about myself."

"Where will you live?"

"I have a little saved. But maybe sleep on the beach until I have enough for a place."

"Hold on."

He goes to the fireplace where he removes a box tucked behind the logs. He hands it to her. "It's money."

"Why are you giving me this?"

"It's twenty thousand."

"No, Wyatt. I don't want to be—"

"What?"

"Beholden."

"Think of it as a payment for what you did for me."

"I'm trying to get out of that racket."

"Not for sleeping together! More like how you uplifted me. I was frozen on the streets when you took me in, remember?"

She fingers the money. "I can't fly with more than ten thousand."

"So put the rest in the bank."

"It's too much."

"I don't want you sleeping on a beach. I want you with a roof over your head. Go on, it's done. The money's yours."

She holds a stack of bills close to her chest. "Thank you."

"You could teach me how to drive in return."

"Drive?"

"Yes, I believe it is something I should know how to do."

They go outside and get in her car, Wyatt behind the wheel. She shows him how to turn on the ignition, drive forward, back up, signal for a turn, check his blind spots, make a U-turn. He adapts quickly, having watched Trav. When they finish, she follows him back inside, standing by the box of bills like she's afraid he might change his mind.

"I don't wanna worry about you is all," he says, and she lets out a heavy exhale.

"I'm more worried about you."

He catches his reflection in the mirror. Tries to smile through but it's difficult.

"You don't look well," she says.

"Haven't been sleeping much."

"You don't look like yourself."

"Who am I anyway? I'm a mixture of some of the past, some of this new present. It ain't a fully realized person. Bits and pieces, you know?"

"That doesn't have to be the case."

"Will you do one more thing for me?" he asks, and disappears into the bathroom. He returns with scissors and an electric shaver. "I wanna lose the beard."

"I'm not sure I'm ready to really see your face."

"I'm not sure I am either." A smile pokes out of his beard. "So see, I don't know how to use this machine thingy. They sold it to me and there are directions."

She takes it out of the box and directs him into the bathroom. Sits him on the toilet.

"Are you ready?" she asks, holding the scissors.

He nods and she cuts a big chunk of beard, capturing it in her fist. A hundred some-odd years of growth, a part of his history. She lets it fall to the floor where it looks like a dead animal. She runs a towel under hot water and pats his face. Then she plugs in the electric shaver and glides it down his cheeks, across his chin, up his neck, until only a fine layer of stubble remains. She dabs another towel under cold water to close his pores. Standing up, she plants him in front of the mirror in the medicine cabinet. He rubs his jawline, mesmerized by the smooth feel. Trav looks back at him, more of an identical twin than ever before.

"Not such a bad mug," she says, sweeping the discarded hair into a garbage bin. She leaves him to take in his new visage. After a while, he joins her outside on the couch where she fingers her new money.

"This is really amazing of you to do for me, Wyatt."

He waves it away like it's nothing.

"I want you to promise me something, though," she says. "Can you be happy finally?"

"I have a plan in mind."

She looks at him crossly. "What does that entail?"

He stares at his palms, lost in the cracks. "I aim to get a new family."

"Well, good." She takes a deep breath, maybe expecting the worst. "I think that's good. But there's not much chance for dating around here. Maybe you should think of moving to a bigger town?"

"No, what I want is right here."

"Your friend's family?"

He gives a solemn nod.

"But they're not yours, Wyatt."

"Who says?"

"Think of how you would've felt if someone came along and took your wife and son away?"

"But they *were* taken—"

"Not like this. He's your friend. And besides, do you know if she even wants that?"

"He's not my friend. He's my…Anyway, I can tell it's meant to be."

"How?"

"Smell her despair. Her need for something different. For me."

"Be careful is all. Sounds like a disaster waiting to happen."

"Or it can be the greatest decision I'll ever make in my life."

She closes the box with her new money, ready to go. "I don't believe it's all your decision."

A shadow haunts the room, darkens Wyatt's face as he adds: "It is my decision." Goose pimples spring up Aylen's arms.

She wonders if she should stay, talk him out of this nonsense, but he's stubborn like her. That's the most they had in common. No one could tell her not to move and leave behind everything she knows. Just like no one will ever come between him and what he desires.

"Okay," she says, because it's getting late and if she wants to hit the bank before her flight she must go.

They say goodbye like business partners, a shake of the hand. There was never really love between them. Sometimes a guide can fall into your life who can mean more than a love. And she'll think of him occasionally, this she swears. The twenty thousand becoming a huge factor in starting her business.

She'll be able to work from her home office, a little studio apartment in Escondido, crime-ridden but nothing she can't handle. And without worrying about putting food on the table, she can focus on her weaving. Selling her wares on the beaches to locals and tourists, catching the eye of a woman who owns a boutique in La Jolla who buys a few blankets that sell out immediately, who soon devotes an entire section of her store to the intricate designs of Aylen Oxendine, who eventually finds a boyfriend, a sweet man twice her age that owns a septic tank business, and treats her well, and one day she'll get pregnant, and he'll marry her while her belly's swelling, and they'll have a small wedding with mostly his family and friends, and when he asks her what to call the baby, she'll say the name Wyatt because she hasn't thought about him in a while, and much like dreams, sometimes we dream about those we have forgotten, our mind's last chance at remembering. Her husband loves this name, and before she can tell him no, it's decided. But she's okay with this. For without Wyatt, she never would've been able to start her business and probably wouldn't have met her husband. She had never tried to contact Wyatt, or vice-versa, but she hopes he found happiness. Whether with the family he craved, or through some other means. But deep down, she's aware that won't happen. She left his house that day knowing chaos would remain. People would get hurt, that's guaranteed. But she had to go. She couldn't take on anyone else's troubles or she'd never be able to flee.

So when she thinks of him, she envisions this other Wyatt, who's able to be with a family he loves. Even though that's likely not the truth, it's enough to keep her moving forward.

56

Travis's been on a bender for a while now. Started drinking before the funeral. Didn't handle Bobby's death this bad, but Grayson was always his brother, the one he chose. Travis never imagined life without him, uncle to Eli, hunting and fishing trips in the wilderness into their eighties. Papa's death hard but understandable, easy to reckon. Grayson ripped away too early. The unfairness, the wasted potential. Travis carried all of this, even in sleep.

First, he honed his anger on the murderer. He went down to the settlement ready to burn Tohopka's trailer. Stood there with a can of gasoline, but he was never really gonna do it. Then he became pissed at Grayson for getting involved in something he shouldn't have. The settlement not in Laner's jurisdiction. It basically had its own. Wild and untamed, meant to be left alone. Bobby made that mistake too.

Alcohol fueled Travis's anger but he wanted to rage. And to avoid taking it out on Callie and Eli, it was better to stay at The Goldmine: dodging nails from the floorboards, the half-painted walls, and the so-so plumbing. The bar had been put in, all he really needed.

It's the state Wyatt found him. Travis so drunk he questions if he's talking to himself, because they look so much alike.

"Are you my fuckin' better version?" Travis asks, when it walks in the door.

Wyatt had been by the Barlows' house after Grayson died to pay his respects. He asked to use the "in-house," and went through the hamper and stole a shirt, jeans, socks, even Trav's boxers. To become this man, he had to smell like him. Live in his skin.

He leaves Trav stinking drunk, yanking him over to the mattress on the floor, a bucket for his puke. Outside he strips down and discards his own clothes, naked blue in the moonlight. He lets the wind dress him in the clothes of another. Once they're on, he has transformed. He knows how to transform because he's done it before, many times. His thoughts now belong to a new version. Travis 2.0. He'd been thrust into a world of machines. And he is a machine as well. Engineered to survive over a hundred years of stasis. Someone created this force for a reason. But he has many lifetimes to discover why. This will be his last chance to be with Adalaide and Little Joe.

Going lupine, he charges to the Barlows'. The moon lighting a crescent pathway. Howls from his throat like earthquakes through the woods. He'd seen them leave a key in a flowerpot by the door. He unlocks it and goes inside. It doesn't smell like his home, but it smells like *a* home. That will have to be enough. The boy is asleep and she's in the bedroom angling toward the window, her back to the door, a thin moonbeam across her face. She sees him in the reflection.

"Travis?"

His nerves are fried, worrying she might know he's an imposter. But there's a half-full bottle of vodka on the night table.

"What are you doing here?"

"I wanted to come home." He takes a breath, speaks from the heart, as if it's Adalaide. That's how he will win her. "Because I've been away for too long. Because you and Eli deserve better. And I've learned how to be better. There's nothing I want more than the two of you, not gold, or I mean, some fish shack. I needed to get over what happened, and I'm getting there. It ain't easy, hell, it might never be easy—"

She's crying. "He was your best friend Travis."

And I killed him, like the other two. Because I had no other choice. The last one a roadblock to you.

"Baby," she says, and they're hugging, and she smells like lilac, like Adalaide. Or maybe she doesn't, but it feels so real the lilac aroma surfaces. She's kissing his neck, his inner ear, their lips touch and he wonders if she knows now, if she even cares. Maybe he's close enough to what she desires. Maybe he's actually what she's desired all along.

"Take whatever time you need," she says, pulling off his shirt, biting down on a nipple. "Eli and I are okay. If you wanna stay at The Goldmine for a while till you get your head together. I want us back when it's right."

Wyatt holds her face in his hands, her red hair cascading through his fingers. "That's just what I want too."

"I love you," she says. "I've only loved you, no one else ever counted."

"No one."

She removes her bra, slides down his pants with her foot.

"You're so hard."

The blood swelling. Once inside her, he has an out-of-body experience. Watching from above all through the night. They make love again and again. She does things he has never experienced before, the 1890s being a prudish time in comparison to Callie's prowess. But he has the stamina to keep up.

She calls out *Travis* over and over. There are moments when it sounds like she's asking for the real Travis to return, scolding his replacement. Other inflections seem like she's encouraging this new snake. After they've exhausted themselves, it's almost morning, the room bathed in a purple twinkle. She's lying on his chest playing with a tuft of hair. Studying the hair as if there's something strange about it, different than the hair she remembers. But they hadn't been intimate in over a month so maybe she figures that chest hair just grows. When he sees this, he moves her hand away. Always on alert of her becoming aware. One day he will tell her. When they are old and gray, or at least before she grows elderly and dies and he simply freezes again until another time, passing through eras in fits and spurts.

He kisses those probing fingers, which probe farther down, but then Eli bursts into the bedroom, excited to see his father because Travis hasn't been home in the mornings since Grayson's death. The boy leaps into bed and snuggles between his parents. He's hugging Wyatt extra tightly. But then he lets go. He looks up, concerned, cocking his head to the side. He pokes Wyatt in the arm, whips his finger back like the arm was made of razorblades. He scooches out of bed, flip-flopping away but staring down this curious stranger, the one who shares a bed with his mom, the one who's primed to take over.

57

The next morning Travis wakes without the need to obliterate himself into a drunken numbness. He collects all the half-empty bottles and leaves them on the curb in a Hefty bag. He spends the day painting the walls, satisfied with the ocean-blue he's chosen. The place still a mess of exposed wires and torn-up floorboards, but with each passing day he can make a dent, keep himself occupied. He stops by Stu and Cora's to check on them, not having seen anyone since the funeral. They've left messages but Stu understands his son needed space, even if Cora's a little hurt. She pours black coffee for them and they sit around the breakfast table in the kitchen. Stu took a few days off after Grayson's death. He promoted Bickley to deputy and they're in the process of hiring a new officer. Despite dealing with the loss of Grayson, Stu seems less rigid, like he's accepted that sometimes life can be awful rather than fighting it. Travis's mother and father sit holding hands, and the way they glance at each other makes him realize that things will eventually be okay. He'll never get his best friend back, but he'll always have family.

"So why have you been staying at the restaurant?" Cora asks.

"Wanted some time to myself."

Stu nods as if that's a completely acceptable reaction.

"And you and Callie?" Cora asks, stirring cream into her coffee. "I know she went to California."

"We've had some bumps. But we'll be okay. I think."

"Oh, sweetie," Cora says, holding onto Travis's hand too. The three of them joined in unison like they're about to say a prayer.

He drives back home afterwards, Cora insisting he takes a rhubarb pie she baked. He's nervous on the way over because he hasn't really seen Callie since she's been back. Things didn't end well, and with all the stuff related to Grayson, there was no chance to have a talk. They spoke on the phone some. He checked in on Eli. The toilet overflowed and in a drunken haze he managed to tell her to get a snake. She had returned from California, a good sign. The question remains whether she's come back for good.

He parks the car, greeted by a tackling Chinook who licks his face once he steps outside. He rolls around on the ground with the dog until Callie opens the door, catching them in mid-wrestle.

"I thought I heard you," she says, with a smile he can't quite read. Excited to see him? Or gearing up before she explodes? He tickles Chinook under the ears and heads in.

"Eli's down for a nap," she says.

She's about to vanish into the kitchen. He grabs her by the arm, spins her around.

"Travis..."

"I missed you."

He kisses her like he did on their wedding, as if a hundred people are watching. It's been about a month since they've kissed more than a peck on the cheek, and he longs for the way her lips allow him to forget his woes.

They're hugging and he continues kissing her neck. She's giggling like a girl as he reaches under her shirt.

"Travis, we can't now. Eli could wake—"

"No," he says, pulling away. "We should talk. We've got some stuff to get through."

He paces the length of the living room.

"I know I shouldn't have left the two of you and stayed at The Goldmine, but I..." The tears come hard, his face swelling. He tries to keep his voice down to not wake Eli. "I had to process what happened alone."

"I told you it was okay. You could stay there as long as you wanted. Eli and I, we're fine. Really. I can't imagine how you're feeling."

"It's like I've been gutted."

"Grayson was...for all his faults he cared about you a lot, about our family. I miss him a lot too."

"I haven't treated you right."

"Now, Travis—"

"No, hear me out, baby. Because I've taken you and Eli for granted. You had every right to escape to California. Every right to leave me even!"

"I'm not leaving you, Travis."

"I took you away from your family and friends. You gave up your whole life to come and live with me in Alaska."

"Wrong, I wanted to. L.A. is a cesspool. There's not a real person there. Not my parents, my old friends. They're all just treading water."

"And with the business, I'm not gonna let it affect me like I had. So we'll be in debt. It's only money. I'll find ways to get it."

"Did Wyatt talk to you?"

"Wyatt?"

Wyatt had been the furthest thing from his mind. A relief to have him gone.

"He wants to invest in your business with some of the money he got from the gold."

"When did he tell you this?"

"When you and Gray were camping, I guess. He stopped by. He'd like to see you succeed."

"How much does he wanna invest?"

"You'll have to talk with him about that."

Travis blows out a long breath. "Would help out a lot."

"See? Just like you said. Nothing for us to worry about."

She rubs her stomach, her face twisting.

"You okay, baby?"

"Stomach's been off these last few days. Must be something I ate."

"Should you see a doctor?"

"No, no, think it's food poisoning. It'll pass."

"Why don't you lie down? Lemme get you a cold compress."

"Travis, really…"

"Nope," he says, rushing into the kitchen and running a towel under cold water. He directs her to their bedroom, lying her down in the warm afternoon light. Dabbing the towel on her forehead.

"Let me take care of Eli these next few days, give you a rest."

"Mm hmm, okay."

"Are we good?"

She gives a hard swallow. "Yes, we will be."

"I'm gonna be more present. This is a new Travis."

"What's that?"

"A new Travis."

A smile trickles up the side of her face. "Like you were the other night."

"Huh?"

"The other night." She closes her eyes. "You wild man."

"I don't know what you mean."

"Sure you don't."

"Maybe you should get some rest, Cal."

"I love you, Bear."

It's what she used to call him when they first met because he was so rock solid and massive and built like a bear. She'd say she'd feel tiny in his arms, protected like she was his cub. That's when they were young and foolish. When life was easy.

"I love you too, Cub."

He kisses her nose and a few freckles along her cheeks. She shuts her eyes and soon they're fluttering and she falls deep into sleep. He sits beside her feeling more love for this woman than he ever has. Perfection with her hands folded over her chest, quiet in slumber. A moment of unadulterated happiness as he creeps to the door, not wanting to disturb their bubble.

The upset stomachs continue for Callie, especially in the mornings, so she picks up a pregnancy test. It's been almost two weeks since she and Travis had their wild night, enough time to fertilize a baby. She'd missed her period and the other symptoms mimicked how she was with Eli. She doesn't tell Travis she's taking the test. If there's no news then she won't say anything. They'd been getting along and falling back into a rhythm. He's been so sweet and seems to be making headway at The Goldmine. There was even a day she spent in bed when he took off work to watch Eli, and all afternoon she could hear Eli's high-pitched laugh, pleased to be back with his father. Her parents called to ask her how things were going and she honestly said they were really good. She'd told them that before but never truly meant it.

Now she squats over a toilet and aims her pee at the stick. Then does calisthenics as she waits for the result. Touching her toes, stretching to the ceiling. Time moves glacially. Outside the door, she hears Travis chasing Eli in the living room. Each time Travis catches him, Eli lets out an ecstatic shriek that stirs her heart. She pictures having another child, maybe a girl to balance out the home. Or another boy so she can remain exalted without any competition. Her family of men that look to her as the rock.

She checks the test, but it's not ready. If pregnant, she and Travis can always talk of the night this child was consummated. They'd reached a low point in their relationship but that night eased them back to where they needed to be. She decides she'll be crushed if it's negative. The ache to have another child with Travis overwhelming. She stares at the stick while caressing the crystal hanging from her neck. Willing the test show a positive. And then, like she's able to guide her wishes, a plus sign appears. She grabs it, whisking out of the bathroom and finding Travis tickling Eli on the couch.

His face goes slack. "What is it?"

She waves the stick in the air, beaming. Rubbing her stomach as if she can feel the baby already growing.

"You're gonna be a daddy again!"

58

Travis doesn't recognize the number on his cell. He picks it up to a voice on the other end that says, "Trav."

It sounds as if the person is light years away.

"Wyatt?" he responds.

"Trav?" the voice asks again, even farther sounding this time.

They go back and forth like this until Travis finally asks, "Are you talking into the wrong end?"

"Don't understand these things," Wyatt says. Travis hears a crackling as Wyatt turns the receiver upside down. When he speaks again, it's loud and booming. "Phone company came and said a landline was already installed in the house. Yours is the first number I'm calling."

Normally Travis would say, "I'm honored," or something along those lines. But he doesn't have it in him.

"Anyhoo," Wyatt says. "Wanted to see how you were doing. With what happened to your friend."

Travis had woken up not thinking about Grayson, a rarity.

"Chugging along," he says, biting his cheek. "Putting one foot forward I guess."

"I'm here if you need a shoulder."

"Kind of you, Wyatt."

The last they'd spoken—except for a week ago when Travis was bombed out of his mind—Wyatt confessed that he was Travis's great-great grandfather frozen in time. Clearly, the man was on heroin.

"In fact, I was thinkin'," Wyatt says, "how about you and I go ice fishing? Right on the lake near Anvil Creek. I have a proposition."

"Callie told me."

"I don't need the money. Maybe a little saved in case, but I would like to invest the rest."

"Could really use it."

"We'll talk specifics when we're there. How about tomorrow?"

"I was gonna watch Eli. Been recently taking the load off Callie. I'm trying to be a better—"

"I'm sure she appreciates. But this is important. It's for the future, our future. Fishing can be good for the soul. Get your mind off other temptations. I know how that is."

"Yeah, man, definitely shouldn't be drinking right now."

"I'm trying to be better too. With my own temptations you see?"

"Uh, okay, okay. I hear ya. Pick you up around dawn?"

"Dawn it is."

When Wyatt hangs up the phone, he untwists a baggie of heroin procured from the settlement before Aylen left. He won't inject it ever again, but a snort suits him just fine. It tingles and centers his brain to get it working right for what he must accomplish tomorrow. The future waiting in bold neon lights.

Travis ends the call, sips some beer, and rises. Callie's at work, having gone back to Pizza Joint. He'd taken the day to bond with Eli, so leaving him with Callie tomorrow or even having Miss Evelyn watch, shouldn't be a problem. He finds Eli playing with his stuffed animals, a wolf and a bear.

"He dead," Eli says, pointing to the bear lying on its back with its paws in the air.

"Looks like. C'mere, kiddo."

He pulls Eli into his lap. The boy has big green eyes much like his own. Looking into them, he visualizes Eli's future. Growing up and taking over The Goldmine where his mom and dad still work too. A little sister or brother waiting tables. A family that gets to spend every day together. Stu and Cora coming in for dinner, sometimes lunch now that Stu's retired. And even Wyatt, a silent partner responsible for The Goldmine's success. Maybe he still lives in Laner and comes over occasionally. Or maybe he's moved on but returns every once in a while for a surprise. Uncle Wyatt. The role Grayson would've held.

He hugs Eli to fight back the tears because he's cried too much in the last few weeks, his body exhausted from the effort.

Eli tries to squirm free. "Daddy, you're hurting me."

But he can't let go. A chill rips down his spine as he thinks about never hugging his son again. When life's going great, the bad can sneak up and wreak havoc. We're never allowed complete bliss without a pinch of sorrow.

"I'm sorry, bud. Just missed you when I was away. I'll never be away like that again."

"Okay."

"Seriously, bud. I haven't always been a good daddy."

Eli taps his chin with his sticky finger. "Uh, yes you have."

"You'll have a better daddy. I promise you."

"I promise doo doo."

"Eli, stop being silly."

"I promise...caca."

"Eli..."

"Pee pee!" Eli shrieks and runs around the room causing a hurricane. Toys flying everywhere.

This child, so content. Travis swears to find that contentedness again, see the world through a baby's green eyes before death and sadness twist it gnarly.

"I love you, bud," he says, and Eli flies into his arms for another hug. The boy always running colder than he remembers.

"Are you sick?"

He feels Eli's forehead that's like sticking his hand in a refrigerator.

"No."

They hear the lock on the front door turn.

"Mama's home!" Eli yelps, and buzzes out of the room.

Travis stays in the peacefulness of his son's space. Breathes it in. The future changing. It's been shifting at a fast pace for a while now. Hard to keep up. Those he's lost. Others to whom he's grown closer. The dust mites dance in the dusk light streaming from the window along with a cool breeze. Who controls these monstrous changes? Led him to gold? Brought him and Callie together again? Took Papa and Grayson from this Earth. Bobby too? Even going back in time, who guided the Barlows to Alaska, to their edge of the world wonder where cold reigns supreme?

He'd be a different Travis had his ancestors settled somewhere else, but he wouldn't have it any other way. Other forked paths could've occurred, except fate decided to trap him in this ice land. A purpose to it all. A purpose to everything.

Callie smells of pizza toppings. She's got a pie for dinner, showing Eli the meatballs on top and telling him it's from a boo. They eat the pizza with wine, milk for Eli. Nothing special about this dinner. Two parents and a child talking about their day. Callie says Lorinda's been doing well, but she wants to have her over later this weekend to cheer her up. Travis tells her about going ice fishing with Wyatt tomorrow and for Lorinda to come over then. A moose had been spotted on Main Street. Old Charlie the drunk saw it. This time Old Charlie was right and not hallucinating. The new deputy Bickley came to lead it out of the road. Miss Evelyn's sick with the croup. Smitty's wife too, something going around. They finish and Eli helps wash the dishes. They make him brush his teeth, twenty times up top, twenty times on the bottom before he gets in his footy pajamas and jumps into bed. Travis covers the blanket with all Eli's stuffed animals.

"Night," Travis says, with a last kiss on Eli's forehead.

They wind back to the couch in the living room, Travis a little tipsy, his lips cracked red from the wine. Callie nestles into his armpit and they interlace fingers.

"Love you, Bear," she says, taken to calling him this again like they're young lovers.

"Grrrr," he says, pawing her, sucking on her neck.

"C'mon, Travis, you'll give me a hickey."

"A lasting image to carry around with you."

He suctions his lips and leaves a circular grape juice stain under her left jaw.

"So gross," she says, wiping off his saliva.

"Grrr, you love it. Now time for some honey."

He tugs down her jeans and underpants, tasting her already wet. Lost in her folds. At sea and not ready to come up for air and end this moment of bliss.

59

As dawn ascends, Wyatt stands in front of the wall mirror waiting for Travis to arrive. He'd gotten up early, having not really slept. The day too important, his mind spinning. Numerous outcomes as to how it will end, but ready for what the future holds. No way he'd be frozen if it wasn't for a greater purpose. Gold not being the reason, worthless when it comes to things that really matter. Family. The ability to create more generations. He'd done his part but was robbed of watching it unfold. That's what makes his ultimate decision justified.

Headlights pull up to his front yard cutting through the muted sunrays. After staying completely still for hours, he rotates his head toward the door. Steps outside of himself once there's a knock. Rises and opens to his destiny.

Wyatt can tell Trav is taken aback upon seeing him, not expecting Wyatt to be clean shaven. Like he opened the door to find himself.

"Been a while, hasn't it?" Wyatt says, embracing him.

"The beard?"

"Too itchy," Wyatt says, going to stroke its phantom bristles and touching pink cheek instead.

"You really..." Travis begins, recalibrates. "Your face..."

Travis touches it, his fingers out of control. He assesses his doppelgänger because it's unlike looking in the mirror. The mirror inexact, only a reflection, not completely him. This vision shows the truth with all its imperfections. And through its emerald green eyes, he sees the inevitable.

"Ready to roll," Wyatt says. "It's something I've heard folks say in this present time. I'm trying to talk more like you all. Say such crazy things, though."

Travis's heart palpitates. An increased vibration pressing against his chest. He gets in the driver's side and Wyatt shotgun.

Theirs is the only car in the road at this time of morning. It's the weekend and the fishermen are usually just starting to wake at this hour. Haven't hauled out yet. Smitty checking on his wife since she has the croup, making her a tea with honey, eggs with rashers for himself. Elson feeding his one-eyed cat Jammy before he opens the bar. Jesse noticing his black eye starting to fade; the phone ringing as Tuck calls saying he's got the croup too. Old Charlie already starting on a hot toddy. Lorinda doing a morning run before she'll head over to Callie late morning. Callie in bed, her and Travis up late last night. He didn't wake her when he left in the morning. In her half-sleep, she grabs for the pillow instead of him now that he's gone.

On the drive over, Wyatt asks Travis to tell a story about Callie, so he does. The day they met. Her cruise ship docked and a sea of lower-forty-eighters spilled forth on Laner. He was taking lunch from the oil refinery on the docks because most of the day he spent inside a windowless room, the sight of the ocean a necessary break. With oil-blackened hands he munched on a Wonder Bread sandwich with bologna and American cheese. She'd been traveling with her parents, two cartoons who waved to her from the boat, uninterested in another boring Alaskan town, so she came over to Travis, popped the headphones out of her ears, and asked him what to do around here. He had work, but just before she docked, he had willed for a girl like her to appear, unlike any he knew in Laner, because it was starting to feel tiny, and he wondered if there might be more for him out there. Then she arrived and so he ditched work and took her for a hike up Ulee Canyon. This wasn't where he went with just any girl, most being fine with brews at Elson's, but this one named California, with a name like that, she was meant to see Alaska at its finest, atop an overlook where the snow twinkles like a million diamonds.

"It's so quiet," she said, and he could see she was in awe. They made love up against a tree, carving their names in it afterwards, T&C, and she never made it back on that cruise ship. She waved to her parents as it sailed away and never returned to California either. Because when the boat was pulling up ashore, she had looked into the great waters and wished for someone like him too.

"I haven't told that story to anyone before," Travis says.

"It'll come in handy," Wyatt says, so softly.

"What was that?"

"Nothing. Nothing at all."

They reach Anvil Creek with the sun now high. Water trickling through the creek beds sounding like glockenspiels. The frozen lake beams before them, majestic in its crystallization. Summertime completely formed. They park the car at the rim and haul the gear toward the center, more fish there than along the edges. They cut a hole, unfold chairs, and dip their rods in the water. Cool out but hot under the rays reflecting off the ice.

"I remember coming up here one time with Stu, Bobby, and Gray," Travis says. "Gray and I were about ten, so Bobby was eight. Mom was at church, but Stu insisted on taking us out since it was the first warm day of the year. That winter being exceptionally harsh. When we got there, Bobby wanted to slide across the ice like he was stealing a base. Stu had already given up on scolding him, even back then. Wasn't worth it. You could yell at that kid till you were blue and he still wouldn't listen.

"So he went sliding around while I sat in a circle with Stu and Gray and none of us spoke. We listened to the silence, save for the cutting sound of Bobby slipping against the ice. It was the first time I caught a fish, and Stu, he was so fuckin' happy. You could hear his excitement echoing across that lake, picked up by the wind. I wonder if you could still hear it in some hidden pocket? And then Gray caught one too. We were like, 'Holy fuck, two big ones.' Stu could've caught his own, too, but called it a day to give us the glory. Bobby whined that he could've gotten an even bigger fish had he tried, but we ignored him, and then Mom cooked up those fish. She was so damn excited.

"And while I was chewing on the bounty I'd brought home, I remembered what I'd thought about during those silent hours on the lake. I willed the fish to bite my line. I made it happen, Grayson's too. I had that power but rarely used it again. Because it scared me, you know? I told you about meeting Callie and willing for her to appear. Like, right before I met you,

I was thinking that something needed to change in my life, and then so much happened, you, the gold, the fish shack, Papa, fuckin' Grayson. Man, I don't know, just some crazy stuff I wrestle with at night. But that's how you found that gold, right, Wyatt? You willed it."

"That's how I survived this past century."

Travis laughs in spurts. Wyatt still sticking to his story of being preserved. He'll play along.

"So are you pleased with how your future brood turned out?"

Wyatt feels a tug on his line.

"I am in a unique position. Most get to witness a grandchild at most. Back in my time, few lived past sixty, so we had to pump out babies early. I was on the later side of my thirties, same age as you. I'd roamed a lot before I met sweet Adalaide. Spent plenty of my twenties panning in California, losing time in opium dens when I couldn't find a nub. She was a farmer's daughter. Can't recall what I was doing in Washington or how we met. Haven't rifled through all my memories yet. But I'm positive we weren't childhood sweethearts or anything. I spent a good portion of my life without knowing her. That's what made it harder when she was taken away from me. It's 'cause we didn't have enough time together."

"Why do you think this happened to you?"

Wyatt goes to rub his phantom beard again. But he's not that person anymore.

"It will be my life's search to find out why. Haunting me like the gold used to. I had to be chosen for a reason."

"Any guesses?"

"Why have any of us been chosen? Million other little sperms could've reached that egg and yet *we* blossomed. Everyone's endless search on Earth being why they're here."

"Do you believe in God?"

"Tricky one. It was more commonplace in my era to believe. Nowadays folks are too distracted for that. I see that on the odd box you call television. This strange portal into others' lives. But even in Laner at the edge of it all, God ain't ruling much. Maybe church on Sundays for just a few. So no, I don't believe. But I do understand there are things in the universe we cannot explain."

"Like how you and I look so much alike."

Wyatt touches his nose. "Well, I told you my theory."

"That you're my great-great grandfather?"

"You got a better one?"

"Yeah, we're probably related somehow, distant cousins or whatever. Plenty of folks around here are, since most don't leave. So the gene pool stays small. And you were in the wilderness and got knocked unconscious and woke with amnesia. Did you ever even try to see a doctor?"

"Medicine can't explain what happened to me."

"Okay, somehow you've got the right chemicals to withstand a hundred some-odd years on ice. And now you've met your family who logically you never should've been able to. Is that why you wanna invest in The Goldmine?"

"Is that so wrong? To help out my progeny?"

"No man, we really need it. You'd be saving my life."

"You don't have to put it that way. Please don't."

"But Wyatt, you would be. I wanna make sure you're doing it for the right reasons. Not because you think we're related. I'd feel bad taking your money if that's the case. Like I hoodwinked you."

"What else will I spend it on?"

"Whatever it is you wanna do."

"I already know. And investing in The Goldmine is a part of that dream."

"How much are we talking?"

"I have about fifty thousand left. All the money from the converted gold. Thank you for taking care of things at the bank by the way, since I have no identification."

"Yeah, that should be enough to get it up and running. And I'll pay you back right when I can. Give you a percentage of the profits too."

"That's unnecessary."

"You have to let me do something for you. I don't like charity."

"You've done enough."

"But c'mon—"

"I said you've done enough!"

There's a throbbing vein on Wyatt's left temple so Travis lets it go. He doesn't fully recognize this Wyatt, more so than simply the man's appearance. In the stillness surrounding this lake, Wyatt should be calm yet he can't stop moving. Twisting from side to side. Hesitant. Jittery. Travis wants to ask if he's on heroin but is afraid of offending.

"I apologize," Wyatt says, then his voice takes on a different tone, more like Travis's. The pitch causing Travis's blood to run like ice, like when you hear a recording of yourself, mystified by the way you sound.

"Who are you?" Wyatt asks, but for a second Travis wonders if he was the one who said it out loud.

"Who am I?"

"At your core? First thing in the morning before the world settles in. If I told you who I was, you would cry."

Wyatt's nervous energy accelerates. He stands and drops the fishing line, pacing from side to side. Travis thinking he's probably on drugs.

"This is the only way."

"What's the only way?"

"I'm telling you there is nothing else that can be done."

"Dude, sit down. You're all over the place."

"I didn't anticipate this conversation. *Saving your life?* Why did you have to go and say that?"

"Because you would be. I've thrown in too much money, The Goldmine'll go under without an investor."

"I'm not talking about money."

Wyatt squeezes his fist, his face wrinkling in pain.

"I did some terrible things in my time. These hands..."

He holds out his palms, the skin pale and cracked, lines like trenches.

"All for riches."

"Well, shit was different back then, right?" Travis laughs, trying to lighten the mood.

"But I am no longer Wyatt Barlow from 1898. That man got trapped in gold and was buried by an avalanche. He didn't ascend. But I did. My heart quietly thumped waiting out the decades. And then that one eye opened, and I saw the wolf, I saw my future, and then I saw you, and you were me."

"Dude, calm down."

"Because I love her. I fuckin' love her. She's what I need."

"I know you miss your wife."

Wyatt clutches the silver mirror around his neck with the floral embroidery. His last link to Adalaide. He will not require it anymore. He rips it off, dangles it over the ice hole, lets go. A current quickly tucks it under, vanished forever.

"What you do that for?"

The blood rushes to Wyatt's cheeks, face red, expression like he was struck by lightning. Travis feels a tug on his line. He hasn't been paying attention. He looks down into the swirling waters, a dark pit with no end.

"I'm gonna be a dad again," Travis says, as if he knows this man's intentions, his survival instincts kicking in. Like taking out your wallet to show a picture of your kids when someone has a gun to your head.

Wyatt breathes this news into his nostrils. "So am I," he whispers.

Travis's ear perks up, catching what Wyatt said.

The fish tugs at the line, monstrous from the strength of its bite.

"I'm gonna be a dad again," Travis says a second time, tears blurring his vision. The future accelerates at a rate faster than he's ever experienced before and he's powerless to its inevitability. Wyatt shaking his head like he feels bad for what's about to occur and the truth is he probably does, even if this man was not his kin, but the two of them aren't meant to exist at the same time, or at least both will never be entirely happy if they do. Hundred and twenty-two years preserved him for this moment. Travis fights the tug on the line, but it's too fierce and tips his balance. Wyatt leaps forward, dragging Travis down on the ice, half of him flung over the edge of the hole. The fishing rod gets yanked under, disappearing in the black, and a demon hovers trying to drown Travis. Travis gets his fingers around its neck, clawing for his life, unwilling to give up. Half of him wet and already doomed, the water cold like a thousand stabbing needles. The universe spoke of this as the defining time of their existences. All else before and after of less importance. The victor continuing, the loser descending. The rush of water hits Travis like a giant slapped him in the face. He plunges into pure nothingness. Above him a ray of light beams from the ice hole, his ancestor peering over the edge, holding him down. He breaks free from the grip, but the current shoots him away, his nose tapping against the surface of the ice shield. He pummels at the barrier with his fists, but his movements underwater are too slow. The cold settling in, skin on fire. Screams nothing more than trapped bubbles. Callie and Eli flicker in his mind and then he's unable to think anymore, brain frozen, body soon following.

Up above, a new Travis walks over his fallen former self. He gets in the pickup, speaking out loud the story of how he and Callie met as he speeds home. He'll keep it in his pocket if ever she gets suspicious. He'd already sent an envelope filled with fifty thousand dollars along with a note to her and old Travis that said he had to leave Laner and for them not to worry because he's found himself again, and they were a huge part of helping to reach that milestone. He wrote that they're the finest people he's ever known.

Then he signed *Wyatt Emmett Barlow* for one final time.

Under the lake by Anvil Creek, a man has been frozen much like another man in the same wilderness had been frozen, in this area of Alaska where silence is the loudest sound. And much like the other man, time leaps forward while he stays petrified. Because it's so quiet, if you place your ear against the ice sheet where the man lies below, you can hear the tiniest beat of his heart, until the lake finally melts and he's free.

ACKNOWLEDGMENTS

This novel was written during a very tough time when my dad passed away. It became my therapy, and even though he isn't any character in the book, he exists and is kept alive on each page. He was always my best and toughest editor and I would not have been able to write this without him.

There are many other people who helped bring this book to life.

I'm indebted to Chris Rhatigan, its brilliant editor, for believing in keeping the novel intact, and having a keen and astute eye.

Sam Hiyate, for singing its praises and giving judicious edits, and for a decade of friendship.

Kat Bedrosian, for being its only other reader and cheerleader, and whose lightning quick turnaround I can always rely on.

Mom, for being a great support and reader of all my works.

Also, to a wonderful group of writers, folks in publishing, and good friends who became a soundboard during this process: Margot Berwin, Jen Close, Vicky Forsberg, Erin Conroy, Marco Rafala, Camellia Phillips, Nat Kimber, and Jeffrey Barken for publishing the first chapter in Monologging.

And, as always, to my tree in Central Park. A lot of this was written in the wintertime indoors, but there were a few times the sun came out enough to create in nature.

Lee Matthew Goldberg is the author of the novels *The Desire Card*, *The Mentor*, and *Slow Down*. He has been published in multiple languages and nominated for the 2018 Prix du Polar. The second book in the Desire Card series, *Prey No More*, is forthcoming, along with his other novels, *Eating the Sun* and *Orange City*. He is the editor-in-chief and co-founder of Fringe, dedicated to publishing fiction that's outside-of-the-box. His pilots and screenplays have been finalists in Script Pipeline, Book Pipeline, Stage 32, We Screenplay, the New York Screenplay, Screencraft, and the Hollywood Screenplay contests. After graduating with an MFA from the New School, his writing has also appeared in the anthology *Dirty Boulevard*, *The Millions*, *Cagibi*, *The Montreal Review*, *The Adirondack Review*, *The New Plains Review*, *Underwood Press* and others. He is the co-curator of The Guerrilla Lit Reading Series and lives in New York City. Follow him at LeeMatthewGoldberg.com.

BOOKS

On the following pages are a few
more great titles from the
Down & Out Books publishing family.

For a complete list of books and to
sign up for our newsletter,
go to DownAndOutBooks.com.

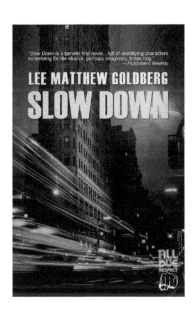

Slow Down
Lee Matthew Goldberg

All Due Respect, an imprint of
Down & Out Books
May 2020
978-1-64396-102-6

How far would you go to make your dreams come true?

For budding writer and filmmaker Noah Spaeth, being a Production Assistant in director Dominick Bambach's new avant-garde film isn't enough. Neither is watching Dominick have an affair with the lead actress, the gorgeous but troubled Nevie Wyeth. For Noah's dream is to get both the film and Nevie in the end, whatever the cost. And this obsession may soon become a reality once Dominick's spurned wife Isadora reveals her femme fatale nature with a seductive plot to get rid of her husband for good.

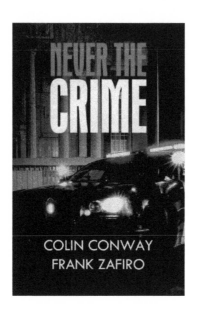

Never the Crime
The Charlie-316 Series
Colin Conway and Frank Zafiro

Down & Out Books
June 2020
978-1-64396-108-8

The greatest danger that Officer Tyler Garrett faces might not be Detective Wardell Clint, who is doggedly trying to prove he's dirty. Instead, the swirling maelstrom of city and department politics threatens to destroy his plans to rebuild after a controversial shooting almost two years ago.

From the mayor to the chief to the officer on the street, everyone seems to have an agenda.

Gutted
A Gus Dury Thriller
Tony Black

Down & Out Books
July 2020
978-1-64396-103-3

When the gangland owner of a pit bull that killed a three-year-old girl is found gutted on an Edinburgh hill Gus Dury is asked to investigate, and soon finds himself up to his neck in the warring underworld of the city's sink estates.

Amidst illegal dog fights, a missing fifty grand and a police force and judiciary desperate to cover their links to a brutal killing, Gus must work fast to root out the truth, whilst the case sinks its teeth ever deeper into him.

Shotgun Honey Presents Volume 4: RECOIL
Ron Earl Phillips, editor

Shotgun Honey, an imprint of
Down & Out Books
May 2020
978-1-64396-138-5

With new and established authors from around the world, Shotgun Honey Presents Volume 4: RECOIL delivers stories that explore a darker side of remorse, revenge, circumstance, and humanity.

Contributors: Rusty Barnes, Susan Benson, Sarah M. Chen, Kristy Claxton, Jen Conley, Brandon Daily, Barbara DeMarco-Barrett, Hector Duarte Jr., Danny Gardner, Tia Ja'nae, Carmen Jaramillo, Nick Kolakowski, JJ Landry, Bethany Maines, Tess Makovesky, Alexander Nachaj, David Nemeth, Cindy O'Quinn, Brandon Sears, Johnny Shaw, Kieran Shea, Gigi Vernon, Patrick Whitehurst.